More Praise for Masterminds & Wingmen

"Rosalind Wiseman is perhaps America's foremost guide through the complex social hierarchies and cruel logics that govern adolescents' lives. And *Masterminds and Wingmen* maps the foreign territory of boys' social and interior emotional lives as deftly and compassionately as Wiseman's earlier book on girls. With clear analysis and down-to-earth practical advice, this book will guide many *many* conversations between parents and their sons."

—MICHAEL KIMMEL, author of *Guyland: The Perilous World Where Boys Become Men*

"In *Masterminds and Wingmen*, Rosalind Wiseman dared the impossible: she asked the most taciturn creatures on earth—teenage boys—to talk about their social lives. The result is a Rosetta Stone for the adolescent male, so even that boy-patented monosyllabic shrug now speaks volumes."

—ASHLEY MERRYMAN, coauthor of *NurtureShock: New Thinking About Children*

"Rosalind Wiseman brings a distinctive perspective and voice to whatever issue she takes up. She did it in *Queen Bees and Wannabes*. Now she's done it again, revealing the inner workings of Boy World. I found the book insightful and useful, as both a father to sons and as a professional working with violent youth who must deal with the most serious life issues facing other people's sons."

—JAMES GARBARINO, PHD, author of *Lost Boys: Why Our Sons Turn Violent and How We Can Save Them*

"The world bombards boys with confusing and destructive messages —the net result is the creation of characters instead of young men with character. *Masterminds and Wingmen* **will help parents, teachers, and coaches understand young boys and make a difference in their lives. An intriguing read.**"

—Dr. Kevin Leman, author of *Have a New Kid by Friday*

Masterminds & Wingmen

Helping Our Boys Cope with Schoolyard Power, Locker-Room Tests, Girlfriends, and the New Rules of Boy World

ROSALIND WISEMAN

HARMONY

BOOKS • NEW YORK

Copyright © 2013 by Rosalind Wiseman

All rights reserved.

Published in the United States by Harmony Books, an imprint of the
Crown Publishing Group, a division of Random House, Inc., New York.

www.crownpublishing.com

Harmony Books is a registered trademark and the circle colophon is a trademark
of Random House, Inc.

Harmony books are available at special discounts for bulk purchases for sales
promotions or corporate use. Special editions, including personalized covers,
excerpts of existing books, or books with corporate logos, can be created in large
quantities for special needs. For more information, contact Premium Sales at
(212) 572-2232 or e-mail specialmarkets@randomhouse.com.

Photos on page 297 by John Loomis.

Cataloging-in-Publication data is on file with the Library of Congress.

ISBN 978-0-307-98665-8
eISBN 978-0-307-98666-5

Printed in the United States of America

Book design by Lauren Dong
Jacket design by Jessie Sayward Bright
Front cover photography by Photo Alto/Alamy

10 9 8 7 6 5 4 3

First Edition

Contents

1

It's Time to Enter Boy World

L ike many parents, I wake every morning with my mind filled with Post-It notes of all the things I'm behind on. On April 12, 2011, I opened my eyes with only one thought: it's time to write a boys' book. For years I've wanted to write a book for boys that would be a complement to one I'd written for girls, *Queen Bees and Wannabes*. When parents and teachers would ask me about the possibility, I'd thank them for their confidence and promise that I'd get around to it one day, not really sure that I would. Ironically, my two children are both boys, which always gets a laugh when I'm introduced as an expert on girls. How can that Queen Bees woman, that Mean Girls woman, be the mother of only boys?

The truth is, I've always taught boys, and they constantly write to me for advice. But up until now I've never publicly shared their struggles and what I've told them. Some of their problems are important but small, like "How can I tell a girl I like her?" or "How do I tell a girl I don't like her?" or "How do I stop my friend from bugging me about how short I am?" Other questions are bigger, like, "I have a coach who screams 'faggot' at one of the kids. Some of the other guys are going after him too. I hate it, but what can I do?" "I want to quit the team but I can't tell my parents." Or, "My dad always, always thinks I'm guilty of something, or lying, or lazy. Every time he lectures me I just want to explode, but I smile and say nothing. My mom makes excuses for him. I can't live like this but I don't know what to do."

I put off writing a book about boys because I wasn't certain I could deliver the level of insight that I'd been praised for in *Queen Bees*. Did I know boys well enough? Could I get them to tell me what I needed to know? I knew that boys are much more complex than popular culture gives them credit for. I knew there was a lot going on beyond their clipped responses like, "I'm fine." But I wasn't sure that I could write something that was equal to what boys, parents, and adults who care about boys need and deserve.

I needed a sign.

I got it when I was least expecting it. In the spring of 2011, I met with Cartoon Network's CEO, Stu Snyder, and Alice Cahn, the network's vice president of social responsibility, to discuss the possibility of working together on their "Stop Bullying: Speak Up" campaign. I'd brought along Emily Gibson, who helps me strategize new partnerships. As usual, Emily got right to the point. "Stu, I'm really glad we're meeting, but I'm not sure I understand why. Rosalind is more known for her work with girls, and we know most of Cartoon Network's viewers are boys, so why her?"

Stu immediately answered. "You can see it in her eyes."

What's in my eyes? I wondered. *Do I have something weird in my eyes?*

"You can see she has boys in her eyes," Stu said. What was he talking about? Then I realized exactly what he was referring to. I'd seen that look. I'd even written about it in another book, *Queen Bee Moms and Kingpin Dads*. I just hadn't realized it was my facial expression too. That look says to others: *"I'm regularly attacked with Nerf guns as a display of affection. I'm not surprised to receive an email or phone call from the principal. There may have been a time, just once, when I realized the boys' principal was calling and I pressed Ignore because I just really didn't want to hear what the boys had done. At any moment I must cope with the following challenges: my children destroying something of high value, hurting themselves doing something mind-blowingly stupid, or facing a hygiene problem so severe that lesser beings would flee or vomit. But because I'm these kids' mother, I'll hold them accountable, patch them back together or bring them to someone who can, while shaking my head at the ridiculous reason we're at this place, seeking help. And yes, I'll force these desecrators of bodily hygiene to clean up after themselves—even if they claim they can't smell anything wrong."*

I returned from my meeting in Atlanta, and the next morning I woke up ready to write. I had just needed someone on the outside to let me know I was ready.

FOR BETTER AND WORSE: HOW I STARTED THE QUEEN BEE/MEAN GIRL CRAZE

There are a few more things to know about me beyond that I have a reputation for working with girls. I've taught in schools for almost twenty years. I started by founding a nonprofit organization that taught kids from fifth to twelfth grade a social justice and ethical leadership course I developed called "Owning Up™." That early work is the basis for the training I still do with educators and administrators. About eight years into teaching, I wrote *Queen Bees and Wannabes,* a book for parents of girls about what the world looks like to a girl and how parents can best guide their daughters through it.

I wrote about girls because I felt that our understanding of girls and the connection between their friendships and their personal development wasn't as good as it needed to be. By 2000, a lot had been written about girls, self-esteem, and body image, but I couldn't find anything intended for a general audience that spoke to girls' group dynamics. I believed that girls' conflicts with others were unfairly dismissed as drama and cattiness. We weren't giving girls real-life skills to handle conflict with their dignity intact. I saw that girls were valued based on their ability to conform to the unwritten rules of what I termed "Girl World," and that these dynamics in turn impacted girls' ability to be socially competent as girls and women.

I can't quite remember the sequence of when and how all this happened, but right before *Queen Bees* was published, I was profiled in a *New York Times Magazine* article entitled "Mean Girls." A few days later, my literary agent asked if I'd talk to a woman named Tina Fey, because she was interested in buying the rights to the book. I had no idea who she was. I'd just had a baby (my oldest son Elijah), so even if I was watching TV, I was so tired I couldn't remember anything I was seeing anyway.

Before you think I was jumping for joy that someone had asked to buy film rights for *Queen Bees,* you should know that I was already jaded enough about media and entertainment that I needed to be convinced. I'd had a couple of strange calls from people asking to buy my life rights—which would have made for an extremely compelling story of a woman desperately trying to raise money for her little nonprofit from fancy foundations while wearing clothes decorated with baby vomit.

But I took the call. Twenty minutes later, I was convinced. If someone was going to do something as crazy as taking a nonfiction, how-to parenting book and turning it into a major motion picture, Tina was the person to do it. All I asked of her was that she not make it stupid. She promised, and I believed her. Not only because she was clearly intelligent, but also because she appeared to be motivated in the same way I was. If you're going to put yourself out there, you can't do it half-assed. (That said, with more than twelve years of parenting under my belt, I'm much more accepting of personal mediocrity.)

With the popularity of *Queen Bees* and *Mean Girls,* I was increasingly called upon to speak on girls' issues, which was great but also made me uncomfortable. While the attention on girls was needed, the message was also sometimes watered down or used as a way to demonize girls.* In addition, with all the conversations about girls, boys, as a distinct group, disappeared. Recently, with the avalanche of attention on bullying and school shootings, the closest we've come to recognizing boys' issues is in our discussions of teen sui-

---

*And, much to my annoyance, even though *Mean Girls* came out more than a decade ago, girls are still dressing up as the Plastics for Halloween.

cides, which we generally attribute to homophobia and lack of gun control. Not that those issues aren't worth discussing—but they're far from the only boys' issues that need to be addressed.

COULD I GET BOYS TO HELP ME?

With every book I write, I ask the people I'm writing about to help me. But when I decided to do a book for boys, I remember wondering if it would be possible to get boys to reveal their deepest feelings, thoughts, and most meaningful experiences. Could I get them to answer my questions day in and day out? Would they really read twenty-page drafts of chapters multiple times for no reason other than that they wanted to? (I did offer to write college recommendations if they worked hard.) Yes. They did, and it was far easier than I expected. First, I put out a few calls to schools—public, charter, private, parochial, international, all boys, big, small, urban, suburban, and rural—and held my breath. Almost immediately, schools of every type were on board. Then a few weeks later, as I was wrapping up a high school presentation, I mentioned to the students that I was working on a boys' book and if anyone wanted to help me, they should please let me know. I couldn't believe the response. Boys walked right up to me and volunteered. (So did girls, by the way.) After that, I made the request after every presentation. What surprised me the most was who came forward. Looking back now, it makes perfect sense that the "golden boys" with the highest social status, like the athletes, volunteered, but they weren't the only ones; many different kids volunteered. By email and Twitter, boys found me and told me they were on board. Within a month, I had over 160 boys contributing to what you're about to read. In their own words, here are a few of them telling you why they did it.

I feel that helping people who are in bad situations I have already been in is a duty. —Mathias, 16

I'm doing it because I want to be part of something bigger that will make a difference for our gender and my "peers," but also because I feel like our "Boys World" is something that's been kept in the dark for too long. —Victor, 17

Sometimes I think working on this book helps me more than the other boys. —Grant, 15

I want this book to inform, educate, and reform the social structure of boys in their natural environments. Things happen in the realm of boys' worlds that are never mentioned in the public eye, or are brought to concern by adults. By contributing to this book, I hope to redefine the way of thinking when it comes to how boys interact. —Cody, 18

Once we began the project, it was nonstop arguing, debating, and laughing—and an occasional tear when boys shared something particularly painful. The boys made me realize that things I'd assumed about them for years were wrong. They told me stories that were so funny and stupid, I cried from laughing. I gave them problems other kids wrote to me about, and they had intense debates about how to help these kids they didn't even know, then emailed me because they were worried about what had happened to the kid in trouble. They shared their most personal stories, feelings, and opinions—all to help you know how to reach out to the boy in your life in the best possible way.

I've also asked parents to share their experiences, concerns, and worries with you. They're going to tell you some stories that I hope will make you laugh and make you remember that you're not alone trying to raise these people who sometimes seem determined to make it as rough on you as possible.

We're going to walk a difficult line in this book. You may read something that challenges you to the core. That's never pleasant. In fact, it's usually a highly anxious experience that leaves you wishing you'd left well enough alone. If this happens to you, I'm asking you to face that challenge without shutting down or beating yourself up for being a bad parent.

You also don't have to like your son or any of the boys he hangs out with. You're allowed to have moments of resentment when you're busting your butt for him and he doesn't seem to notice. You're allowed to be angry that the child who used to give you hugs and kisses turns away from you. You're allowed to fantasize about the fabulous carefree life you'd have if you weren't driving him to games all weekend. You aren't a bad parent if you go out with good friends and admit these feelings out loud. If you don't acknowledge them, then you will become one of those parents who robotically smile as they tell you that their kids are perfect, but in reality can't laugh at themselves or ask for help when they come up against the real-life, no-holds-barred, humbling work that it takes to raise a boy into an honorable man.

HOW ARE YOU REALLY COMING ACROSS TO YOUR SON?

I've sat with a lot of parents who insist that they've talked to their sons about how important honesty and integrity are to them and been completely confused when the boys haven't acted in ways that reflect those values. In their confusion, they tend to blame others. While it certainly can be true that parents talk to their sons about values, I've realized that parents often speak to their sons about their family values without placing them in a context where these values will be called upon. It isn't enough to say "Be honest" or "Do the right thing," because in moments of conflict many of us lack the skills to move through the fear and put our values into action. The context of the situation really matters more than a catchphrase. What's way more useful for boys is to talk to them about what integrity looks like to you under duress. This book will bring these moments of conflict front and center and then show you how to make your values meaningful within the problem your son is facing.

This gets us to role-modeling, one of the most-talked-about concepts in parenting and teaching, but also one that frequently isn't supported with our actions. Our children aren't stupid, and they're not naive. They see when adults around them act hypocritically. They see what we value and believe by our actions, not our words. If we try to present a perfect image of ourselves, they will see through it. In order to earn our boys' respect, we must examine our own behavior. It doesn't matter if you're a parent, a teacher, an uncle, an aunt, an administrator, or a coach. How do boys see you express anger? Sadness? Disappointment? How do you express affection? How do you acknowledge when you've made a mistake? Are there areas in your life where you say one thing and do another?

Our boys are watching. They may appear cynical and seem to brush off how much they care when they don't respect how we conduct ourselves. Don't let their appearance of complacency fool you. They care deeply. Boys profoundly want strong, comforting, honorable adults who admit how messy life is.

WELCOME TO BOY WORLD

In this book, I'm going to describe and give suggestions for the most common dynamics and challenges you'll probably face with boys. How can you help your son when he's struggling? How can you get a better understanding of how he sees the world and his place in it? How can you reach out to him without his shutting you out?

We're going to start by understanding the unwritten rules of Boy World and how they define for a boy who has power, who intimidates him or vice versa, or where he can let down his guard and be himself. Understanding Boy World can help you assess him as well. What is he being teased about? Why would other kids turn on him? Or even harder to admit, why would he be cruel to others? What would make him lie or sneak around behind your back? Understand Boy World and you'll understand where he's coming from.

Boys don't all respond the same way to Boy World. When I name behaviors by labeling them (like Queen Bee or, in this book, the Mastermind), I'm doing this to create a common language about behavior we often see but can't easily put into words. I'm not doing this to stick boys with labels they can never peel off. For this book to be useful for you, you'll have to balance what I write with the boy you know. I could be wrong. He could see things differently from what I'm writing here. But whether or not he perfectly fits the behaviors I'm describing, what's far more important is that you have a conversation with him and he's able to tell you what's going on in his world. As far as I'm concerned, regardless of whether you end up accepting my terminology, if this book can help open up a line of honest communication with your son about what he thinks and cares about, then I've done my job.

THINGS TO REMEMBER AS YOU READ

I'm a "parenting" expert and a mother. What this means is that it's much easier for me to think through a problem that's not about my own children. When one of my boys is involved, my initial reaction is to get angry, disappointed, frustrated, or anxious and to think of the worst possible outcomes, like: *My child will be scarred for life, he'll never learn from the experience, he'll end up with severe mental health issues, everyone will hate him* . . . the list goes on and on. When other people's children are having a problem, I can see the situation much more clearly and think through possible challenges and strategies.

This doesn't mean I'm a useless mother. What it does mean is that I try to be mindful of how my initial reactions exacerbate the problem when my own children are struggling. I have learned to give myself a little time to process the anxiety, anger, and fear coursing through my veins until I can think again and consult with someone who likes and knows my kids. Throughout the course of this book, I'll ask you to do the same thing. Sometimes our love and worry stops us from providing the help our boys need. As a mother, one of the most difficult lessons I've learned while writing this book is how much parental anxiety can repel boys and come between them and their parents. This book is about bringing you closer together and helping you create and maintain the support system you and your son need.

This Book Covers a Wide Range of Ages

You may be reading this after your ten-year-old son didn't get invited to a friend's birthday party and you have no idea why. Or you may be reading this because at 2:00 AM last night you got a nasty phone call from a father who found your teenage son sneaking into his daughter's bedroom. If you're on the younger side of things, skip over the parts for older parents if the issues covered there stress you out too much; those parts will still be there when you need them.

Read This Book When You Can

This book is organized to fit the pace of your life. While you're more than welcome to sit down and read it all cover to cover, I doubt that's going to work for everyone. I've organized this book so you can read what you need when you need it. It's also designed to be read in small bites for those times when you're waiting in a carpool line, sitting on those cold uncomfortable bleachers, or waiting outside the principal's office. Your child has a friend you think is a terrible influence and you need to know what to say without it becoming a battle of wills? Go to page 89. Your son has a girlfriend and she's texting him five hundred times a day? Read pages 349–350.

Most chapters begin with a thorough analysis and description of a specific aspect of Boy World. You'll also see sections called "Checking Your Baggage" and "Landmines." "Checking Your Baggage" is where I challenge you to answer a few questions to help you understand your reactions. "Landmines" are things parents do and say, usually with the best of intentions, that make their son shut down. Like landmines in real life, they're usually right in front of you, but you don't realize they're there until they've blown up in your face. As you read this you may be thinking that pointing out landmines is a lost cause, since anything you do—like looking in his direction or asking one innocent question—makes your son zone out, roll his eyes, look down at his phone, walk away, or put his headphones on, but I promise that you will learn ways here to improve communication with him. Then I'll give you specific, step-by-step strategies to help him through the common situations that my boy editors have chosen.

If He Sees That You're Reading This Book...

Especially if you're one of those parents who read every parenting book they can get their hands on, here's a suggestion. He's probably going to take one look at the book and immediately roll his eyes and say something like, "Mom, I don't want to talk about whatever is in there." Even if this is the first book like this you've ever read, you'll still get the eye-roll. Just tell him this: "It says in here that most parents ask way too many questions when their sons get into the car, like when I pick you up from school. It's telling me how to know when you need more space." If he laughs or says, "Really? Let me see that," you have a couple of choices.

You can show him the book, but you can also tell him I wrote another book specifically for him, a "survival guide" pitched directly at boys. I wrote *The Guide* because I think boys need a book written just for them.

As for those of you who have sons who don't make snarky comments and are actually willing to talk to you . . . have some sympathy for the rest of us.

If you're a teacher, coach, or counselor who works with boys, someone who wants to work with boys, or an aunt, uncle, or grandparent who has taken a boy under your wing, I'm grateful that you're taking the time to read this. My hope is that somewhere in these pages you'll find ways to empower the boys you care about to become honorable, emotionally secure, strong men. Never forget how important you are to these boys. I've watched the power of another adult reaching out to a boy. It's life-changing for both. So I'm putting some pressure on you, because the boys you're helping need your guidance and support. And please don't hesitate to answer the "Check Your Baggage" sections or to think about the impact of your experiences with the parenting styles in chapter 8 on how you relate to the boys in your life. Whoever you are, I hope this book is worth the read.

Before you turn to the next page, keep the following in mind:

1. Boys are a lot smarter than most people realize.
2. Boys can have really complicated problems with their friends and families.
3. Boys usually say, "I'm fine, don't worry about it," when they're really feeling the complete opposite.
4. Some boys love death and destruction. This doesn't mean they're crazy or mean.
5. Some boys don't love death and destruction. This doesn't mean they're weak or weird.

There is one thing I won't be able to do. I'll never be able to tell you how to get boys to stop leaving their dirty socks around the house. If you know the answer to this problem, please let me know. In the meantime, we're going to raise our exhausted heads, rise up, and be as strong, smart, open-hearted, and self-reflective as our boys need us to be.

2

Why Doesn't Batman Ever Smile?

Boys are just so different from girls. They just don't fight the way girls do. When it's done it's done. It's just so much simpler with boys.

You have boys??!! Isn't that funny that you have boys when you do all this stuff with girls? Let me tell you, you are so lucky to have two boys! Boys are so much harder than girls when they're little, but just you wait. When they get older, boys become so easy compared to girls!

I've lost track of how many times people have said the above to me. But over the years that I've worked with boys, I'm convinced that what looks like their "easiness" is actually our own ignorance. If you've ever picked up a boy from school and asked him how his day was, you may know what I'm talking about. If you don't, let me explain it to you this way.

When a fourteen-year-old girl screams at you for not "getting" a problem she just described to you in detail for the last fifteen minutes, at least you heard a name and a few nouns and adjectives that gave you an inkling of what she was so upset about before she ran upstairs and threw herself on her bed. Boys' problems can slip under the radar precisely because there's usually no early warning system. What you thought was easiness turns out to be your own cluelessness, which you only figure out when someone drops a "bad news" bomb on you that makes you doubt someone's sanity—yours, your son's, or that of the person who's telling you. What then ensues can be tremendously frustrating. You sit across the kitchen table from your boy (who's slumped in his chair or precariously balanced on its back legs), and his only response to your worried questions is, "It's fine. Don't worry about it." You finish the conversation exactly as you started, except now you're even more frustrated.

After twenty years of teaching and working with teens, I realize that we often make the mistake of believing that if a boy doesn't come to us with problems, then he doesn't have them. We believe this for various reasons. Boys don't demand our attention in the same ways that girls do. We don't give them a language for talking about their worries and experiences like we do with girls. And we really don't think enough about what our culture—and ourselves by extension—demands and expects of boys and how it frames their emotional lives, decision-making, self-esteem, and social competence. When we do notice boys, it's usually because they're somehow failing or they're acting out in ways that appear thoughtless, reckless, disrespectful, threatening, or frightening.

As a result, by the time boys reach adolescence, most have adopted an appearance of calm detachment and seem to be disengaged from their most meaningful relationships, their future academic or professional success, and any desire to make the world a better place. This is the "slacker" attitude that people so often note in describing boys. Our reactions to this attitude are equally problematic because we usually dance between two extremes: getting angry with them because they're unfocused and "lazy" or dismissing the problem as "typical boy behavior" (i.e., not anything that needs to be addressed).

The reality is that most boys' days are filled with many of the same social challenges that girls face, and what they learn from those experiences matters now and for their futures, as it does for girls. We just aren't trained to see it because boys' problems can look deceptively simple and we can't interpret the signs when they're calling out to us for help. Frankly, we find it really challenging to admit how much we contribute to boys' alienation. But make no mistake—under that detached facade, boys are desperate for meaning in their lives and for relationships they can count on for support and love.

Do you remember the moment when you realized you were going to have a son? Stop reading and really think about that moment. Remember your feelings and thoughts and what people said to you. I'll tell you what mine were. I remember being five months pregnant and walking through a park watching a group of ten-year-old boys scream and throw themselves on each other. As I watched them I distinctly recall thinking, *There's not a lot going on in those brains.* I remember my in-laws liking me a lot more because I was giving them a grandson. I remember people telling me how loud my house would be and how I'd better start saving money for all the things he'd break. (By the way, that money is called my sons' savings accounts, and I do withdraw their money when they break things.) But that was it.

Compare this to someone who is having a daughter. From the moment they find out they're having a girl, most parents know that the culture we live in will present specific challenges to their daughter's self-esteem. As a girl matures it's assumed that her parents need to worry about, prepare for, and then talk to her about body image, mean girls, bullying, eating disorders, physical safety, negative portrayals of girls in the media, and sexual vulnerability. Parents of girls also get a lot of support. If you want to find a conference, book, or seminar on any of these issues, it's not hard to find, regardless of where you live and what your income is.

Equally important, because both educators and parents of girls are aware of these Girl World issues, we can protest the unhealthy messages. We don't just accept them. Maybe you've seen what mommy bloggers do when a clothing company has the audacity to sell a T-shirt marketed to girls that says, I HATE ALGEBRA! Besides protest, we also include girls in our mission. We enlist them in the fight so that at very early ages many girls can cross their arms and lecture you about how even if they like purple, girls can like any other colors too. All of this is great for girls and a huge improvement from what girls experienced even a generation ago. While we still have a lot more to do (a *whole* lot more to do), girls have a general understanding that the complicated, mixed-message culture we live in not only gives them terrible messages about their sexuality and self-worth but also includes empowering messages that support them as they come into their full, authentic potential.

We don't do any of this for boys. We don't collectively challenge boy culture. We either buy into it ourselves or don't notice it. We don't see boys as complex, nuanced individuals. We don't think a boy who loves shooting Nerf guns (at age seven), air-soft (at age eleven), or paint guns (at age thirteen and over) also wants to read romantic adventure stories. Instead, people often say, "Boys don't read." We are part of the problem when we say this. We are contributing to boys' alienation.

Here's a concrete example. If you have a seventh-grade daughter, you probably know that girls are often self-conscious about their bodies at this age, especially if they have larger breasts or weigh more than other girls they hang out with. When your daughter is invited to a swim party, you probably understand why she's anxious about what she's going to wear without her having to tell you, "Mom, girls can be very mean to girls who develop early. I'm feeling very self-conscious about my breasts, so I really need some help and support, and I'm not sure if I want to go to this party." If you're her dad and don't get it right away, her mom can tell you in two seconds, and then you'll get it.

Now imagine that your son is a seventh-grader who has "moobs" (man boobs) and that he's invited to the same swim party. Two weeks before the party, he casually asks you to get him a swim shirt, but he doesn't say anything about needing it in time for this party. Understandably, you file away *Get him swim shirt* in the back of your mind and don't get the swim shirt. When it's time to leave for the party, you have to yell at him four times because he won't stop playing video games. When you finally get him into the car, you assume he's sullen because he's going through video-game withdrawal. You drive him to the party, lecturing him about screen time and getting even more annoyed because he's not listening to you. Meanwhile, your son is fantasizing that the moob teaser broke his arm at practice today and is currently getting metal pins inserted in his bones without anesthesia so he'll be missing the party.

Two hours later, you pick him up from the party determined to start fresh. You enthusiastically ask if he had a good time. He says, "It was fine." You ignore his sullen attitude. You cheerily ask him who was there. He answers, "I don't know. Some people from school." In two minutes you're back to feeling angry and rejected. But he's not mad at you. Well, he is, because you didn't get him the swim shirt. But he's miserable because the moob teaser didn't break his arm and miss the party. Instead, that kid took a picture of your son with his shirt off and showed it to all the other guys, who laughed and called him "Boob Boy." But you won't know any of this. Which means that when you get home and he goes right back to the TV and chooses the most violent game he has and starts destroying his enemies in the most gruesome way possible, you'll go right back to yelling at him that he's addicted to those horrible games and worry that the games are turning him into a violent freak.

He isn't running to play that video game for no reason. He's running to distract himself from the shame he feels that he was ridiculed for his body, from his deeply wired belief that he can't tell you what happened, and it feels good to shoot something that he can pretend is his tormentor.

We assume boys are easy because they keep quiet, and in the process we sentence them to a lifetime of being misunderstood. If we don't recognize and appreciate the challenges they're facing, no matter how much we love them and want to help them, they won't see us as a resource. Instead, they'll see us as an essential part of the problem. You don't need to take my word for it. Listen to them.

There is no way I'm telling my parents about my problems. There's no point. My dad especially freaks out, starts yelling at me, and makes everything worse. —Ethan, 14

*This girl in my class must be the most annoying girl on the planet.
Last week she would not stop talking about who liked who in the
class. After school, she wouldn't stop teasing me. I finally snapped
and poured water on her head. Of course I was the only one who got
sent to the principal's office. My parents want to kill me. This week
this girl's right back to doing the same thing because she knows she
can get away with it. WHAT DO I DO????* —Evan, 13

*When my mom gets mad at me, she tells me I'm being like my dad.
She hates my dad. Can you imagine what that's like? It's like being
cut with a knife. And this is the person who I'm supposed to tell my
problems to.* —Sean, 16

In addition to what the boys say, there's significant research that
clearly shows how boys are struggling:

- For every 100 girls age 6 to 14 with a learning disability, 160
  boys have a learning disability (US Census Bureau, "Ameri-
  cans with Disabilities: 2002," May 2006).
- For every 100 females age 15 to 19 who commit suicide,
  549 males in the same age range kill themselves (Centers for
  Disease Control and Prevention, http://www.cdc.gov/nchs
  /data/dvs/LCWK1_2002.pdf).
- For every 100 girls in correctional facilities, 879 boys are
  behind bars (http://www.census.gov/population/www/cen
  2000/briefs/phc-t26/index.html).

Adding to these statistics, 70 percent of high school valedictori-
ans are now female. My colleagues in college admissions tell me that
the ratio of male applicants to female applicants has continued to
weaken so much that now they believe that for every eight qualified
female applicants there are only two male applicants. Eight to two.
They won't admit that publicly, but it's something they discuss
among themselves. The last time I spoke to a group of college admissions professionals (and there were representatives of Ivy League

and other select colleges in the room), one of the attendees asked me, "Should we accept a male student who does well on his standardized tests but doesn't get good grades and does the bare minimum with extracurricular activities? We can accept him because we need boys, but we have no indication that he'll be a productive member of our community." So while people are worried about racial affirmative action, the biggest affirmative action problem is right in front of us. If you're still having a hard time believing me, check out this graph from Collegestats:

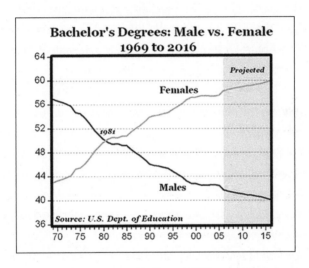

In that context, this comment from Will, a sophomore at Georgetown and one of my primary research and editorial assistants, makes perfect sense.

In my AP classes, I was always one of five guys. The same five guys in a classroom of girls. I had plenty of guy friends who could have taken those classes, but they didn't want to do it. They'd rather be the best among the mediocre. Really, my friends would rather look stupid. They weren't secure enough to compete with the girls.

We owe it to boys to do better. We owe it to the girls who are growing up with these boys to do better. Because even if you don't have boys, you don't want girls having to put up with insecure, intellectually stunted, emotionally disengaged, immature guys. Worse is when some boys' insecurity combines with arrogance and privilege. Then we're dealing with guys who believe that the right to amuse themselves by degrading girls is more important than behaving with common decency—or they don't even realize how stupid they'll look when they get caught. For example, when a fraternity at self-described "elite" Amherst College in Massachusetts (not a big university in the South where we stereotypically assume these things occur) designed a T-shirt for their pig roast party of a pig smoking a cigar and watching a naked woman roast on a spit with the words ROASTING FAT ONES SINCE 1847, the guys didn't understand why that was such a problem. Here's Dana Bloger, a female student at Amherst, explaining why the T-shirt is a problem:

> *The woman on the shirt is depicted as an animal—or rather, as inferior to an animal, since she has not only replaced the pig on the spit but is being roasted by it. She is objectified as a literal piece of meat, whose thoughts, feelings, and humanity are rendered nonexistent and her consent therefore irrelevant. The hypersexualization of her body links violence with sex, thus perpetuating the notion that violence is sexy and sexuality violent. While I am not suggesting that this image would ever directly cause the infliction of violence on any individual woman, dehumanization is always the first step toward justifying such violence.*

The guys' official response, after they tried to blow it off by saying they were drunk when they came up with the idea? "We didn't mean to offend anyone."*

All I have to say is: eight to two. It's not good for anyone.

For all of us, including the guys who made that T-shirt, the stakes are high. So here's what I'm asking. Just as I challenged people in

---

*There were many male students who commented on Bloger's blog in support of her article and who called out the other guys. But as they pointed out, Bloger was the one who came out publicly and attached her name to the problem—which meant she took the heat from the guys who wanted her to shut up.

Queen Bees to examine girls' social lives more closely and be honest about how they contribute to the pressures on girls, I'm asking us to do the same for boys. Despite the fact that some extraordinary people like Bill Pollock, James Garbarino, Leonard Sax, Michael Gurian, Paul Kivel, Michael Thompson, Jackson Katz, Don McPherson, Michael Kimmel, and many others have been doing some extraordinary work on boys' issues for a long time, the reality is that the impact of Boy World and boys' social dynamics on their emotional well-being has been left out of the national conversation. We don't acknowledge that boys wage sophisticated power plays and can be relentlessly targeted for humiliation, or that so many feel insecure about their bodies. We don't notice when some boys abuse power and then get allies to back them up while other boys seethe in silence. And we really struggle to see how our own behavior with boys reinforces these dynamics.

The big question is this: how did those frat boys—who probably wrote "I love you!" Mother's Day cards when they were eight—get to be such jerks? Did their parents know that their sons were capable of such callousness? On the other side, I believe there were guys in that Amherst fraternity who didn't want to go along with the T-shirt but didn't say anything. Why did they stay silent?

WHY BATMAN NEVER SMILES

I'd bet any amount of money that you've never said to a boy, "If you have a big problem and admit you're really upset and worried, I'll be ashamed of you and you'll grow up to be a poor excuse for a man." But somehow most boys have this message to some degree wired into their brains by the time they reach older childhood. Where does this message come from? It's not like someone has been beaming things into their brains all day since they were little kids about when it's okay for a guy to ask for help.

Except that's exactly what's going on. Think back to when your son was five or six and what toys he was given and what he liked to play with. I'm not about to launch into an argument about trying to get boys to play with dolls instead of trucks, and this isn't about what color clothes you put him in as a toddler. Just go with me here. Did he get or play with toys that looked like this?

Do you remember the first time he got a superhero costume? Who got it for him? Did he jump off couches? When you walked through the door, did he attack you? Do you remember how exciting it was for him to be the all-powerful superhero? When you're a young boy and you're flying around the room with a Batman cape your grandma gave you, it's intoxicating. You're the hero. You don't have to listen to anyone. You have unlimited power—which, when you're five, is particularly cool because the reality is that you have very little control over your life.

Now I want you to imagine what this Batman looks like when he's incredibly happy and excited. Imagine him in love. Does Batman ever look like anything other than what he looks like above? No. Batman's emotional range is always somewhere between serious, detached, sullen, and angry. No matter how physically hurt he is, Batman shakes it off. If he's angry, he either clenches his jaw or exacts revenge with utter physical domination. If he really needs advice or he's being stubborn, Alfred seems to always know what to say to make Batman feel better or set his head straight. Alfred teaches boys that the people who are closest to them should innately know when they're upset, why they're upset, and what to do to make them feel better. But if people don't get it, boys give up, because otherwise they would have to admit having messy feelings of "weakness" that Batman never shows. When you're dealing with a boy, it's like you have one silver bullet to kill the bad thing that's upsetting him.

Now imagine you're an eleven-year-old boy, and even though Batman is still cool, you and your friends start hanging out with this guy:

And now you're thirteen and you like this guy:

The first picture is from *Halo,* one of the more popular video games for guys of all ages. The second picture is from *Assassin's Creed,* one of the more popular, interesting games that middle school and high school guys play.

When I show these pictures to the boys at the beginning of my presentations, they respond by roaring. There's no other way to describe it. They roar. It doesn't matter if they're in middle or high school. They jump up and down. They throw their arms in the air. When I ask them if they remember their superhero outfits, they grin and for a moment you can see the five-year-old boy each one of them used to be. Then I ask variations of the same questions I've asked you. What would the *Halo* guy act like if his parents were going through a bad divorce? How would the guy in *Assassin's Creed* show he was sad because he just got dumped? What would he do if his friends were spreading horrible rumors about a girl and he knew they weren't true?

Boys should want to act heroically at certain points in their lives. Being independent and self-reliant, getting up after having been knocked down—these are absolutely critical skills. But because these characters never show sadness, fear, anxiety, or obvious enthusiasm and love, they constantly teach and reinforce that boys should limit their emotions, and they even tell boys which ones they're allowed to have. They don't show how a man should speak out in a morally complex situation when his loyalties are torn between friends and ethics.

But as much as the boys love them, these characters (and by extension, the media at large) aren't entirely responsible for defining and suppressing boys' emotional range. The adults around them nurture and reinforce those limitations as well. It comes down to this. Many of us talk a really good game, but we aren't being honest with ourselves. I have watched countless parents say they don't want their son to bury his feelings, then tell him to "get yourself under control." I've seen parents say nothing when their sons' coaches call them "pussies," "fags," "little girls," or "ladies," or their sons report that they're being accused of "running like they have sand in their vaginas." I've seen teachers and school administrators interpret boys' frustration as disrespect and punish them for it. Make no mistake: when our boys see that we aren't saying anything in their defense, they believe that either we agree or we're powerless to stand up to this kind of treatment. Either way, if a boy is growing up in this atmosphere, why would he ever ask us for help?

THE POWER OF THE GROUP

We all want to feel a sense of belonging. This isn't a character flaw. It's fundamental to the human experience. Our finest achievements are possible when people come together to work for a common cause. School spirit, the rightful pride we feel in our community, our heritage, our religion, and our families, all come from the value we place on belonging to a group. But it's also true that our need to belong can be the cause of our greatest inhumanity. It can be our collective Achilles' heel as it pushes us to say nothing when faced with injustice, or to join in the abuse of people the group has identified as different and therefore deserving of unequal treatment.

What I'm talking about is how we maintain our ethics and moral compass when we're in a group. Why? Because conflict is inevitable, and at some point one person will abuse his or her power over another person. When conflicts and power plays arise, a cascade of decisions are made by every other individual in the group based on their own personal characteristics and history. It's critical to realize that it's these decisions that develop both our collective and individual ethical framework, moral courage, authentic voice, and social competence.

For most boys, the goals of being ethical and honorable, while valued, are vague. In the short term, it's the experiences a boy has in a group that will teach him about friendship and what kind of boy is accepted or rejected by the group. His experiences in groups will influence how hard he tries in school, how he presents himself, his level of respect for women (including his mother) and girls, when and how he makes choices about sexual activity, and how he faces situations such as bullying, drinking, and drugs.

> *Each group has certain "morals," and to be part of that group a guy has to follow the group code. If he doesn't, he's out.* —Brian, 16

Within these moments are ethical choices and complex dynamics that frame the way a boy will act throughout his life. Should he say anything when someone is being excluded and treated cruelly? What's the price of speaking out? What's the price of silence? If a person speaks out, is he disloyal? Does he believe that seeking revenge or teaching someone "his place" justifies humiliating someone? What issues are more important than that?

THE ACT-LIKE-A-MAN BOX*

Group dynamics have distinct but unwritten rules. Understanding what those rules are and how they're created is critical to understanding boys' social dynamics. To do that, I'm going to begin with how we define culture. The dictionary defines "culture" as "the attitudes and behavior characteristics of a particular social group." I define it as everything you intuitively know about how a person in your community should think and act to be accepted.

Of course, each of us lives in more than one community. The largest, loudest culture we all live in is our national culture, and we get constant messages from the media about what is valued (and not valued) within it. But we also live in smaller communities. Where we live, our ethnicity or religion, our economic class—all have their own cultural guidelines that react to or reinforce the value messages we get from the overall culture. But almost all cultures, no matter how big or small, base their greatest expectations for how a person is supposed to act on whether they're male or female. If you're born a

---

*Paul Kivel created this paradigm to explain how masculinity "boxes" men in.

boy, you have to act X way. If you're born a girl, you must act Y way. These specific, detailed gender rules are often the invisible puppet strings controlling people's social behavior.

Not every guy reacts to these rules in the same way. Some guys really drink the Kool-Aid. Others openly despise or rebel against the rules. Some guys are in the middle. But one thing is always true: in order for a boy to come into his own, he has to come to grips with how these messages exist inside his head and how they influence what he thinks, says, and does.

Let's go back to my classroom and the boys high-fiving each other after they see the pictures of Batman, Halo, or whatever image I think is most credible to my students at the time. I ask guys if these images represent the way they think guys are supposed to act. Not surprisingly, they don't think that's what these images represent—or maybe they do, but only a little bit. Then I ask this question: "Describe a guy who can influence people or has high social status. This is a person everyone knows, and if he has an opinion, everyone listens and agrees. What does he look like, and how does he act?"

I write their responses on the board like this, inside the box:

Funny	*Money*
Strong	*Tall*
Good with girls	*Cut*
Always relaxed	*Confident*
Independent	*Good at comebacks*
Good at "right" sports	*Detached*
	Tough
Slacker attitude even if he does well at school	

Then I say, "Describe a guy who doesn't have high social status. This is someone who is likely to be teased, ridiculed, or ignored. What does he look like? How does he act?"

I write their responses around the first set of answers like this, outside the box:

	Acts like a girl	Tries too hard	Awkward
Sensitive, easily upset			
	Funny	Money	Snitch
Poor	Strong	Tall	Rule Follower
Weak	Good with girls	Confident	
Bad style	Always relaxed	Good at comebacks	"Flaunting" being gay
Fat	Independent	Detached	Disabilities
Shows pain	Good at "right" sports	Tough	Controlled by girls
	Slacker attitude even if he does well at school		

In this exercise, called "The Act-Like-a-Man Box" (from now on I'll abbreviate it to ALMB), I write down all the normally unwritten rules for boys. Even after I've written them down, boys can still have a hard time admitting how much control the ALMB has over their lives. Some get upset about the unfairness of it. For example, money can make them angry. Which is exactly the point. It's not fair, but it's still true that it's easier to have more status if you have more money. Then I ask them what they would do in the following situations:

1. Four guys are friends. One guy in the group gets teased a lot and hates it, but doesn't say anything.
2. A star athlete wants to quit the team, but feels he can't.
3. A guy won't tell his friends that he got an A on his science test and that he studies really hard.
4. A guy won't tell his friends that his girlfriend puts him down all the time.

5. A guy is really struggling in school, but doesn't want to admit to anyone how much it bothers him.

Then everyone in the room gets serious, because they see how the box traps them. Doing the ALMB exercise isn't about the boys figuring out how to increase their social status or where they fit in the Act-Like-a-Man Box. Instead, it's about understanding how these invisible rules convince them what emotions they're allowed to have and how to express them. It stops them from asking for help. But its impact is even bigger. It teaches boys to value a person who has more in-the-box characteristics and devalue a person who doesn't. It's about understanding that power and privilege are at work when one person believes he has the right to speak for everyone and no one contradicts him. It's about how people with power abuse it and why they choose the specific weapons they do to humiliate or isolate others. Because, if everyone believes that people with a lot of the in-the-box qualities are better or have more power, then it follows that the people who don't must have qualities that are inferior and must have less power. This is the foundation of how we all learn the different "isms" that separate us, like sexism, racism, classism, and other types of bigotry against people who are different (i.e., outside our particular cultural box).

Guys in the box (and often their parents as well), like any other group of privileged people, often don't recognize their privilege. Privilege can make people blind. Many parents have been convinced that they're raising their son to achieve future success, and are being good parents, if they steer him toward having as many ALMB characteristics as possible. It never occurs to them that putting their son in the ALMB has costs. Either he'll feel immense pressure to conform to these expectations and believe that the only way his parents will truly approve of him is if he stays in the box, or he'll believe his placement in the box makes him better than others (and no, he won't say that, but his behavior will reveal this belief). As Brad and Jack describe it here, it doesn't feel so great if you're a boy who feels this internal conflict.

What's weird is that in ninth grade I think we were all trying to be in the box. That's all we wanted. But by senior year it feels like such a trap and all you want to do is get out. I look at me and my friends who are trying to always keep up with what people expect of us and it's exhausting. —Brad, 18

In the eighth grade I went to a Catholic boys school where the real religion was homophobia. The toughest guy in school called me gay, and I lost a fight with him about it and was pretty much history for the rest of the year. So I changed schools and stopped doing anything remotely brainy or fruity like writing for the school paper or playing chess and now spend my time playing hockey and acting like Bluto from Animal House. *I bet every second guy in every high school acts like me. Maybe it doesn't excuse it, but I'll bet nobody really changes either. Besides, college is two years away, I guess I will become that great guy then. In the meantime, my mom, my girlfriend, and my six-year-old sister (and now possibly you) are the only ones who can really know my dark secret. That I'm only a stupid jerk half of the time. —Jack, 16*

Remember, every boy is an individual. The boy you know may not care about conforming to what's inside the box. He may despise it, but he still interacts with people who judge both him and themselves according to its rules. He's getting a constant stream of messages from the culture about what a real man is like.

One of the clearest lessons the ALMB teaches is that the easiest way to prove your "in-the-boxness" is to demean and dismiss girls and out-of-the-box boys. And we contribute to it. In boys' daily lives, adults still often motivate them by equating bad performance or weakness with femininity. Without even realizing what we're doing, we say to boys, "Don't throw like a girl!" or "You're screaming like a little girl!" or "Don't cry! You're a big boy!" (which implies that girls cry and crying is always bad and weak). Some people excuse these comments by saying, "But it's true. Most boys throw better than most girls. Little girls scream at a higher pitch. Girls cry more easily than boys." When people say those things to boys, though, they lead boys to draw a connection between acting incompetently or in a way that people can ridicule and being like a girl.

Obviously, going after boys who are outside the box is usually connected to being called gay. It's the knee-jerk reaction to condemn and marginalize anyone who is acting outside the narrow range of the ALMB. Of course, rarely do any of these behaviors have anything to do with sexual orientation or sexuality. Specifically, the word "fag" is no longer exclusively used as a put-down against boys. I'm regularly accused of being a fag by some boys and young men when I speak out about racism or violence against women. Here are a few recent examples from my Twitter account:

@rosalindwiseman I beg she got raped by a whale cock and the jizz turned her into a fag. Everyone tweet @rosalind wiseman is a fag

@rosaline wiseman F****** fag

This is all happening at a time when official tolerance for homophobia is decreasing in the arenas that often mean the most to boys. In the past year the National Football League and the National Hockey League have both taken official action against homophobia. Pro basketball player Jason Collins has come out as the first active professional athlete from one of the top four team sports, and there'll be more athletes who come out after him. But homophobia is still the dominant hand in Boy World that compels boys to be silent in the face of cruelty and teaches that they will be punished for speaking out. Just as important, boys feel that they can go after one another in this way either because they see adults use these terms in similar ways or because adults won't say anything if they hear it (unlike racist put-downs, which boys know they should usually say only among their peers and which I'll discuss later).

Boys start hearing the word "gay" or words like it on the playground by the time they're in fourth grade, and they instantly know that the word is shorthand for a put-down. By middle school, most boys have a clearer understanding of what gay means in the context of Boy World. They know that whatever behavior triggers this accusation must be stopped immediately. Wearing fuzzy multicolored socks, liking the Disney Channel, getting upset when someone's mean, or defending someone who wears fuzzy socks or likes the Disney Channel makes them a target. In high school, this dynamic is so powerful and pervasive that most boys don't realize its viselike grip on their behavior. If they see a boy being teased for wearing something not included in the Boy World code of appearance or for complaining about people being mean to him, or if, in older adolescence, they watch a friend take advantage of a girl so he can sexually coerce her, they know they can't say anything or they'll be labeled as gay.*

> *Last week ten close friends of mine were bullying this kid who is exactly like we've described him by not having high social status: fat, bad style, weak, etc. I told them to cut it out and that they should leave him alone, and while eight of them stopped, two told me to "stop being a fag." —Carl, 16*

To equate speaking out about abuse of power and social injustice with being sexually attracted to other men makes no sense. If it did, heterosexual men would be defined as those who do nothing or who join in when someone's being abused. Then only gay men would have the courage to stand up. Not only is that inaccurate—gay men have challenges about speaking out similar to everyone else's—but it's insulting to straight men.

What's so frustrating and ironic is that homophobia represses boys' courage—not the courage to fight someone if challenged, but the moral courage to raise one's voice when someone is being degraded. Will knows how frustrating this can be.

> *I know many gay people and have many family friends who are gay, and I have to say, one of the most frustrating things about going to my school is how they use terms like "fag" and "gay." The even more*

---

*This is one of the reasons effeminate boys often align themselves with high-social-status girls. Such girls are an effeminate boy's best protection against boys who want to go after him, because if they do, they'll have to answer to the girls.

aggravating part is how, if I imply that we shouldn't be derogatory to gay people, I'm somehow "gay." —Will, 15

Thank you, Will. The same way someone who advocates animal rights isn't an animal, a person who advocates gay rights isn't necessarily gay. —Matt, 16

We really could stop this. By "we" I mean parents, teachers, administrators, and any adult who works with kids. How we do this is by being honest about our own behavior. Certainly there are some adults who are actively part of the problem. But many more of us are bystanders.

The simple definition of a bystander is a person who's present at an event but doesn't take part. In reality, it's a lot more complicated. Bystanders are convinced to join the person abusing power because they believe they'll sacrifice their position in the group if they speak out. If bystanders are silent (which some define as being neutral), their "non-action" either looks like support for what the bully is doing or sends the message that they're powerless to stop him. This isn't to say that being a bystander who speaks out is easy. Far from it. Speaking out against the ALMB power dynamics is terrifying, and boys know this like they know how to breathe. And so do you.

Let me give you an example. Imagine you're driving a group of boys back from practice. Your child is sitting shotgun, constantly scanning the radio or his phone for everyone's perfect song. The other three boys are rehashing their day. Everything is good until you hear one of the boys, Josh, say to another, "Mike, you're so retarded in basketball! Do you have any idea how gay you looked shooting in PE class today! The girls were kicking your butt!" You immediately tense, look in the rearview mirror to gauge the kids' reactions, and wonder if you should say something. In that instant, several thoughts go through your head. You know it was bad but kids say words like that all the time. All the other kids are laughing. If you say something, you're going to embarrass your child and you're going to be known as the uptight parent. It's inappropriate to set rules for other people's kids. Or worse, what if the other kids get mad at your son because of what you say? And then the moment passes.

The hard truth is that this is the adult behavior that makes children believe adults support bullies or are powerless to stop them. These are also the actions that come across as not wanting to be "the parent" in difficult situations. Here's how you can handle it differently: Take a deep breath, focus on what you're about to say as you pull the car over, and put it in park. Take your seat belt off, turn to face the kids in the backseat, and ignore your son's silent begging or death stares. As you make eye contact with all of them, say:

> You: Guys, using the words "retarded" and "gay" to put people down is unacceptable.
>
> Josh: It's just what we say! It doesn't mean the same thing now! Mike doesn't mind. Mike, tell her you don't mind that we call you retarded.
>
> Mike: It's fine. Josh's just messing with me.
>
> You *(still ignoring your son's death stares)*: No matter what, it's unacceptable to call someone gay or retarded to put them down. I know I can't control what you say, but this is important to me. If any of you want to talk to your parents about what I just said, please do so. *(Josh stares at you like you're crazy, and your son stares out the window pretending he was born into a different family.)* Everybody got it? Good—what was the station we were just listening to?

There are three things to point out before we can leave this situation behind. First, please note that Mike had no choice but to agree with Josh. Second, it's important to end by encouraging the kids to talk to their parents about what you said. Not only because it's smart to be transparent when you have these teachable moments with other people's children, but also because you want to avoid any of the kids going home and accusing you of "screaming and totally freaking out" to their parents. Third, I know many parents are very worried that doing something like this will backfire onto their son. The truth is, kids don't go after a child just because he has a strict parent who has no problem setting limits on other kids. The Joshes in your child's world go after him because of a combination of factors, like your son tries too hard, is a pleaser, or has low social skills. Also, these kids have to respect and fear you to the extent that they know you won't let them get away with bad behavior. Today it's put-downs in the car, tomorrow it's hanging out at your house when you're not there. They need to take you seriously.

Don't worry if you've been in this situation and didn't handle it well. The good thing about hanging out with kids is that if you make a mistake, there's a 100 percent chance you'll have another opportunity to try again. Or you can always go back and address it later by starting with, "You know, something was said in the car yesterday that I've been thinking about and want to discuss. . . ."

WHAT IF OTHER PEOPLE ARE DRAGGING YOU AND YOUR SON INTO THE ALMB?

It's not if, it's when. Parents of girls have lots of experience with intervening when other people try to put their daughters into the Act-Like-a-Woman Box. For example, if someone in your family says anything about your six-year-old daughter's weight, you tell them to back off and then talk to your daughter about it. But again, we rarely think to intervene when it's our boys. For example, your mother constantly refers to your son as "the bruiser." Or you go to the grocery store, your son picks up a box of cereal, and a nice lady says, "He's so big and strong!" Or your son is eight and cries after striking out in his pee wee baseball game and a well-intentioned dad says, "Stop crying! Only babies cry! You're not a baby, are you?" In any one of these moments, you're confronted with two big problems. One, someone is forcing your son into the ALMB. And two, what are you going to do about it?

I'm not suggesting that you yell at your mom or the nice lady at the store, "Stop putting my baby in the ALMB!" Or that you grab your son, shake your finger at this dad, and say, "Don't you dare tell my son he can't cry! He can cry if he wants to!"

But you do need to say something. I know no one wants to do this, especially dads. (If you're a dad, maybe you'd do it, but you know I'm accurately describing most dads.) First you have to prepare. Don't wait until the moment it's actually happening to think of what to say. Here are a few suggestions. "Mom, I know you love him and want what's best for him. Instead of talking about how tough he is, can you talk to him about something he's doing that you think is great?" To strangers, I'd say, "Thanks, but you know what's the coolest thing about him? He draws animals incredibly well!" Yes, the other person may think you're strange for saying something so random, but your son will hear you complimenting something specific to him, a skill of his that you admire. He'll know that the most important people in his life value him for who he is individually.

Why not just blow it off? If we're talking about a grandparent who sees your kid once a year, then I'd let it go. But if this is someone your son has consistent contact with, then you say something because this person is helping you raise your child. With the dad at the baseball game, you say something like, "He's upset, give him a break," because he's not just saying that to your son, he's saying it to all the boys. If you really don't feel comfortable saying something, then you can talk to the coach. If you want more help with that, go to page 292.

This is messy stuff, and you don't have to fight every single battle that comes your way. If you're too tired to have these conversations on a particular day, don't sweat it. Like it or not, you'll always have another day. But be proud that you're taking this on. I see way too many sons whose parents haven't provided this guidance and support, and so these boys truly believe their self-value is based on fitting in the ALMB. They can lose themselves so easily. When you take on this challenge, your son will know where you and he stand. Proud. For the right reasons.

The purpose of this book, and of all the work I do with boys, is to give them a strategic methodology to rebel against the ALMB so they can come into their own as authentic, strong, and emotionally engaged men. I want boys to rebel and reinvent themselves in a way that makes them feel empowered through the process. Yes, it will be messy. It'll probably be highly unpleasant on occasion. But if they go on this journey with the right skills and support, they'll develop insight into their own motivations and the motivations of other people. They'll be better able to predict the conflicts they'll get into, and they'll have the courage to look in the mirror and see what's staring back at them. They will come into their own as the men they want to be. They won't be stripped of their passion and go through life accepting mediocrity in themselves and others.

The stakes are so high. Our boys deserve meaningful relationships, the freedom to pursue what interests and challenges them, a feeling of belonging and social connection to others, and a sense that they're contributing to something larger than themselves. Those four criteria make up the definition of happiness. If we allow our boys to pursue these four goals, I believe they will grow into men who will make us—and themselves—proud.

CHECK YOUR BAGGAGE

When you were growing up, what got you high social status as a guy in your community?

Were you intimidated by another kid or an adult when you were growing up? Did you ever ask for help? What happened if you did?

3

Popularity and Groups

O ne of the most common questions that girls ask is, "Why are the popular girls popular? People don't even like them." In all the years I've taught, no boy has ever asked me that question—not because guys are unaware of the power of popularity and social status, but because the definition of both are incredibly obvious to them. They know that being popular doesn't mean that people like you. It means that people know you and realize it's not worth confronting you in a conflict. Unlike the way groups of girls actively compete with others for social supremacy, dynamics between boys' groups are usually tension-free because boys are resigned to them. But don't be fooled—social status is still exerting its power. Boys' social structures are just as powerful and controlling as those of girls, especially in moments of conflict or abuse of power. In this chapter, we're going to look at how popularity and status influence boys' overall social hierarchies and how boys behave in their individual groups.

CHECK YOUR BAGGAGE

What activities did you participate in? Why? Did you love them? Did you avoid things because you thought you'd lose social status if you did them?

What activities do you steer your son toward?

THE BREAKDOWN

Most guys I talk to believe there's an elite 10 percent who look like they fit into the ALMB the most, followed by the 75 percent who make up the general population and the 10 percent who hang out at the bottom but have a strong group, leaving 5 percent of kids who, for a variety of reasons, satellite around everyone else from the outer perimeter. Every group has a corresponding girls' group to the point that some are entirely coed, but for the most part there's limited social interaction between these larger groups of boys.

The 10 Percenters

For the top 10 percent, conforming to the ALMB is law. Those in this group aren't individuals, they're pieces of a machine. There are four defining characteristics of this top 10 percent. One, they look like they're good (less important is actually being good) in at least one Boy World sport—football, basketball, soccer, hockey, lacrosse, or water polo (depending on your geographic location). Two, their hair, clothes, walk, swagger, and slang are the same. That look becomes their social uniform. (Think of how they all shave their heads before a game.) Three, their parents are so invested in their sons' status that they allow any "bad boy" behavior from them by supporting it outright, looking the other way, making excuses for it, or denying it altogether. Four—and maybe the most important—these guys have an intense desire to be in, and remain in, that 10 percent group.

The "10 Percenters" are usually identified by seventh grade. By eighth grade, it's absolutely clear to all the other boys in the grade who is in the top 10 percent. While some of the 10 Percenters may have leftover friends who didn't make the cut, the public nature of these friendships will gradually disappear and will only be resurrected by necessity. (Maybe they're related, or their parents are friends and their families socialize, or they have a class with the guy and no other guy in the 10 percent is in the class with him.) Listen to what guys say about the 10 percent.

> *They constantly put up a front, and they build it up in school. They walk around with this scowl and attitude of, "I'm so cold and tired of everything." If I go up to a normal person and say, "Hey, what's up?" they'll say, "Hey, what's up?" back to me. But with the kids we're talking about, they don't mingle in the other groups because they think, "Why should I?" —Ethan, 16*

> *It's like a cult. Every year a couple graduate, so they add a few. It's a continuous cycle. —Auguste, 18*

> *At my school, I'm in that 10 percent elite, but I honestly feel like I have to fight for it. I'm not the meathead jock who plays lacrosse and football and gets the praise handed down to them. To be up in the 10 percent elite, I have to be bold and make some moves that I personally wouldn't make but have to in order to fit in. We [the 10 percenters] are the ones with the parties and the booze, the hot girls, and I feel like, if I wasn't fighting to be in this group, I would just blend in with the rest of the crowd and high school would be pretty crappy. I wish I didn't care as much about my social standing, but no matter what any guy says, they truly care. —Sean, 17*

The Majority

While the 10 Percenters feel self-conscious about socializing outside of their tribe, the guys of "the Majority" usually feel that they can hang out with kids in other groups. The 75 percent is made up of different groups of about five to ten kids each. Regardless of their social status, all guys are still subject to the pressure to live up to our culture's standards of masculinity, so the guys in the Majority can be self-conscious—but they don't constantly think about their image in terms of the ALMB, the way the 10 percent guys above them do. The only time a guy in the Majority intensely cares about his image is when he decides to fight his way into the 10 percent. The parents of these boys don't tend to invest in their kid's social status or to make intense efforts to steer them into ALMB activities.

> *The 75 percent is much more open to change. I try to move around in the 75 percent group. What I've found is that it's a lot easier to be sitting at one table with one group in the 75 percent and go to another table the next day, because they aren't as territorial as the upper 10 percent. —Will, 15*

> *I'm in a pretty high group. Not the highest but pretty high. This may sound weird, but honestly, what I'm about to say really meant something to me. In tenth grade, I had gotten into theater, and one day the theater kids invited me to a party, and that felt incredible. Some people would say that those kids invited me because I'm in a higher group than they are, but that's not true. They're happy to keep to their group. When they did that, it was a huge feeling of acceptance. —Hunter, 17*

CHECK YOUR BAGGAGE

What did people write in your yearbooks?

If you didn't have yearbooks, what do you think people remember about you when you were a teen?

Are there kids you want your son to be friends with (or not) because of social status? Why do you think his life will be better if he's hanging out with these kids? How do you know you're right?

What does your son say?

The Bottom Rung

Adults often assume that guys on "the Bottom Rung" are miserable, lonely, depressed, and the subject of the most bullying. It's not true. Bullying between boys usually happens when they jockey for power within a group or when someone goes after a kid in the Outer Perimeter (see the next section). Guys on the Bottom Rung know their low social position, know they can appear odd to others, and don't care as long as they have at least one strong friendship. Many of them believe that because they aren't even in the running for high social status, they have more dependable friends. That's debatable, but what is true is that the members of the group are usually very connected to each other and don't feel like they have to constantly prove themselves to anyone.

While most boys don't mind being low in the pecking order, most parents either don't believe their son ranks so low or are so unhappy about it that they can't stop interfering in their son's life to improve his social standing. When this happens, a boy may know his parents mean well, but their efforts make him feel that his parents either think he's a loser, don't understand him, or value social standing more than what and who he values. Of course, sometimes the boys themselves are unhappy with their place in the pecking order; if they don't have much luck with girls, for example, they may feel like being "cooler" or more popular would solve the problem. But the last thing even these boys want is to have their parents interfering to help them "be cool" or "get a girlfriend." Nothing will embarrass a boy quite so much as the idea that he needs his parents to get him dates or manage his reputation.

Parents sometimes lack the ability to distinguish between a kid who's on the bottom rung and has a group of friends and a kid who's more of a loner and fighting to retain friends in general. They aren't unpopular in the same way. The loner really may need the parent to get him some help, but the other kid is fine. —Will, 15

I think the parents on the bottom rung either don't care or try so hard to raise their son's social standing because they might feel as if they have failed as parents. But that's not the case at all. Some of the kids on the bottom rung may have two really good friends who may be better than fifty crappy friends. —Miles, 16

My friends and I in elementary school were in the bottom rung. We didn't do sports and we acted silly, but we had each other. We were called stupid all the time by the other kids, but we reminded each other that we weren't. —Marcus. 11

The Outer Perimeter

The Outer Perimeter (OP) is made up of guys who are seen by their peers as existing apart from the entire social system. It's populated with anarchists, pranksters, politicians, obsessed single-subject or single-sport high-achievers, and kids seriously lacking in social skills. I'm grouping a lot of people in the OP who have very different characteristics and can be at either the highest or the lowest level of social status.

A boy can choose to be in the OP because he understands the ALMB (even though he's not going to call it that), sees no value in joining the social system, and has strong friendships outside of school. This kid can be exceptionally good at blending into the background. Other kids don't find him irritating; they just don't know what to make of him and sometimes don't know he's there.

There are also guys in the OP whose position is inflexible. With limited skills in forming and maintaining basic social relationships, they have a really hard time understanding how they come across to others and an equally hard time reading social cues that are obvious to everybody else. These kids are either ignored or targeted for ridicule because they can be so weird to the other kids.

Rick, our sixteen-year-old, was diagnosed last year with a mild form of Asperger's [syndrome]. He has outgrown most of the things, like sensitivity to sounds and textures, but he still has the social aspect. He is very immature and delayed when it comes to his peers.

I have cried so many times for this poor kid because he is so alone.
—Kathy

*Since I am really bad at making friends, I have to keep any that I
make. Right now I have one friend, but they don't want me making
other friends. I don't know what to do. I'm stuck. —Michael, 16*

*My freshman year I had a roommate who just had no social skills.
He literally made other people hate him. When I tried to talk to him
about it, he was completely unwilling to take other guys' advice to
get along better with everybody else. —Ned, 16*

Chapter 14, "No Man's Land," will address the challenges associated with kids who have low social skills, are socially anxious
or sensitive, or have social disabilities. If your child doesn't have
these deficits, please read the chapter anyway. Many of these kids
are mainstreamed into schools with your children, and they're often
the targets of bullies your child interacts with or can be the bullies
themselves.

There are a few notable exceptions when the groups tend to in-
termingle. The most common one is when boys are drinking or
smoking pot. The day after I wrote this section, I got this email
from sixteen-year-old Brian.

*I have proof of it from yesterday! In my school, you have all the typi-
cal groups that during the day tend not to mix and hang out with each
other. Everybody pretty much stays within their own group. However,
yesterday my friend (slacker) was telling me before a party at night
that he, along with 2 hipsters, 1 jock, 1 musician, 2 drug dealers, and
another slacker, all got together to smoke pot. At first I was super-
amazed to find out that some of these kids smoked pot, but also
that the jock—who you'd think would be "too cool" to hang out with
others who weren't from his group—was actually willing to hang out
with the hipsters and vice versa. —Brian, 16*

CHECK YOUR BAGGAGE

What group did you fit in with in middle school?

Where did you fit in high school?

What did you get from being in this group?

Did you ever want to leave your group behind but felt like you couldn't?

THE MASTERMIND AND HIS MINIONS

So far I've presented a picture of how the boy groups work in relation to each other. Now we're going to go deeper and examine the individual roles within the group. Within any one group, most boys have a best friend, a three- to five-boy inner-circle core group, and then a few more guys who they associate with as part of their group but who they're not close to—that is, they don't do things one-on-one. Boys have assured me that these roles can be found in every group, regardless of social status. The boys and I came up with the following list to describe these roles. If the majority of items describing a role sound like the boy you're reading this for, you've identified his role in his social structure. But also give the boys some credit; few of them are walking around obviously and precisely fitting into these roles.

Here are the different roles that guys can play:

Mastermind	*Conscience*
Associate	*Punching Bag*
Bouncer	*Fly*
Entertainer	*Champion*

In middle school, the ALMB forces boys to fit into one of these roles, which are obvious and constant as they interact with each other. In high school, some guys are trapped by their role as much as they were when they were younger. But for most high school guys the roles are not so rigid all the time. Think of it this way: Everyone, even the guy with the highest social status, has moments in his life of trying to please someone with more power. But what's really important to pay attention to is that with older boys (and men) the roles emerge when there's conflict in the group. Instantaneously, each person's role comes out full force. The behavior behind these roles is the boys' programming, and that programming is defined by the ALMB.

Now let's break down what these roles are.

The Mastermind

"The Mastermind" is charismatic and naturally good at figuring out people's weaknesses based on what would cause the maximum amount of public humiliation. He decides what's funny, stupid, cool, etc., and has the absolute right to dismiss any opposing viewpoint or opinion. This can apply to anything from sneaker color to real-world political issues. While he may not talk to girls a lot, he's good at getting and holding girls' attention without looking like he cares. In middle school, he's the kid who decides when the group should get up from the lunch table. In high school, he's excellent at arguing, and he's especially good at arguing with girls and making them feel stupid. Adults who love the ALMB love him. Despite what we're calling him, the Mastermind doesn't often look and act as calculating and intelligent as the name might imply, but his ability to influence others is what counts. It's hard to know how much of a deliberate "mastermind" any particular guy is until the moment someone publicly and effectively threatens his authority. In that moment, he instantly goes from having a careless attitude to becoming a self-righteous, crusading political operative.

> *If the Mastermind talks badly about a less popular person, then all the other guys won't like him. But if the unpopular person talks badly about the Mastermind, it won't matter. —Ryan, 11*

He's excellent with the side comments. The ones you can't quite hear but you know are bad. —Max, 15

He never looks like he doesn't know what to do. —Ryan, 14

What does the Mastermind gain? Power and control.

What does the Mastermind lose? He won't admit it, but he constantly feels the pressure to maintain his position. He won't take risks that might go against his image. He can't admit to anyone when he's in over his head. His relationships are weak because his friends' loyalty is based on fear and power.

The Associate

Although "the Mastermind" and "the Associate" can look similar, the Associate is much more talkative and well liked. He's interested in other people's business and what advantages he and the Mastermind can get from it.

He's the one that the Mastermind respects the most. He can be honest with the Mastermind without having to worry about getting the shit kicked out of him. He's harder to tell by a simple glance, but if you watch the interactions within the group, he's the guy that the Mastermind will pay most attention to. —Ian, 17

More people like him more than the Mastermind. Plus, he usually knows all the information. Like if a bunch of guys are hanging out, the Associate gets the texts about where people are hanging out. Then he tells the Mastermind what's going on, and then it just takes the Mastermind saying, "Yeah, let's go," and the group is going. —Keith, 14

What does the Associate gain? Power by association.

What does the Associate lose? Any identity separate from that of the Mastermind.

The Bouncer

Like a bouncer at a club, "the Bouncer" within a group is big, tall, intimidating, and willing to sacrifice himself as one of his job responsibilities. The Bouncer really starts to show himself by seventh grade. He isn't good at verbally defending himself and can't read or understand people's motivations. The Mastermind or the Associate can easily convince him to get in trouble or take the fall for them because he's always eager to show his loyalty to them. He can be rude to guys who are outside their group, and he'll say stupid, perverted things to girls because the Mastermind or Associate tells him to. The girls in his social group don't like him, and he doesn't understand why. He's often the odd man out in situations with girls, or the guys set him up with someone who is similarly socially vulnerable.

> *The Bouncer has to be tall compared to everyone else. The Mastermind has to be physically strong, but he doesn't really have to use it. Sometimes I think the Bouncer isn't that smart. But he always acts like he doesn't care about school, so it's hard to know what's really going on. —Oliver, 16*

What does the Bouncer gain? He has social status and power in a way he never would have without the Mastermind and Associate.

What does the Bouncer lose? Respect and the ability to have healthy social relationships. His blind loyalty stops him from seeing how the Mastermind and Associate are using him. Other kids don't like him and don't feel comfortable around him.

All three of these roles have the following common characteristics:

1. Everyone is aware of their presence. For example, they always sit in a designated spot in school that gives them the ability to see and be seen by everyone else.

2. They can make racist, sexist, homophobic comments to other students and then laugh at anyone (other guys, girls, adults) who tells them to stop.
3. They like to break small rules in school so it looks like they're beyond the authority of the adults.
4. When they are sent to a school administrator (like the principal or assistant principal) to be disciplined, they walk out of the office making faces or jokes that clearly communicate to everyone around them that they don't take the situation or the administrator seriously. In extreme cases, they will seek revenge against the adult and their original victim.
5. They have little or no respect for female authority figures or men outside the ALMB.

The Entertainer

When there's tension in the group, "the Entertainer" diffuses it. He's willing to make fun of himself and do awkward things to refocus the attention. He loves debating, but never takes it seriously or personally. He responds to the bragging and aggression of other members of his group by bragging himself in ways that are clearly absurd and untrue. He's good at making people feel comfortable, but he also can have a hard time stopping the jokes when he's on a roll.

When he wants to be serious, people turn their heads and say, "Stop." They never take him seriously because they're always waiting for the laugh. —Toby, 18

What does the Entertainer gain? A sense of inclusion, belonging, and security in the group because he's funny. He has membership in the group but doesn't have to act like an ass or feel desperate to be in.

What does the Entertainer lose? He always has to keep up the act to feel valuable in the group. He has trouble being taken seriously about anything.

The Conscience

"The Conscience" worries about getting caught and the consequences. Depending on how vocal he is, the other guys can find the Conscience very annoying because he's like having a chaperone. If they have a lot of history with him, they'll put up with it. Because he wants to follow the rules, he's much more likely to always do his schoolwork, follow the rules to the letter, and take care of his responsibilities, which leaves him vulnerable to both sharing his work with his friends and doing work for them, then being ridiculed for having done his work in the first place. Sometimes he'll get tired of his nice-guy reputation and do something to prove he's not as nice and innocent as his friends laughingly assume. Because he's trustworthy, he is used as a smokescreen when dealing with parents and authority figures. As when he says, sincerely, "I'm so sorry, officer. I know my friends were really loud. We'll keep the music down, I promise. No, sir, I haven't had any alcohol."

> *I'm the Conscience, and I hate it. I always feel torn when the other guys do something I know is wrong but I'm always the one who says something. —Bill, 16*

What does the Conscience gain? Considered a "nice" guy by teachers, administrators, and parents, he has that extra layer of trust that the other guys might not have.

What does the Conscience lose? Considered a "nice" guy by the other boys, sometimes the group excludes him. Guys in the group will leave him out of certain things because he'll point out when they're doing something mean, stupid, or dangerous. He's at risk of being seen as a snitch, which can hurt his friendships.

The Punching Bag

In almost every group of guys, there's one guy in the group who the other guys love but relentlessly ridicule. It's like when someone says,

"No one beats up my little brother but me." If someone outside the group goes after "the Punching Bag," the other guys will defend him to the death. Whoever he dates, his friends will harass him for it. Despite all of this, he hates conflict and just wants people to get along.

What does the Punching Bag gain? Not a lot. He has friends, but the price is high.

What does the Punching Bag lose? He can feel that he has no choice but to accept his friends' behavior.

The Fly

"The Fly" is the kid who hovers outside the group, either the larger social group or an individual group of guys.* He doesn't understand how annoying he is. If his parents have money, he'll try to build his friendships by bragging or buying. Guys can tolerate a Fly for a while, but usually the frustration builds and at some point the other guys have had enough and lash out. There's no guilt when excluding him because he's seen as bringing it on himself.

> *There are no benefits of being the Fly. And parents just don't or can't see that their kid is the Fly. They keep buying more things so other kids will like him. We don't like him. We use him. Parents can't see the difference.* —Chris, 15

What does the Fly gain? NOTHING.
What does the Fly lose? A LOT.

The Champion

"The Champion" is a guy who isn't controlled by the Boy World box but has enough of its positive characteristics that people respect him.

---

*If you cross an Entertainer with a Fly, you get a Showboat. The more Fly characteristics he has the more annoying he is, therefore the more of a Showboat he is.

People like him. He can take criticism, doesn't make people choose friends, and doesn't blow off someone for a better offer. When people are harassed or demeaned, he intervenes. He's comfortable hanging out with guys who are both inside and outside the box. He holds his own opinion, but still listens to others.

What does the Champion gain? People genuinely like him and respect him.

What does the Champion lose? It can be lonely. People will sometimes turn on him for doing the right thing or not upholding the box. He can feel older and distant from his peers.

> *Rosalind, I'm not sure you should put the Champions stuff in here for the parents because as soon as they read it, they're going to think their son is one. How are we going to convince them that they're probably wrong? —Calvin, 15*

I think Calvin just said it better than I ever could.

LANDMINE!

Don't tell your son what position you think he is—even if you're 100 percent sure. Keep that to yourself. If you want to know his opinion, ask him to read this chapter and tell you if he thinks I'm completely wrong, mostly wrong, occasionally have a point, or basically know what I'm talking about. Then ask him to explain why he came to that conclusion. Also, under no circumstances should you use the words "clique" or "posse"! Boys will immediately believe that you're saying they're behaving like the most annoying girls they know.

REBELLING AGAINST THE ALMB

Boys' roles aren't life sentences. Masterminds can realize the price of their arrogance, Punching Bags can learn to stand up to their friends, and Flies can realize that people will like them if they stop trying so hard. And strange as it may seem, Champions don't usually like walking around thinking they are these morally upstanding young men all the time. That would be exhausting and weird.

At the same time, I acknowledge that the boy you are reading this for has his own unique set of circumstances and friends. He may go to a school where everyone looks like him and basically has the same amount of money, a truly diverse school where twenty-five languages are spoken in the hallways, a tiny school where he's known every single person in the school since he was five, or a huge school where most people only know him by the school ID he wears around his neck. However, feelings of power, disempowerment, and struggling with friendships are universal. There will always be a group that has the trappings of power. There will always be people in the middle. Outliers will have moments when they should confront people who have more power and whose voices have more influence over others. All boys will have moments when they see someone being trapped in the box or punished for not conforming to it, but not know what to do. They need to know what to do.

When you combine the ALMB, popularity, and the group breakdown, you're looking at something that spans generations. The men in most boys' lives can probably relate to all of this. (Whether they remember it or will admit it is another issue.) But this generation of boys does have a unique relationship to the Boy World social structure. While the popular stereotype of the ALMB guy is a jock type, these days, jocks don't have a universal monopoly on the ALMB. Other paths to high social status include being a musician, skater, hipster, or even drug dealer. Especially in big diverse schools, there isn't one social hierarchy but many hierarchies. But here's the catch. No matter what a guy does or what he has that brings him high social status, that status can easily give him a really fat head. Why? Because having social power easily convinces you that you have the right to do what you want to other people. Popularity and social power in themselves aren't bad (just like football and lacrosse in and of themselves aren't bad). Being an arrogant, entitled young man, however, is. And when you're a parent who is so proud of your son for his achievements and how well he fits into the ALMB, it can be easy to forget how much harder it may be for him to develop into the man of honor and moral courage you want him to be.

SO WHAT DO YOU DO ABOUT IT?

We will spend a lot of time on this, but for right now I want you to accept the following.

You have to get out of your denial. Your son will make poor choices, behave in cruel or cowardly ways, or be on the receiving end of these behaviors. If you want to raise a son who survives adolescence, you have to accept that he will be in tricky ethical situations and probably make decisions that surprise you.

There's always a good reason in his mind for what he did. It may not be a good reason to you, but I guarantee that in the moment it seemed like an excellent reason and his best option.

He acts differently around his friends than he does around you. And you should hope so. By the time he's in fourth grade, he should know to behave better around adults than he does around his friends. That doesn't mean he turns into a fake suck-up whenever adults are around. It does mean he watches his language, says "thank you" more often, and doesn't tell adults the dirtiest joke his friend just told him. You have to acknowledge the very real possibility that your son has a foul mouth and does really disgusting things when he's not around you.

He reveals and hides different things with you than with his friends. If your son is over twelve years of age, does he still sleep with his favorite stuffed animal? Do you think the guys he hangs out with know that? What you know about him is different from what his friends know. Not better or worse. Just different.

All of this means you'll often have to depend on secondhand information, either from what other parents, teachers, or coaches tell you or from what you overhear from other kids. Your influence is limited to what you can do before and after. The only people who are guaranteed to be there in the moment are his peers. Even if you're looking at your son's texts, tweets, and posts every night, you still won't get the full picture. He will have to stand up for himself with your support, but usually not your physical presence.

Now that you know how boys see their social structures, we're going to examine the issue that is always in the background but never gets discussed in relation to boys—body image. As Michael says, "I hear my parents talk to my sister all the time about feeling good about how she looks. I don't think they even think about it with me." But we need to think of looks as a boy issue because the pressure on boys to physically fit into the ALMB box can be over-whelming. Now we'll look at why.

4

Six-Packing

Girls never feel confident about their bodies. They're always eating
lettuce. I overhear my parents talking to my sister about this stuff
but never to me. But guys can feel really badly about it. —Luke, 11

For many years we've been talking to girls about the unhealthy images they're bombarded with on a daily basis. There's a constant stream of campaigns, documentaries, and websites devoted to counteracting the super-sexy image that's held up as the definition of feminine beauty. Combined, these efforts educate girls and teach them to get angry at these messages and turn that anger into advocacy for themselves and other girls. Now, of course, all girls don't drink the "pro-girl" Kool-Aid. There are plenty of girls who watch these things and are still more than happy to be sucked into the hypersexualized messages that companies constantly direct at them. But even these girls know the mantra.

There's no comparable advocacy for boys. Despite some excellent books, videos, and advocacy campaigns,* as a culture we have

---

*http://www.commonsensemedia.org/advice-for-parents/boys-and-body-image
-tips. Even though nonprofits have created campaigns that include boys, they're usually organizations that advocate for girls. Their orientation is naturally girl-oriented and so their campaigns aren't compelling to boys. In my research, I haven't come across any large boy-serving nonprofits that addresses these issues. The only one is International Boys' Schools Coalition, but they serve all-boys schools.

never been comfortable with or able to comprehend the impact of the masculine images we constantly bombard our boys with. We're too invested in boys' fitting into the ALMB to challenge it. Even when we do, it's usually through the lens of girls. For example, there are 132,000 links on Google for "body image girls" and 72,000 links for "body image boys." You may look at that and think that, although there's a big difference between those numbers, it still looks like that's a lot of information dedicated to boys and body image. Not really. After the first page, the resources include girls. When I looked up "boys body image documentaries," the first two were related to boys. After that, the resources were directed at girls and women.

As with girls, boys' toys have gotten more gendered over the generations. Many years ago, my friend and colleague Jackson Katz showed me the difference between the bodies of boys' toys in the fifties and sixties and what was then marketed to boys. It took my breath away. These are G.I. Joes with and without clothes from the 1960s:

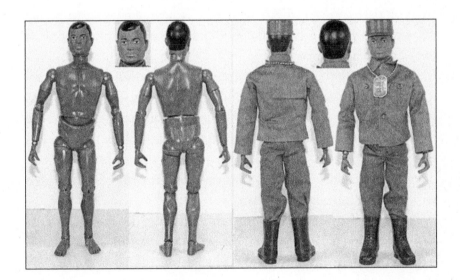

Here are naked and clothed G.I. Joes now:*

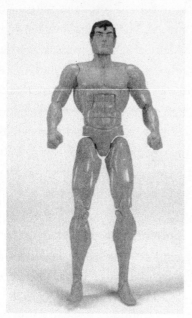 

See the difference between the naked G.I. Joes' legs? It's insane. Or just remember Batman in the seventies. He was a seriously flabby guy compared to the MMA fighter he is now. These days the toy definition of what a "man" should look like is increasingly muscular to the point of absurdity.

But absurd or not, body image is incredibly important in Boy World. The appearance of masculinity matters to boys. Boys and girls will mercilessly tease boys for being too fat or too skinny. By the time they're seven (or younger), most boys know what a six-pack is and that they should have one. If they haven't figured it out on their own by then, they will when they get their first Halloween costume with a six-pack sewn into it.

In the midst of all this, your son will make choices about how he wants to present himself to the world. I know this may sound strange if you have a son who looks like the last thing he spends any

---

*The clothed G.I. Joe to the right was part of a cross-marketing campaign with the 2009 movie *G.I. Joe: Rise of the Cobra*.

time thinking about is his personal style. But if you have this kind of boy, just think about how he would react if you asked him to wear "skinny" jeans. See? He cares—he just doesn't come across like he cares as he picks up the gym shorts he wore yesterday.

Let's break down a little more how the ALMB affects how boys present themselves, specifically in relation to a boy's background and identity development. In the African American community, it has generally been the case that men are expected to pay attention to their clothes, hair, and general appearance, and they aren't going to be teased for being gay or effeminate for caring about how they look. No matter what race a kid is, if he comes from a relatively poorer family than his peers and/or attends a wealthy school, he knows he has to dress well to represent himself and create the armor that makes it harder for the other kids to identify him as "other." In contrast, it's the wealthiest kids I've worked with who have the "privilege" of wearing rags. Yes, sometimes kids wear those clothes to make a statement about not being as materialistic as some of their socioeconomic-class peers, but it's still a choice. In poorer schools, some kids have to wear the same thing every day. The other kids notice and inevitably tease them for it.

Style can also signal a boy's sexual orientation or a boy's processing of his gender identity in relation to his culture. We are living in a time where two things are going on simultaneously, where some boys (and girls) are pushing us to accept more fluid gender definitions and identity. They're literally breaking the gender appearance box that we are all so usually confined by. Other kids are responding to that in a variety of ways, but one of those ways is to accept it. That's one of the reasons why we're seeing some "traditional" straight boys have openly out male gay friends. Or why the girl who looks like a boy on my ten-year-old son's highly competitive soccer team is completely accepted by the other boys on the team. But that acceptance really depends on your community and how the adults role-model (or not) allowing children to exist outside the gender expectations.

Gay boys who are afraid to come out can try hard to look as

straight as possible to protect them from other people's homophobia. Or they can dress against the ALMB to signal that they're gay and people have to acknowledge and notice them. One of the bravest students I've ever known was a black male high school student attending a conservative school who would occasionally wear a shiny black unitard to class. But not all gender nonconforming boys are going to wear unitards. As Ian points out, you can't assume that gay kids all have the same uniform style, any more than you can assume straight guys all have the same style:

> *When it comes to style, gay teens can range from being very preppy with polos and pastel shorts to as grunge as a flannel shirt and ripped jeans to as lazy as sweatpants and a T-shirt off the floor. Typically (or stereotypically) gay teens will wear nicer clothes, or at least will put together outfits. I think when it comes to gay teens, parents will generally wonder about attitude. Some gay teens will have that flamboyant pizzazz, while others will be as apathetic as any teens, and others can be very composed and reserved.*

People ask me all the time if school uniforms would help reduce the social competition in schools. Not really. Although it does make it easier to dress in the morning and I personally hate it when my kids wear sweats to school every day, the way boys wear their uniforms communicates their social status and identity. What's more relevant to you is observing what kind of clothes he wears outside school, where he has the freedom to choose how he appears to others. If he wants to wear all black and dye his hair black too, that doesn't necessarily mean he's depressed. Similarly, you can't assume that a kid wearing a polo shirt is happy and well-adjusted.

If he changes his style, this means he's trying out different identities. He's thinking and questioning the world. This is a good thing. So no sarcastic remarks about whose funeral he's going to and no asking if he's bumping into walls because he can't see through his hair. Ask him with genuine curiosity what's behind the change. If he shrugs you off, don't hound him about it. But see the dress choice as an invitation to really look at him and think about what message he's trying to send. As is often the case in this book, I'm not telling you about this aspect of Boy World so that you will talk to your son about it. The goal is to understand and know your son better, and you're probably not going to get there by having a heart-to-heart talk with him about how he feels about his body. The best thing for him is to see men he respects presenting themselves outside the ALMB, have meaningful friendships with those men, or, at least, not insulting men who have made that choice.

What If Your Son Is Way Out There?

Parents can really struggle when their son doesn't fit into our culture's rules for what a boy should look like. An unusual appearance can be a lot harder for people to deal with than a boy's sexual orientation. Our culture wants boys looking and acting like boys the same way it wants girls looking and acting like girls. But however he chooses to present himself, you have to respect his decision. That's what feels true to him. If you disapprove of it, he's going to believe you're ashamed of who he is. I know this can be hard. It can feel like everyone is looking at your kid and making judgments about him. It can feel like you don't have anything in common with him. But you do. You love each other.

Puberty

Imagine you're a thirteen-year-old boy and you're looking in the mirror. First, you look at yourself to see how you're developing. Second, you figure out how to cover whatever part of your body embarrasses you, like the weird length of your arms or the skinniness of your legs (remember G.I. Joe). Third, you size up how your style matches that of your friends. So as you cover up whatever seems unacceptable or embarrassing, you have to do it in a way your group thinks is cool. Now you have finally arrived at your "personal" style—which of course has been determined for you by your peers and culture.

Too Early

I got facial hair really early. Like by seventh grade I was shaving, and I got so much crap for it from the other guys. I hated it. —Cody, 17

Developing earlier than his male peers has consequences. Within his age group, his size and physical maturity may empower him to dominate his peers and decide who gets game controllers or where they ride their bikes—which I know doesn't seem like a big deal but it is to boys. When he interacts with adults, they may struggle to remember how old he actually is and treat him as a young man instead of a boy.

He may get attention from girls, especially older girls. Then he has two choices: run away or hang out with the girls, which will inevitably inflate his ego. He's either going to like the attention or he'll withdraw, hunch his shoulders, and try to appear smaller than he is.* He's also likely to be in positions of trying to hold his own with those boys, which may lead him to say things he doesn't necessarily believe or do things he doesn't want to do. So here's what you can say, depending on how he's dealing with the situation:

He's getting a big head.

Okay, I'm going to keep this short. We both know you look older than you are. Sometimes older girls will pay attention to you more because of that. It can be very flattering, but it also can be overwhelming, so remember that you never have to do anything you

---

*This is similar to the girls who developed early. They either love the attention and feed off of it or hide in big sweatshirts.

don't want to do. And if you get a big head because of all the atten-
tion, you know I'm going to have something to say about that.

He's hunching over.

You know the other guys are going to catch up to you, right? I know
it can feel a little weird to be taller than the other guys and you don't
have to talk about it if you don't want, but if you do, I'm here (or: Do
you know Uncle John went through a similar experience?).

Too Late

Boys don't think they've really gone through puberty until other
people can see the physical signs. If a boy is really short or developing much later than his peers, he may feel like he has to fight to be
taken seriously. Girls will often treat him like a pet, which he will
understandably hate. Consequently, he may look for other paths to
social power by being socially aggressive and dominating his other
friends and/or projecting the toughest image he can.

DO YOU EVER TALK TO HIM ABOUT ANY OF THIS?

Yes and no. He's probably embarrassed that you've noticed. Remember, you have the luxury of taking the long-term view since you've
gone through puberty. You know it eventually happens. He's not
sure. He may be worrying that he'll have some weird condition.
He probably won't tell you if he's worried that he's developing too
quickly or too slowly, so you should also never tease him or comment on his body, and you have to stop your other children from
teasing him as well.

If he's upset, he's not going to come out and say something; he'll
do the things I describe in the parenting-communication chapter.
Don't say, *It's okay. You'll get through it. It happens to everyone.* Instead, wrap it into the more general conversation I suggested. *You*

know it's really common for guys to tease each other so much that sometimes it goes over the line. So if that ever happens to you, you know you can talk to me. Or if you don't want to talk to me, let's think of someone that you would like to talk to.

If it becomes clear that he's really upset about his physical development, then you can say, *I'm really sorry. You will get through this. But it's still really annoying while you're going through it. You know I'm always here to talk if you want to.* Then don't stand around waiting for him to say something. Instead, immediately do something else to lessen his discomfort, like turn on the TV or tell him you're getting something to drink/eat and ask if he wants anything.

Hygiene

Boys need to be clean. Not only is it polite, it's healthy.

My boys started to smell bad around age seven. Five years later, their feet alone are so powerful that they make a car uninhabitable in minutes (and that doesn't even take into account the deliberate farting). As soon as you think your child may be starting puberty, buy him some deodorant and leave it in his bathroom. Don't talk about it, just leave it there. If he starts to break out, go get him some skin cleanser, leave it in the bathroom, and text him the following:

> *Hey, I left some stuff for you in the bathroom. If you don't like it or it's not working for you let me know.*

Too much cologne

When my son comes downstairs in the morning, I swear I think he's trying to poison us. That or he has no sense of smell. He even bathed the dog in it once. —Diana

This problem usually afflicts middle school boys the worst. In high school, girls tell boys to stop bathing in it, and that usually does the trick. But if you can't breathe when he passes you in the morning, tell him. Dads, this is your time to shine. Drag him into the bathroom and show him how much is an appropriate amount to use. As in, a small dab on the neck should suffice.

As you can see, there will be countless times when we need to talk with our boys about embarrassing and awkward topics. Even when we're talking about the most everyday subjects, boys can be really tricky to communicate with. If boys are going to listen to us, respect us, and come to us for guidance, we have to examine our interactions with them and what we think we know about them. The biggest hurdle you and I have with boys is convincing them that pulling back the curtain on Boy World isn't a waste of time and won't make their lives worse. If you want a meaningful and positive relationship with your son and you want him to listen to you, you have to really examine yourself. That's not easy, so it's what we'll discuss next.

5

Breaking Through the Wall

We have to build up this mental wall between us and the world or else we would go crazy. Every guy puts on this persona, especially toward his parents and people they don't really know. —Rafael, 17

Anything lower than a scream and my teen interprets my requests, demands, and decisions as merely a "suggestion." —Alicia

You know from the way he opens the car door. He's in a foul mood. So you ask him what any loving parent would: "Is everything okay?" Followed by the equally understandable question: "Do you want to talk about it?" To which he mumbles, "No, I'm good." If you press him, he responds by looking away, reclining the seat, and zoning out.

You know how parents say to their kids, "Life's not fair"? Well, let's apply that here. Parenting boys isn't fair. When your son is upset or angry, it can feel like you're given one chance with very limited information to say exactly the right thing. If you don't get it right, his expression says, *This is why I never tell you anything. And now I will never tell you anything again.*

Your chances of getting it right are about on par with winning the Powerball lottery. Except it's worse. When you play the lottery, you're only out a couple of dollars, and no one makes you feel stupid for not picking the right numbers. But when you don't get the "numbers" right with a boy, not only do you often feel incompetent, but the stakes are higher because there's a possibility he really does need guidance and comfort.

In this chapter, I'll give you general strategies to help you see your son more clearly. Once you can do that, you can communicate more effectively with him and translate what his words and body language mean. But before I get boys to share the when, how, and why of talking to you, let's run down the reasons he doesn't.

1. He believes that, at best, talking to you won't make a difference and will probably make the situation worse.
2. He doesn't want you to get angry with him.
3. He doesn't want you getting angry with the person he's having a problem with because then you won't let him hang out with that person anymore or he'll have to hide from you the fact that he is.
4. He doesn't want you to think he has bad judgment.
5. He doesn't want to hear the reasons you think he has bad judgment.
6. He doesn't want to get into trouble.
7. He doesn't want you to worry.
8. He doesn't want you to become involved and cause him public humiliation.
9. He doesn't want you to react by taking over and therefore taking away his ability to solve the problem on his own.
10. He doesn't want you taking away his technology.
11. Don't *you* avoid conflict whenever possible?

After reading this list, it would be reasonable to think there's no point in trying to have honest communication with your son because he'll always have a perfectly logical reason in his mind why telling you anything remotely difficult or embarrassing is a very bad idea. We have to convince boys that while we don't need to know every detail of their personal lives, it's not an entirely terrible idea to let us in once in a while. In fact, there's always a possibility that we can help. But here's the problem. The boys have good reasons to shut us out, and unfortunately, those reasons are reflected back to us when we look in the mirror.

While it's true that overall we want to emotionally connect with them, in our daily interaction with them we often don't come across that way. We don't see them. We don't take the time to really look at this person in our presence. We force bonding moments, micromanage, judge, assume, lecture, or try to control. Ironically, as our boys push us away, what they want most is for us to recognize and acknowledge them. They just don't have any idea how to ask for what they want. Even if they did, they often fear that we'll shut them down.

First, let's look at one of the classic dynamics between children and their parents. It's the "You're embarrassing me!" complaint. It's more than fine to "embarrass" your son in a good way. As in, you demand that he recognize your feelings, you role-model how to treat people with dignity when it's hard and how to show emotion in a healthy way, you respectfully speak out when he'd rather you keep your opinions to yourself, and you're comfortable with making a fool of yourself.

HOW TO EMBARRASS A BOY

Examples of "Good" Embarrassment
1. Singing along to the radio (including when you drive carpool)
2. Giving him a hug or kiss when you see him in public
3. Brushing your fingers through his hair to get it out of his eyes
4. Apologizing on his behalf when he's being a butt-head
5. Signing up to be a chaperone at his school dance and then enforcing the rules

Have you seen the sixth Harry Potter *movie? Remember that part in the cave when the hand reaches out of the water and drags Harry in? My mom screamed at the top of her lungs in the middle of the crowded theater. A friend was with us in the theater, and she thought the scream was part of the movie, not something emanating from my mom's mouth. I also hate going to athletic events with my mom because she always screams at the top of her lungs. I try to ignore her, but that seems to make her more passionate. —Brian T.S., 16*

But these are not the only ways we embarrass our kids, and this is where it starts getting a lot harder for us. Sometimes we lose sight of how we're coming across and blow off our children's complaints because they seem to be embarrassed by everything we do. While it's hard to admit, our kids have the right to be angry and embarrassed if we discuss aspects of their lives that they consider personal. They don't want to be labeled and dismissed as moody teens. They want you to respect their privacy, and that means treating them respectfully in public. Here are the ways parents embarrass their kids, and if you see it from their perspective, I think you'll agree . . . they have every reason to deny knowing us.

Introducing Your Child by His Deficits

Imagine if your kid introduced you by saying, "This is my mother, Rosalind. She's really shy." Is it any wonder that the fifteen-year-old boy whose mother recently introduced him to me like this ran into his room? Yes, he might be shy, but what else would anyone in his place want to do? After you teach him how to introduce himself, it's up to him to say his name and create his own image.

Oversharing

"It's amazing how early puberty starts these days! He's breaking out everywhere!"

You shouldn't be talking to people about your child's physical development, the latest fight you got into with him, or his latest accomplishment or failure as if it's a part of his identity. ("Hi, this is

my son John. His team just won state. We're just so proud of him.")
This includes people in the grocery checkout line, people at parties,
strangers you strike up a conversation with, or even good friends if
your child is around. When you're having a problem that you really
want to talk to another adult about, do it privately—away from your
child. Remember, it's up to him to introduce himself.

If you're guilty of any of the above, go to your child and say, "I've
realized that sometimes I talk for you and don't give you the opportunity to speak for yourself. From now on, I'm going to really try to
stop myself. But if I don't, I want you to say politely, 'Mom/Dad, it's
okay. I've got it.' I promise I'll stop. If I overshare, you can politely
tell me to stop, and I will."

I know we all fall back on talking about our kids, but can we try
to give it a rest? Do you have any hobbies? Are you doing anything
interesting? You have your own life separate from your children, and
there's nothing wrong with talking about that. It's actually pretty
cool. And it's really good for your child to have interesting parents
with their own interests and passions.

"Having a Moment"

Have you ever temporarily lost your mind and succumbed to being
an anxious or overinvolved, self-righteous mess of a parent? Honestly, I haven't met a parent who at some point hasn't done this. The
key is recognizing when you're "having a moment" and changing
it up.

Examples of "Having a Moment"
1. Yelling obscenities during a game at anyone on the field or in
   the bleachers
2. Gossiping about other children
3. Approaching another parent, coach, teacher, camp counselor,
   or school administrator and immediately launching into the
   problem you need to discuss without saying hello or giving
   them any kind of introduction to what you need to discuss

(I've done this, only to stop myself mid-rant, pause, and say, "Wait, I'm sorry. Can I start that again? Good morning! Can I talk to you for a minute?")

OF COURSE, THIS GOES BOTH WAYS

As much as we might embarrass our boys from time to time, the painful truth (which not everyone wants to admit) is that sometimes *they* embarrass *us*. There's the "good" kind of embarrassment, like when they are really goofy in public and we think everyone notices. But there's also the "bad" kind, when they display such terrible manners or poor understanding of courtesy that we don't even really want to admit we know them. Just as boys have the right to expect parents not to act in inappropriate ways that humiliate them, parents have the right to expect their sons to uphold certain values, including basic courtesy. Yes, our children really do need the space to create their own image. But we still have to teach them the fundamental skills to make a good impression. I'm sure you'll have your own ideas about what those are, but the following three are the ones I consider a good foundation for ensuring that your son knows how to act in a way that *won't* leave you humiliated and apologetic for his behavior.

Greetings

When he's around five to seven, teach your son how to shake hands, make eye contact, and say the basics in social situations, such as, *Nice to meet you. Thank you for inviting me. Good-bye and thanks for having me.* First role-play it with him between five and ten times at home. Then the first few times you're going somewhere, explain to him that you'll do it first and then he'll follow. If he's feeling shy, that's okay. Any part he does is a success and will make you proud of him. If he falters, don't make excuses for him with the other person. Afterward, praise him for a small thing he did successfully and then role-play three times what he can do better next time. When you congratulate him, he'll be proud that he was being mature. By the time he's ten, he should be able to do it himself. You'll still have to remind him a few hundred times, but the building blocks will be there.

Holding Doors

Yes, this is a "gentlemanly" thing to do, but it's the right thing to do regardless of gender. It's also a good exercise in remembering that your child exists with other people. Boys move fast. They can move so fast that they literally don't see the people around them. Our job as parents is to condition them to the point that when they see a door, they automatically slow themselves down.

This is important not only for the sake of politeness but also for other people's safety. I'll never forget waiting for my boys to come out of a community center when they raced by a woman who must have been eighty years old. Not only did they rush by her, they didn't keep the door open for her. Just closed it in her face. I calmly walked over to them (okay, that's a lie, I was highly annoyed) and explained what they had done. They hadn't noticed her at all. I couldn't find the woman to have them apologize to her, but I did make them open and hold the door for the next ten minutes for everyone who was coming through that door.

Giving Up Seats

Your son should offer his seat to anyone who looks like they may need to sit down more than he does. This could be on a bus, at a party or school function, or anywhere else people gather. Since he may have difficulty determining whom he should yield his seat to, you'll probably have to prompt him, but obviously the starting guidelines are the elderly, pregnant women, and people with small children and/or large packages.

WHY DO WE WANT TO TALK TO OUR BOYS
SO MUCH ANYWAY?

I try to open the lines of communication, but I keep feeling like I'm actually slamming the doors shut. I want him to open up. So then I try to come up with other questions because maybe I haven't asked him in the right way, but that doesn't work either. —James

James isn't alone. So many dads (and moms) have shared similar feelings with me. It's also entirely reasonable to want to communicate with your son—to be able to exchange information in a way that makes both of you feel good for having engaged in the conversation. It's really not too much to ask to be filled in on some details about your son's life. Any details. You have no intention of wanting to know everything, but a few scraps would be great. We need to be honest, though. We have a lot of communication agendas beyond wanting to have feel-good conversations with our boys or help them when they've had a bad day. In general, there are four common parenting-communication agendas.

1. Genuine curiosity—we want to know what's going on in their lives.
2. We want them to pay attention when we need them to do something.
3. We're worried, and we want them to talk to us.
4. We believe they're about to do something stupid, wrong, or dangerous. Or they've already done something stupid, wrong, or dangerous. Either way, we need to know what's up to minimize the damage and/or hold them accountable.

All of these agendas intertwine to impact our relationship with our boys. Our seemingly inconsequential daily conversations matter. They're the foundation of our relationships. If we can't listen to each other in the small moments, we'll never listen to each other in the big ones.

I define listening as being prepared to be changed by what you hear. If you want a good relationship with your son, you have to listen to him and respect his world. While his overall concerns and challenges are largely the same as when you were his age, he's really living in a different world than you did. You lived in a time when you had the luxury of making the common mistakes we all made as teens in relative privacy. He doesn't. When you were a teen, your most embarrassing and humiliating moments weren't up for public discussion and used to entertain everyone you knew. Take a second and remember the moment when you were his age that you'd never want anyone to know about. There's no protection. There's no privacy. This is his regular, ever-present reality. This isn't necessarily a bad thing; it just means that your son is growing up with a different definition of what's public and what's private.

LANDMINE!

Stay away from comments like, "You don't realize how easy you have it. All you have to do is go to school and hang out with your friends." No kid hears this and feels better about his life or believes that this comment is helpful or relevant.

Agenda 1: You Just Want to Know What's Up with Him

No matter what the situation, if there's one thing all the boy editors want to make sure you understand from reading this book, it's this: when parents barrage their son with a torrent of questions at first sight, he'll completely tune out and answer with the most noninformative answers he can think of in the hope that they'll give up and stop. It doesn't matter where the boys come from, whether they're wealthy or poor, whether they go to public, private, or parochial school, whether they're twelve or eighteen, what ethnicity or religion they are—they all jump up and start imitating their parents the moment the subject comes up. To witness the fervor that comes over all boys when one boy describes his personal experience is like watching a religious sermon with people spontaneously getting to their feet proclaiming, "Amen, brother! The man speaks the truth!"

Believe me, I've repeatedly explained to boys that parents usually have the best of intentions. We love them and therefore want to know what's going on in their lives. We also believe that knowing the details of their daily lives will strengthen our relationship. But here's what the boys have explained to me. As soon as we see them the questions begin. Whether it's when we pick them up from school or after practice or when we walk into the house from work, our questions feel like a physical assault.

> *The first thing my mom says to me every day after school is, "Tell me five things that happened at school today." Five. She exhausts me.*
> *—Jake, 16*

Honestly, can you remember five specific things you did today? When Jake can't come up with five things, it comes across as if he's withholding information from his mom, which simultaneously makes him feel annoyed and bad because he doesn't want to hurt her feelings.

Here's how I want you to approach the challenge of finding out about a boy's day: take a step back. When he's at school, he's part of a complicated social dynamic with many different kinds of people. He's interacting with Masterminds, Bouncers, people he has crushes on, people he hates, authority figures who wield their power with varying degrees of professionalism, all while keeping up with his academics and extracurricular activities. Even on the best of days, dealing with all of this can be emotionally and physically exhausting. To get through it, your son develops his own personal brand of armor and wears it throughout the day.

When your son gets into your car, the last thing he wants to do is have an intense conversation. He wants to unwind and decompress.

He may not want to think, talk, or do anything but listen to music and stare out the window. I'm not saying he gets to be rude to you in response to your well-meaning inquiries. Nor does he get to play video games, text, or keep his earbuds in the whole time either. I just want you to see it from his perspective so it's easier for you all to enjoy each other's company and create the environment where pleasant, even meaningful conversation is possible.

Your goal is to make the first few minutes stress-free. If you do this, he'll be much more likely to tell you about how his day was on his own. Try asking no questions when you see him.* Let him choose the music—within reason, of course. I'm not saying you have to put up with music that gives you a headache or offends you. If he hasn't said anything for a few minutes, you can use Walter's suggestion:

> *I would probably respond best if she asked me something that could be answered in a short time, but be just as good for her to hear about. An example would be "Okay—best and worst parts of your day in sixty seconds! Go!" It makes the mood more engaging, and I would be more interested in her being interested if it didn't seem like the same classic "how was your day," because, in my mind anyway, repetition equals disinterest. —Walter, 14*

The Most Common and Futile Parent Questions

1. *Seeing your son right after school:* "How was your day? What did you learn? Anything interesting?" "Did you get into trouble?"

2. *Picking up/seeing your son after practice:* "How was practice? What did you do? Was it hard? Did you score? Did you win? Did you try your best?"

3. *Picking up your son at a party (elementary through middle school):* "What did you do? Did you have fun? Did you have a good time? Who else was there?"

---

*You can ask him one time if he's hungry. One time. Not three times. One time.

4. *Picking up or seeing your son after a party (high school):* "Who was there? Were the parents home? Did you talk to them? You didn't do anything dumb, did you?"
5. *Seeing your son in general, coming back home at night:* "Where'd you go? What'd you do? Who was there? Was it fun?"

For younger boys, the best time to talk to them is when they're in bed, the lights are out, and you can talk for a few minutes before they go to sleep. For older boys, the best time is also at night. Of course, this is very hard for most parents because we can't keep our eyes open past 9:30 PM and our boys are just getting started. But try to manage once every two weeks to stay up to 10:00 PM and drop by your son's room for a talk.

Parents can also talk to us and ask questions while we're having dinner, but under no circumstances should parents ask about girls then, especially if any brothers or sisters are around. Oh, and don't ask us questions first thing in the morning because I'm terrible in the morning. So right before bed, that's definitely the best time. —Ryan, 18

They Aren't Always Really Sleeping

When I get into the car, I put on my headphones and gradually pretend to fall asleep. I don't want to hurt my mom's feelings, but she can be really intense with all the questions. —Justin, 14

I fake sleeping. That's my main tactic. Every time my mom or dad comes into the house, they both have these voices and I jump. They don't know how to have a normal conversation. Everything is yelling. —Tyler, 14

It's why noise-canceling headphones were invented. —Thomas, 14

When my mom asks embarrassing questions, I pretend she's invisible. —Quentin, 12

If you're looking for ways to connect with your son, the general rule is that it can't feel forced. You want to do something else while you're having the conversation or be fine hanging out with him without carrying on an intense conversation in the first place. Boys really do bond with you by doing things with you (and by the way, this works with girls too). Whether you're a mom or dad, going on a hike or fishing, working on something together, playing basketball, throwing a baseball, driving and listening to music, or just hanging out in the same room reading can all be very meaningful bonding moments without a lot of words exchanged. Don't be afraid of silence. With all the noise we get from TV, phones, and everything else, we can all forget how great silence is.

Plus, remember, if your son is too young to drive, you're probably his key to accessing the things he loves. Say he isn't into cartoons, but he likes to build airplane models. Offer to take him to one of the best model stores around. You don't have to have some intense conversation on the way there or back. Just taking him there is appreciated—and you don't need to buy him anything.

If you've never done something like this before, or if you're trying to reconnect after there's been some distance or hostility between you, you have to be prepared for some serious push-back. For example, you tell him about a comic book convention coming to your area and suggest that you could go together. He responds with, "Whatever," as if he has no interest in comic books and that's a totally stupid idea even though he has four thousand graphic novels and comic books in his room. Or he may be more aggressive and say something like "Why do you care all of a sudden? I'm not going on some bonding trip" or "Why would I want to go with you when I can go with my friends?"

Who could blame you for giving up on the whole thing because you think your kid's never going to give you a break? But as hard as it is to feel this kind of rejection, you can't shut down yourself. Reengage with him instead: "I'm not asking you to hang out with me and tell me all your feelings. I think it'd be cool to learn what you know. You don't have to tell me now, but let's talk about it later."

If your son doesn't want to hang out with you as he used to, that can also feel like a deeply painful rejection. But you get to request that you spend time with him. Try to stay away from using the phrase "spending time together." As in, "I'd just like to spend some time together" or "We should spend some time together" or, even worse, "I feel like I don't see you enough anymore." Instead, ask, "Do you want to go to lunch?" Lunch has a definite beginning and end. Plus, you're feeding him. If you have an older teen, lunch is good because it's not at night, so there's no chance it'll interfere with any of his social plans. If you do ask him if he wants to do something at night and he responds with, "I don't know, it depends on what's going on," don't take it personally. He's suffering from FOMO—Fear Of Missing Out. That's not an acceptable excuse for him to bail on previous obligations, but I just want you to realize his motivation.

If you take this advice and try several times to "spontaneously" get your kid to do something and he always says no, then you have to switch your strategy: "You always seem too busy to do something together, so let's plan something." If he keeps pushing you away, then you're within your rights to sit him down and ask what's up.

How to Stop the Eye-Rolling

If your son excels in the art of eye-rolling or sighing, this may be annoying to you. Here's my suggestion for addressing the problem. At base, your son wants something from you—either he wants to do something or he wants you to appreciate his opinion. This is what you say:

"Miles, here's the deal. You want (X) from me. When you roll your eyes and sigh when I'm speaking, there's no chance you'll get what you want out of me because your behavior is so irritating. But if we can have this conversation without eye-rolling, there's a chance we can come to some kind of agreement. Eye-rolling, you have no chance. No eye-rolling, you have a shot. So excuse yourself, think about what I've said, and when you're ready, we can have the conversation again."

Of course, sometimes the eye-rolling happens, not when they're coming to you with a favor to ask, but when you want them to do something. Teenage boys are masters of making your requests seem like Herculean labor. As long as they aren't overtly rude and they're doing what you tell them, ignore the eye-rolls and foot-dragging. As annoying as it is, they're generally just trying to goad you into an argument as a way to avoid doing what they have to do. If they really want to discuss it with you, schedule the argument for after they complete your request. I do it all the time with my sons. I schedule arguments for later in the day because it always seems like these fights happen when they haven't done their chores or we need to leave the house.

Agenda 2: You Need for Him to Pay Attention

Now let's move on to a scenario where you go from being in a great mood to a highly irritated one—the moment when you walk through the door and see him becoming one with the couch. I know how irritating it is to come home from a long day of work or to walk in the door weighed down with bags of groceries to see your son's eyes glued to the TV. Seriously, wouldn't any decent person in your son's place leap off the couch to help you? What kind of horrible child have you raised? Does he want you to yell at him and be in a foul mood? Apparently he does, because he doesn't move. You look at the dog who is desperate to be walked, the trash that obviously needs to be taken out, his dirty socks on the floor next to his nasty shoes that you can smell from the front door, and it appears as if you don't exist. Of course you get annoyed and think he's a spoiled, ungrateful, lazy brat. So you start shooting questions at him like "Have done your homework?," "How was your test today?," "Did you bring in that form you've forgotten three times already for the field trip next week?," using the "I'm so annoyed that I should get a parenting prize for not hitting you on the back of the head right now" tone of voice.

As hard as this is (and I admit it's very hard), I'm asking that you think of the situation from his perspective:

Imagine you come home every day from work and I bombarded you with questions as soon as I saw you. Like . . . "What did you get done at work? Do you have more to do? Do you have more emails you need to look at? Were people nice to you at the office? Isn't that big project due tomorrow?" All you want to do is sit on the sofa, watch TV, and chill out, but you can't. It's exactly the same with us. —Luke, 16

My mom calls me nonstop. "Dion, do this," "Dion, do that." I do it. I'm thinking I'm done so I sit down, and then she calls me again. So I ask her, "Why couldn't you have asked me to do that too when I was up?" You know what she says? "Because I wasn't thinking about it then. Now I am." —Dion, 16

Let's take a step back and examine the situation. You don't need to know anything about your son's school obligations right now. You need his butt off the couch, helping with the grocery bags. You need the poor dog walked. In moments like these, humor and action are essential. You can start by walking over and putting the grocery bags on his lap. Or tell him his choice is either to walk the dog or clean up the rug after the dog has had an accident on the carpet. What you absolutely shouldn't do is use the martyr strategy. It's passive-aggressive, you'll get resentful, and all he'll think is that you're annoying. Even if you get him to take in the grocery bags, this strategy hurts you in the long run because your son will lose respect for you. If you lose his respect, you can't be a credible authority figure to him. So drop the bags in his lap and take a few minutes to unwind from your day before you make dinner, look at homework, fold laundry (with his help), and collapse.

Chores to Power Wars

Do these conversations sound familiar?

DAD: Did you put out the trash?
SON: Yes, I did.

DAD: Is the lid on the trash can?
SON: Yes.
DAD: Is it on the right side of the driveway? Is it off the curb?
SON: Yes. It's fine.
DAD: Did you mow the lawn?
SON: I'm getting to it.
DAD: Really? Have you been getting to it the whole afternoon?
SON: Dad, I said I'd do it.
DAD: Did you weed-whack? Did you wrap the hose the right way? Did you put the gas cap back on when you refilled the mower?
SON: Yeah, Dad, whatever you say.

Like in the car, this conversation often takes place within the first moments of seeing each other. The questions come across as interrogation and cause the boy to shut down and get away from his parent as fast as possible.

Don't get me wrong. Our boys need to pull their weight and develop a sense of responsibility. But we have to ask ourselves if the way we're communicating with our boys is effective.

Listen to seventeen-year-old Mark:

I came home from practice, and I had tons of homework to do. So then my dad tells me to take out the trash. I say fine, but I ask if my brother can help out by taking out the recycling. My dad's response is, "Fine. You can take out the garbage for a month." It's just so stupid. Everything is a power trip with him, and I can't say anything without him doing something to make my life worse.

Taking out the trash is an entirely reasonable request. It's also more than possible that Mark occasionally said to his dad that he'd take care of something and he forgot. It's also possible that Mark and his dad have different definitions of what "soon" or "in a minute" means. Nevertheless, it's also exactly these seemingly small power struggles that undermine a boy's relationship with his parent. Many, many boys respond to these conflicts with anger, frustration, and ultimately resignation because all they hear is that they're lazy, ungrateful, and irresponsible. If we want our children to listen to us, we have to really acknowledge why they don't.

Mark's dad comes across as being disrespectful to his son. A lot of people would disagree with that, believing that, as Mark's dad, he has the right to demand what he wants and say what he likes to his son. Were you raised to respect your elders? If you're having a hard time with how I'm approaching this situation or thinking that I'm coddling Mark, here's another way of looking at it. Respect in Latin means "to look at someone's conduct and admire them." When people say to kids, "Respect your elders," they're often really saying, "Obey your elders." But the amazing thing is that kids inherently know the real meaning of respect, and far too often they see adults who don't merit it—not only public figures, like hypocritical politicians and athletes, but the adults they interact with on a daily basis. This is hard to write, but for some boys it could be one of their parents. It also could be a school administrator, a school resource officer, a teacher, a coach, or a clergyperson. Our children know that they can't depend on adults to do the right thing just because they're adults. All of these experiences contribute to this powerful feeling among young people that there aren't many adults who they can truly respect. I know challenging the inherent respect of one's elders can go against some people's deeply held cultural values. But again, I am challenging you to think about the cost of not admitting when adults don't speak and treat children with dignity. Even if those children look like they're treating those adults with respect, they aren't. They're acting out of fear and powerlessness.

Still not convinced? Think of the worst boss you've ever had. You know the one, that jerk who was just awful to work for. How did he treat you? Did he treat you with respect? Or did he assume that because he was in a position of authority, he could be as disrespectful as he wanted to those under him? I'm guessing he didn't treat you with respect, and I'm also guessing you didn't like it very much. Well, if you didn't like being treated in a disrespectful manner by an authority figure, why would your son feel any differently?

Many boys understandably rebel against this hypocrisy. When this happens with parents, the power struggle can be about anything. Big things or little things. Things the boy can anticipate, things he can't. What usually happens is that he gets angry and bottles up his rage. When he finally explodes he looks immature, and that infuriates him even more because he knows it confirms the negative image his parent has of him. What a boy wants to know is how to formulate an argument and not be accused of talking back; otherwise, he'll end up shutting down.

> There were so many times I clenched my jaw and said, "Believe whatever you want." —Aiden, 20

> If you don't get how angry I am when I'm looking you in the eye, then I have lost all ability to think of you as someone that I trust and respect. The only thing you can do is make my life worse." —Charlie, 24

What's amazing to me about talking to dads and boys is that so many dads seem to have forgotten what it's like to be a boy. They come across as if they believe that boys don't have deep feelings or care deeply about their relationships. What's also so sad about this dynamic is that dads like Mark's, Aiden's, or Charlie's don't usually have any idea how irritating they are or realize that their son stopped listening a long time ago. What's even sadder is that many of these dads really want a good relationship with their sons, but in their efforts to raise a responsible son their disrespect has made their son turn away.

Agenda 3: You're Worried Something's Wrong

In any conversation where your goal is to find out information from a boy, to encourage him to share his thoughts or feelings, or to give him advice, your goal is to demonstrate that you're a nonjudgmental listener (but please note I didn't say non-opinionated), as well as a good resource for advice and comfort when needed. If you can create this foundation, that gets you to the second goal: helping him develop critical thinking skills so that he can come up with realistic strategies to confront his problems effectively. You'll never accomplish the second goal without the first.

Unfortunately, you can't depend on your son to come to you when he's upset. The older he gets, the less he'll want to involve you in his problems (often because he considers you a main source of them). You can't depend on your son to announce that he needs to talk to you. Instead, he may broadcast signals that he wants your help without actually saying it. Here are some signs to watch for:

1. He hangs around where you are but doesn't say anything.
2. He says he doesn't feel well and wants to stay home, but there doesn't seem to be anything physically wrong.
3. You're about to drive somewhere on an errand, and he volunteers to go with you.
4. He asks to watch a show with you.
5. He slips a very casual reference to his problem into the conversation.
6. He begins to revert back to younger behavior.
7. He tries to get other people out of the house except you.

LANDMINE!

If your son does any of these things, don't immediately lean in and intensely ask "What's wrong?" or "What's bothering you?" Just a casual "What's up? Anything you want to tell me?" is good. If they say no, follow it up with "Okay, but if you change your mind, I'm here."

When Your Son Tells You He's Having a Problem with Someone

In general, when a boy tells you he's having a problem with someone, there are a few things I suggest not saying. Unfortunately, they're also the responses that boys hear most often from their parents, teachers, and coaches. I'm going to list the most common ones the boys reported and explain how these often well-intentioned responses come across.

- *"He's jealous of you. He's insecure":* This response is ineffective because there's nothing the boy can do with this information. Even if it's true, that doesn't stop the other kid from making him miserable.
- *"He probably comes from a bad home. You should feel sorry for him":* While it's sad that some kids have really tough home situations, that doesn't give them an excuse to lash out at other kids.
- *"Are you sure? Maybe you took it the wrong way":* Now you're coming across as if you don't believe him or you think he's overly sensitive or overreacting.
- *"Use your words":* How? What words? What happens if the person doesn't listen?
- *"Just ignore it. Walk away":* By the time he comes to you for advice, he's probably been trying to ignore or walk away from the problem, but it hasn't worked. That's why he's coming to you.
- *"Don't let him see that it bothers you":* But what if it does? How long is he supposed to just take it? Forever? Does he ever have the right to let it bother him?
- *"He's not worth your time. Forget about it":* The message is, if he can't forget about it, then he must be weak.
- *"Punch him in the face":* I'll go more into this in chapter 12 on "Frontal Assault," but as tempting as that can be, it's not as simple as fighting it out and it's over. He knows this.

Here's what you say when your son approaches you with a problem:

> *"I'm so sorry that happened."*
> *"Thank you for telling me."*
> *"Let's think about it together."*

You don't have to say these things in this exact order. At some point, just get those concepts across. Also, remember that your son will probably start with generalities or only part of the story to see if you're going to freak out. For example, if he comes to you and says, "These guys are sort of bothering me," the more quietly and casually he says this the more you should pay attention. I'd suggest responding with, "Can you tell me a few specifics? I don't want to make any assumptions."

Boys choose very carefully which adult they're going to talk to and for what reason. Take a moment right now to reflect on who your son has confided in and why you think that is. One thing is certain: boys won't talk to people who they think will patronize them or overreact, no matter how good their intentions may be.

LANDMINE!

Don't say, "Why did you wait so long to tell me?" Even if you have no intention of coming across as accusatory, you probably will. If you really want the answer to that, say something a few hours later like, "Hey, I've been thinking about what you told me and I was wondering: is there a specific reason why you didn't tell me before?"

It's important to allow him to have a wide range of feelings. Moms, if he's feeling so angry that he wants to release his anger by punching a pillow or a punching bag, or going into his room and yelling at the top of his lungs, or playing really loud music, or even playing a violent video game, let him do it. If he punches the wall, that's okay too, as long as he isn't threatening someone else when he's doing it. Plus, after he's calmed down, he can then learn the skill of drywall patching. The bottom line is that a lot of women can be intimidated in the presence of men's anger (with good reason). But at the same time, your son needs a healthy outlet to express his anger without feeling like you think he's a violent, crazy person for having his feelings.

Dads, you also need to allow your son to have a wide range

of feelings, including feeling stuck, frightened, intimidated, and helpless—without you telling him what to do. You must tell him that it's okay to ask for help. I know a lot of dads say that they're cool with these displays of emotion, but check yourself to make sure you're really acting that way in the moment.

When He Says, "Mom, Dad, I'm Going to Tell You Something, but You Have to Promise Me You Won't Do Anything"

Okay, this is one of those times that prove how incredibly confusing parenting is. Common sense would dictate that you want to make that promise because if you don't, your son won't talk to you. If he won't talk to you, then you can't help him. But what if you make that promise and he tells you something you need to do something about? Then you'd be forced to break a promise.

Tell your son that while you'd love to make that promise, you can't because if he or someone else needs help, you may need to tell someone who knows more than you about the problem. But you can promise that, if you involve someone else, you and your son will decide who the best person would be and he'll be the first to know that person is getting involved. In my experience, kids don't stop talking to their parents when their parents make decisions they don't like—as long as they're respected and brought into the process. It's moments like this—when parents show that asking for help from others isn't a weakness but a skill and nothing to be ashamed of— that they're simultaneously the source of comfort and guidance that their son truly needs.

Here's the short list to remember in an emergency. If it's helpful, you can put it in your phone's notes or in your wallet for immediate access.

1. *Is this situation really a crisis?* Is someone going to be hurt or killed if you don't get immediately involved? If not, focus on role-modeling social competency and dignity in the moment.

2. *Strategic timing and location:* Are you and your son in a place and time where he can listen to you and you can listen to him?
3. *Affirm feelings:* Say, "I'm really sorry that happened to you." Ask if he's just venting or actually wants advice.
4. *Don't tell him what you would have done if you were in his situation.*

Be prepared to be changed by what you hear.

Judging

Parents have their good list and bad list. If they can get information from another parent, they will automatically use it to judge one of my friends. —John, 16

My mom is very judgmental. She denies it, but whatever she hears from another parent, she'll believe it. But she doesn't know the kid like I do. Nothing I'm going to say will make a difference to her. So I tell her nothing about my life. —Anthony, 15

Parents communicate with their sons without a word being said. An arched eyebrow or arms crossed, followed by a sigh, clearly indicates your opinion about what your child is doing and who they're doing it with. Before you even realize it, you're asking leading questions and interrogating your son, which only makes him want to get away from you as fast as he can. You can tell if you're doing this because you'll get the noninformative one-word answers that I described at the beginning of this chapter.

If you don't like someone your child is hanging out with, your child probably knows how you feel. He may even agree with you about what you don't like about the kid. But it's also true that there's something about this kid that your child likes. Maybe he's a very loyal friend. Maybe he's really fun to be around. Maybe he has a terrible home life, so your child doesn't excuse his bad behavior but understands the context for it. Since you don't see it and your son isn't telling you, it can be easy to assume that he's blind to what's going on and therefore it's your responsibility as his parent to point it out to him. I guarantee that strategy will backfire, because your son thinks you think he's naive and he knows your judgments are based on not understanding the situation like he does.

It can still be incredibly difficult to keep yourself under control. So how do you do it? First, be honest with yourself about your agenda and goals. For example, suppose that for years your son has had a friend you never liked—in fact, you've never trusted one hair on his gelled head. In the last year or so your son has drifted away from this friend, and you couldn't be happier. But the last three times you've picked him up from school he's been hanging with this kid again. What follows is what the boys tell me they've experienced with their parents.

> You: I've noticed you've been hanging out with Jason more recently?
>
> Your son Toby *(silent for one second)*
>
> You: I just don't want to see you get dragged down again.
>
> Toby: Mom, don't worry about it. *(He takes his phone out of his pocket.)*
>
> You: I'm just worried about you. The last time you went through this, I know you felt really bad about how he treated you. I just wouldn't want you to have that experience again.
>
> Toby *(sighing, refusing to look at you, and starting to play a game on his phone)*: Mom, can you please give it a rest? Jason's fine. You're being paranoid.
>
> You: Honey, I'm your mother. My job is to look out for you. *(You notice he isn't paying attention to you in the least.)* Toby, do you hear me talking to you? *(Nothing. Your voice rises in anger.)* Can you please look at me when I'm talking to you?
>
> Toby *(very slowly raising his eyes to you, giving you a blank, bored expression)*: Mom, I know what you think. I get it. Can you drop it now?

You're now facing the impenetrable wall of your son's emotional and physical disengagement. People think girls are hard. Give me a girl screaming and slamming the door of her room over that detached face any day.

What do you do? If you're a woman, when you see that face it can be very easy to react as if he's like other emotionally detached men you may have struggled through a disagreement with. If you're a man, his response can come across as a challenge to your authority. (That's true if you're a woman too.) At this moment, you have to stop talking. What started out as a genuine attempt on your part to reach out to him about something you have every reason to be worried about has turned into a minefield resulting in the opposite of what you want. He doesn't feel listened to. You don't feel listened to. He doesn't feel respected. You don't feel respected. You want him to listen to you so he doesn't make the same kinds of mistakes you made when you were his age. He wants to get away from you.

Pretty much any parent or person who works with boys is going to have at least one conversation with a boy that goes down like this. But you can change the dynamic in the moment, and at the very least you don't have to make a habit of this kind of conversation. You can change the pattern, but only when you realize that any hope for success in this situation starts with you.

First, you have to admit that your goal is not "finding out what's up," but instead, communicating your mistrust of Jason. You may be absolutely right that Jason is a bad influence, but if you talk to your son like the parent in the conversation above, you'll exacerbate the problem. Your son will now be less likely to tell you anything about Jason, or anyone else for that matter, because you weren't really trying to connect with him. You were leading the conversation to confirm your own suspicions and force him to agree with you. Boys see through this easily and will shut down. Anyone would.

Instead, let go of your agenda and allow your son to take the lead. Here's a suggested script for how this could go down if you've already had the conversation above:

You: Hey, Toby, I'd like to try again with the conversation we had yesterday.

Son: Mom, can we please drop this?

You: Actually, I need to apologize. I thought about what I said, and I realized I wasn't listening to you. Besides the fact that I can't control who you hang out with, maybe there are good reasons you like him again and I need to listen to you about that. So can we try this again?

If you're starting from scratch:

You: Do you mind if I talk to you for a second about Jason?

Son: Mom, I know what you're going to say, so you don't need to say it.

You: Okay, what am I going to say?

Son: You don't trust Jason.

You: Why do you think I'd say that?

Son: Because of what happened last year. You probably think he's like a drug addict now. But it's fine. *(He looks around, desperate for an escape.)*

You: If you want me to leave you alone about this, you're going to have to give me some evidence to back it up. What's Jason doing differently now?

Son: I don't know. It's just better. Do we really have to talk about this? I have a ton more homework to do.

You: Can you tell me a little more specifics to help me understand?

Son *(sighs)*: Okay. . . . He doesn't brag all the time or put me down like he used to.

You: Okay, that makes sense. On the chance that he could slip back into his old habits, have you thought about how you'd handle it if he did?

Son *(sighs again)*: I guess.

You: I just want you to be prepared.

SON: You're really not going to leave me alone about this, are you?

YOU: No.

SON: Mom, you know how annoying this conversation is, right?

YOU: Yes, I do.

Or here's another suggestion, from fifteen-year-old Ethan:

Just as I'm about to leave, she'll say, "Are you sure you should be hanging out with these guys?" So that way I don't forget and it's on my mind right when I see them. She says she trusts me, but sometimes I wonder if that's a lie and she's just saying that to put guilt on me so I won't break her so-called trust. Mothers are very tricky.

Neither of these strategies feels good in the moment. They don't guarantee that your son is going to stop hanging out with this kid you don't like. But you don't have that guarantee anyway. The hard fact is that kids have to develop boundaries with people by going through the process of having those boundaries crossed until it's so annoying or painful that they can see that the cost of being in the friendship is higher than the cost of severing the tie.

LANDMINE!

Be really careful about judging, because sometimes your gut can give way to your biases. For example, have you liked a kid in your son's social circle because he comes from such a nice family? How do you know that? Because he looks nice? Because his family's life looks nice? Because he fits into the ALMB and his parents fit into their respective good parenting boxes? Countless times, after something bad has happened and it looks like one of those "nice kids" was responsible, parents have said to me, "But he comes from such a nice family." Exactly—and that's why he thought he could get away with it.

The Ally

Your son may feel more comfortable talking about some subjects with another adult. Even if you have a great relationship with your son, he may want to turn to someone else sometimes, so please don't take it as a rejection or as a statement that you don't know how to handle your parenting business. I call this person an "Ally." He or she can be a trusted relative (perhaps an older sibling, aunt, or uncle), another parent in the neighborhood, a teacher, a member of the clergy, a coach, or a guidance counselor.

The following is a list of the qualities of a good Ally. If your son goes to someone with these qualities for advice, then he's going to the right person and also showing that he has good relationships with other adults. You should be proud of him for exhibiting good judgment.

A good Ally is:

> *Opinionated but not judgmental*
> *Honest and willing to say things that may be hard for your son*
>   *to hear*
> *Reliable and always ready to set aside time to listen to your son*

There's nothing wrong with you reaching out to an Ally as well. It's probably inevitable that your son will face a situation that's so guaranteed to trigger your specific anxieties that you wouldn't be able to think clearly. If you get to a place where you realize that it's too uncomfortable for your son or the issues he's facing are making you so crazy and anxious that your input is only making the problem worse, go get an Ally to help you. Both you and your son will be grateful.

Whenever you're trying to reach out to your son, here's the overall guide.

- *Don't act like a truth cop:* Don't ask him a million questions right away in an attempt to verify the accuracy of everything he tells you. Don't barrage him with questions about who was there, where were the adults, what did he do, etc. The facts will come out over time, but your son's emotional truth is what is important, and you should support that.

- *Don't force the Hallmark moment:* If you go into a conversation with your son expecting that he'll completely open up to you, thank you for reaching out, and give you a hug, you're setting the bar way too high. The very nature of having the conversation can be so intense for your son that all he can do right afterwards is walk into his room and listen to music.

- *Don't use the slang your son uses:* There's nothing more ridiculous to a teen than an adult who tries to be hip by using teen slang. Slang changes so fast that it's impossible to keep up anyway. Nevertheless, some parents think that if they use it, they'll relate to their son better. Not true. It only looks like you're trying too hard—and there's nothing worse to a teen. If he uses a word you don't understand, ask him to explain it to you. He may laugh at you, but it shows that you're really listening and you want to fully understand what he is describing.

- *Selectively share your own stories from when you were his age:* That means don't start conversations with "When I played football . . . ," "When I was in high school . . . ," or "When I was applying to college . . ." You share something in response to something he's talking to you about.

- *Maintain boundaries by trying to avoid telling him stories about your adult experiences:* Even though the purpose of such storytelling is to empathize ("I know what you've been through because something similar happened to me"), be careful not to preach or make it about yourself.

- *Don't tell him how you would have handled the situation unless he asks you:* You're different from him. Maybe you're extroverted, or you've developed the skills to advocate for yourself, while he's more introverted. If he shares something with you and you respond with "You should have . . ." or "Why didn't you . . . ," you're coming across as telling him that whatever he did wasn't good enough.

- *Don't say things that only increase his anxiety:* For instance, avoid saying things like "Whatever you do now will affect the rest of your life" or "This is your future we're talking about." Boys already feel this pressure.

- *Stop trying to fix the problem:* Sometimes your son just wants to voice his concerns about something and isn't looking to fix it right away. Ask him, "Are you telling me because you want to get it off your chest, or do you want advice? You can always change your mind, but I just want to be clear about what you want right now." If you don't know if you're the "fixer" kind of person, ask your spouse or your siblings. And don't argue with them if they say you're the fixer.

- *If he asks for advice, don't turn it around and say, "What would you like me to say? What do you think is best?":* Yes, you want your child to think through his problems, but when he actually asks you what you think, he really is asking you. He wants you to be the adult and tell him what you think.

- *Give him ownership of what he does (both good and bad) and let him make mistakes:* Unless he's going to do something that will hurt himself or others, the fact that it's his idea means that he's working toward independence. Encouraging that is more important than making sure he tries the best (i.e., your) solution.

- *Remember to accept silence:* You're his parent. This means that when you discuss difficult or uncomfortable topics with your son, he may not respond right away. Don't think you always need to fill the silence. You can ask him about it after a while by saying, "You got really quiet when we talked about (X). Why was that?"

- *Don't make fun of his problems:* You may be tempted to make fun of the situation in a well-meaning attempt to make him realize that his problem isn't the end of the world. If you do, you will look like you're mocking him. Keep the joking comments to yourself and substitute supportive questions. Dads—pay attention to this. There's a fine line between good teasing here and making him feel that it was a stupid idea to confide in you.

Agenda 4: He's Done Something Wrong and You Need to Find Out What Happened

We're now in really tricky territory—especially if your child is socially intelligent, highly verbal, and persistent and has a good memory. Obviously, having these attributes is helpful for anyone's future success, but when you're dealing with a boy who has them, it's understandable if sometimes you wish he weren't so smart and determined. I remember that when I first had the idea of writing this book, I kept telling people I knew that boys are smarter than we give them credit for and that they're just as calculating as girls, and people would laugh and make comments like, "Boys can't even tie their shoes without help!" Here's the thing. Boys don't care about tying their shoes, but most of them really, really care about keeping us clueless about what they're doing, when they're doing it, and who they're doing it with.

Boys are frighteningly good at being confusing, charming, distracting, and even intimidating to get adults to back off—most notably their mothers. But before you read about all this, I want you to stop reading. Seriously, this has been a long chapter, and I want you fresh and ready for listening to the boys tell you what they lie to you about and why. So put the book down and go get a cup of coffee, pour a glass of wine, or walk the dog. When you're ready, come on back and I'll be right here.

6

Lying and Reconnaissance

We lie about if we like someone, what we did last night, and how we really feel all the time. It's ridiculous. —Daniel, 13

Guys lie about all kinds of stuff. School, friends, family, you name it. Maybe it is because there is an excitement. You're living an alter ego, another person. Also, another thing is that most of the time guys feel, in some way, invulnerable. As a result, there is a level of "what can she do about it" and "they won't know." Unfortunately, the phrase "look before you jump" is lost on our collective mind. Being a guy is like being at an amusement park: you go and do stupid stuff, and you laugh no matter how scared [you] are. —Michael, 16

It's a common thing for boys to lie, even more than girls if we are talking about boys to parents. It's because boys do much dumber things than girls, and they don't want their parents to know. —Max, 15

We are living in a world where the entire concept of honesty and truth is under cultural assault. We've come to expect that people in leadership positions within our financial and political institutions will bend the truth. The distinction between spinning, twisting the truth, and outright lying has been blurred.

"Teaching my son to be honest is incredibly important to me. It's our most important family value. He's an honest kid," the mother said emphatically as she sat down next to me. I've heard variations on this statement, spoken just as passionately, from parents all over the country. She told me this in preparation for a *Dateline TV* shoot I was working on about children and cheating. When I sat next to her a few minutes later, squirming in my seat as I watched her son cheat and lie on hidden cameras, it was a unique experience for me. As a teacher, I've known that children and teens lie way more often than their parents believe. But I'd never witnessed a parent's conviction about her child's honesty shattered in front of her.

This mother was not unusual; in fact, she was in the majority of parents. Most parents understandably define honesty as a virtue, connect it to their family values, and communicate this belief system to their children—with the expectation that their children won't lie. But most children and teens do lie. According to one of my absolute favorite parenting books of all time, *NurtureShock* by Po Bronson and Ashley Merryman, although parents list honesty as the trait they most want to see in their children, studies show that 96 percent of kids lie to their parents. If you're now assuring yourself that your child is part of that 4 percent, check yourself and let go of your certainty. By the way, no researchers seem to have ever asked about the percentage of parents who lie to their kids. I've lied to my sons, and each time I've done it I've had a very good reason for deceiving them. From our children's perspective, they're lying to us for the same reason we lie to them. Because they think they have a very good reason.

Getting a handle on why boys lie can be difficult because we usually assume either that our own son won't lie to us if we have a good relationship with him and "he's a good kid" or the opposite—that he is always lying to us and can't be trusted. Either of these assumptions has a profound impact on your relationship with your son— and an even larger impact on his motivation to believe in being honest and therefore developing a personal standard of honesty and integrity. This is complicated, to say the least. So keep these things in mind:

- *To be a good liar, you must be socially intelligent, highly verbal, and able to control "leakage" (the inconsistencies that reveal the lie).* The Mastermind, Associate, and Entertainer have the easiest time lying. The Bouncer and the Fly can try to lie, but they'll make mistakes. The Conscience, Punching Bag, and Champion can lie to you but usually will be too nervous to try, or they'll lie and then admit it.
- *Different lies need different responses.* For example, lying to cover up unethical behavior is completely different from lying when a child feels overwhelmed.
- *Don't take your son's lies personally.* If you do take his lies personally, your anger, embarrassment, and frustration will stop you from teaching him that being truthful is worthwhile and you will teach him instead to hide and deceive more.
- *Boys lie to their parents about completely different things than what they lie to their peers about.* This may sound obvious, but when a boy is caught lying to his peers, his parents can have a hard time believing it when the behavior sounds so different from what they know of their son.

Let's first look at one of the most common and completely understandable things parents say to their kids: "If you make a mistake (or do something wrong), I'd rather you be honest with me than lie about it." When parents say this, they're appealing to their son's sense of honor in relation to the family's moral code and correctly communicating that lying after you've done something wrong makes the situation worse. For some boys, this strategy works. But for the vast majority I work with, it doesn't—at least not in the moment when they make the decision to deceive. Why?

If you look at it from the boy's perspective, you can see the answer. The rewards for being truthful—his parents are happy with him, and he gains the personal satisfaction that comes from being an honest person—are abstract and long-term. In contrast, the rewards for lying are concrete and immediate.

For example, your son just broke a neighbor's window. Here's his thinking: *If I tell the truth, my parents are going to be mad, they're going to force me to have a conversation about why I did it, and they may make me fix the problem. If I lie, I don't have to have a stressful conversation with my parents, and there's no chance I'll have to pay for the window out of my allowance or that Mom or Dad will make me go over to the weird neighbor's house to apologize.*

In parents' minds, when we say, "Just tell me, you won't get in trouble," we aren't defining trouble the way our boys do. Talking to parents and having them be disappointed in you and then talking to the weird neighbor is all under the umbrella of how a boy defines trouble. If you see it this way, taking the chance that lying will allow him to avoid the whole situation begins to make sense.

> It's just taking a gamble. If I get caught, I still get punished or have to clean up, skip dessert, or whatever else is the consequence. But if I'm successful in lying to my mom, then I can avoid any consequence. —Lee, 12

I'm not saying that your child is a dishonest person, even when he lies about breaking the window. I'm not saying he has poor character—remember, 96 percent of kids lie, but that doesn't mean they're all somehow bad people. It's critical to understand the various reasons why boys lie so that, without excusing it, you can respond effectively when your son lies and he'll be more likely to learn that the future benefits of being honest outweigh the immediate benefits of avoiding trouble in all its forms. And importantly, what I have realized through talking with boys is that how we respond when they lie or when we falsely accuse them is a direct reflection of how healthy our relationship with them is, both now and for the future. Here are the real issues: Do they know what we stand for? And how seriously do they take us?

> Lying in my eyes is the easy way out of things, and in fact it usually works, but then again, lying gives you guilt and can be hard to get over if you're the only one that knows the real truth. —Gabe, 14

CHECK YOUR BAGGAGE

What was the biggest lie you told to your parents when you were young? Why did you lie? Did they find out?

Has your child ever seen you lie? I don't mean lying about how good the chicken was at your in-laws' house when it tasted like leather. You know what I'm talking about.

Have you ever lied *for* your child?

HOW CAN YOU TELL WHEN HE'S LYING?

Some parents believe they have the magical power to look their son in the eye and make the truth spill out of him using their stern, unflinching parental lie detector. But a good liar can pass this test easily. A good liar is cool and collected and continues to hold his ground no matter what.

A good lie is always told calm. I maintain eye contact. —Seth, 15

The truth is, parents often can't tell when their children lie. They just think they can. Worse, kids who are good at lying are particularly good at the "look them in the eye test," and therefore their parents will believe they're honest. What is most frustrating for kids is parents thinking they're lying when they're telling the truth, but believing them when in fact they're lying. It drives kids crazy that parents can't tell the difference. Ironically, it's much more likely that a parent will catch a bad liar and then mistakenly believe that child is less honest. This is a huge mistake that doesn't just hurt your relationship with your child but can also have larger negative consequences within your family.

My mom thinks my older brother is the more truthful person, and he lies all the time. He just knows how to get away with it. When I lie, I

always get caught. I'm a terrible liar. After he lies, I'll go to him and say, "Why did you lie?" and he'll say, "Because I'm just that good." I get so mad. I want to tell my mom, but she's already laid down the law and she doesn't want to hear it. And then when she thinks I'm lying, it feels like I'm trapped. So I just say, "Obviously, you think I'm lying, you got what you wished, so just give me the punishment." But I do hold a grudge about it, and that's why I don't tell her anything.
—Avery, 15

Just so we're clear, Avery is a great kid. He's thoughtful and conscientious. But his mom's belief that she has correctly determined which of her children is honest has had far-reaching consequences. Not only does Avery know she's wrong, but Avery feels like she won't listen to him and doesn't think he's an honorable person. So he pulls away. How he pulls away is by putting a smile on his face and shrugging his shoulders, which she sees as being disrespectful or indifferent. Children who believe that someone expects them not to be honest will meet that expectation or give up on the relationship. Plus, that expectation encourages them to lie or deceive because they're already dealing with a parent who thinks the worst of them and they have nothing to lose by being as dishonest as it's assumed they'll be anyway.

CHECK YOUR BAGGAGE

Did anything Avery said ring true for you?

Do you use the "look them in the eye" test?

Have you already decided about your son's guilt before you ask him if he's telling the truth?

If you have more than one child, do you believe one is more honest than another? What are you basing that assessment on?

WHY BOYS LIE TO YOU

Reason 1: Self-Delusion

I lie if my parents ask if I cleaned my room. I say I did and close my door and then leave for school. It's because I am going to clean my room later. —Jake, 13

Why do boys do this when they know how easy it is for you to check whether they're telling the truth or not? I want to share with you something Anthony Wolf, PhD, explains about lying in these situations. He calls this a "lie of the future self." The boy lies because he genuinely believes that in the future he'll do the things he's supposed to have already done. So when boys say, "I walked the dog," "I cleaned my room," or "I did my homework," they don't think they're technically lying because they believe they'll eventually do it. Understanding this concept and therefore confirming that my children are confused about the time-space continuum has dramatically decreased the yelling I do at them. I still have to get after them to do their chores and homework, but I don't think they're dragging their heels on purpose to make me crazy.

Reason 2: Managing Parental Interference

Boys believe that parents overreact to problems, and they want to manage their problems themselves. Their best strategy is to keep you on a need-to-know basis by limiting and manipulating what you know. From schoolwork to after-school activities and athletics, boys will go to great lengths to keep parental interference to a minimum. From the parent's perspective, this doesn't make sense, because who better than a parent, the person who wants the best for the child, to help and give guidance? Parents can help only if they know about the problem. But the reality is that parents' reactions often cause only more anxiety, frustration, and anger for the boy.

When my parents find out I haven't done well, they say, "This world is getting harder and harder. You better do well because it's harder to get a good job." Or "You'll have a bad job," or "You'll have a sucky life." So why wouldn't I lie to them? I don't want to hear it. —Max, 15

When I come home from school and I tell her I did my homework at school, her automatic reaction is, "No, you didn't. You're lying. Go do it." Thanks, Mom. —Anthony, 15

Why would boys lie about something if they know they're going to get caught? Dre's answer sums it up nicely and had every boy in our editors' group nodding his head in agreement.

I'd rather get yelled at one time instead of every day. If I tell them the truth, then I'm grounded every weekend instead of just getting mad at the end of one test. —Drew, 15

LANDMINE!

Don't follow up these conversations with any remarks like these:
"Sam [your son's friend] got an A, and you got a C. How is that possible?"
"How did your friends do?"
"Couldn't you have studied more? Couldn't you have gotten a better grade on that?"
"We never had these problems with your sister/brother."
"If you just applied yourself, you would succeed."
"Your brother may get it quicker, but if you work harder and put in the time, then you'll be just as successful as him."

Parents never understand the context. It's just like me saying, "Couldn't you make more money?," "Couldn't you have gotten that promotion?," "What did you do wrong to get laid off?" —Dylan, 14

Reason 3: Protection

You may think that lying for protection is only about a boy protecting himself from taking responsibility for something. We'll get to that, but that's not what I'm talking about here. Boys lie to protect themselves or their friends from harm, or in some cases to protect others from the truth. Boys are often terrified of people (including you) finding out their true self or of the judgments and assumptions you'll make.

> *I lied to my parents about my friend. He's a really good kid, but he's always getting into trouble. His home situation is pretty bad, like his dad drinks and he's never home, so I know my parents wouldn't want me going over there, but we just hang out in his room and it's fine. —Ryan, 13*

> *I had to lie about me being gay to my parents. It was a hard time for me, but now I don't lie to them anymore. I had to lie about myself not being gay because I thought my parents would hate me for that, but I told them and I feel great about it. When guys or girls are gay, they have to lie about their true feelings and who they are because they think that no one will accept them for who they are. —Ian, 17*

Reason 4: Freedom and Independence

> *I tell my mom I'm going to hang out with some friends—which technically I'm doing. I'm just not telling her exactly what I'm doing because am I really going to tell her that I'm hanging out with people she doesn't trust, getting into a car with way more than five people in it, or possibly drinking? I don't know for sure that I'm doing it anyway. —Kyle, 16*

Boys want freedom to go where they want to go and believe they can assess danger and risk more accurately than their parents. Parents want them to be safe and believe they're better at assessing danger and risk in their sons' lives. For example, younger boys believe they're better at assessing the danger of going up on the roof of their house to shoot water from high-powered Super Soakers at passing cars ("Mom, it's fine, no one is going to get hurt") because they haven't seen someone get into an accident yet. Your belief that they could fall off the roof or cause someone to get into an accident is needless worrying to them, especially since you don't know how good they are at climbing on the roof or what a good shot they are because their plan isn't to actually shoot at the car, just near the car.

Likewise, using similar logic, older boys who drive or have friends who drive know that parents don't want seven kids in a car piled onto each other's laps. Of course, it's against the law in many states too. But boys drive with too many people or get into crammed cars because they believe they know who's a good driver and who isn't and because they want the independence that comes with not relying on their parents for rides. Therefore, they believe they're in a better position to gauge the safety of getting into a particular person's car; parents don't understand the specific situation, so their perspective is unreasonable. What's scary about boys lying for freedom is that often they rationalize lying to you because they don't want you to worry.

> *Guys will lie in order to keep their parents from worrying. Some may see this as a positive aspect of lying because the guy is doing it for the benefit of his parents.* —Bill, 15

> *When it comes to lying, I don't like lying to my mom. So if I do something bad and don't want her to find out, I'll try to avoid her or the topic. But sometimes I do lie just so she won't worry. I also lie to my mom when I have people in my house and she's not home. And I lie to my mom about relationships sometimes.* —Vince, 16

Of course, the other reason why boys lie in these situations is that they know the possible consequences of their actions but believe they'll never encounter them. If they're thinking about their past when it comes to lying, they may be remembering the times they didn't get caught and got away with lying rather than the times they did get caught and were punished.

Teens think they're invincible—or so adults love to say. Undoubtedly this is true, but before we move on, look in the mirror. Do you talk on your phone or text while driving? Have you ever drunk a couple of beers or glasses of wine and driven home, even when your kids were in the car with you? I'm just saying that young people aren't the only ones who are in denial about consequences hitting them upside the head.

Reason 5: Cover-up

After a party, my mom will question me about what happened, who did what, or who was smoking or drinking. So I tell her, "If you don't believe me, ask Drew" (one of my friends I know she likes). When I do that, I know Drew will back whatever I'm saying. —Jordan, 15

You have to coordinate with friends. But you only do that with guys who are really close to you. They're sticking their neck out for you. They're going to go down with you. —Will, 16

What's really important to keep in mind here is that most boys differentiate between lying and deceiving. Lying to you is clearly unethical and punishable. Deceiving is more ethically ambiguous, because it relies on you making assumptions for which he's not necessarily responsible.

WHAT MAKES A GOOD LIAR?

It's like he thinks of it as civil disobedience. —T.J., 17

Every lie is based on a grain of truth. A "truthlet" can be used later by a boy if he is caught to justify his actions. This is why he can be so self-righteous when he's caught.

Boys recognize who they can lie to and to what extent. If a kid smells an ounce of hypocrisy on an adult, it's easy for him to lie because he doesn't respect the person. He also believes that the adult would have a harder time calling him out. Conversely, lying to someone whose integrity he respects is way harder.

In either event, a good liar usually resorts to the following tactics and rationales:

1. He overloads you with details so you leave the conversation completely confused.
2. He approaches you when you're distracted or tired.
3. He collaborates with accessories to back up his story.
4. He truly believes he has a higher purpose that justifies the lie.
5. He's angry with you for something else, so he feels justified in lying.

LANDMINE!

Don't ask questions that force a lie. You have the right to ask your child where he'll be and with whom, but this question is often a setup: he may not know all the details, or things may change and he won't have total control over the outcome. When you're trying to get information about where he's going, ask yourself what your underlying concern is. Probably like most parents, I have two main concerns: I want him to be safe. And I want him to not act like a jackass in a way that hurts people.

RECONNAISSANCE STRATEGIES

My mother has a mom network. It's really bad. They knew some-
thing that happened before it happened. —J.D., 17

You can call it a support system or parental covert operations. As soon as you become a parent, it's absolutely critical to your sanity and your kid's safety to get information from other parents when you need it. I mean it. It doesn't matter how on top of things you are as a parent, you need other trusted eyes and ears to back you up. The best operatives are people who really like your kids, people who for better and for worse know what your kids are capable of, and people your kids respect and are a little afraid of making angry.

The best way to create your own network is to connect with the parents of your son's friends and associates. Whether he participates on a team or in an activity, the theater, or the robotics club, get to know the parents of the other kids involved. (Actually, you don't have a choice because you'll be hanging out together watching your children or carpooling them places together.) You don't have to be BFFs, but you do need to know how to get ahold of them when necessary, and you have to let go of any embarrassment or hesitation you might have in admitting you're having a problem with your kid. Every parent will have the experience at least once of not knowing something important that's going on with their kid and having to ask other adults for help.

It's also good to develop your child's paranoia. The more he thinks you're talking to his friends' parents, the less confident he'll be that he can deceive you. Get as complete a list as possible of cellphone numbers for your son's friends and their parents and keep them in your cell phone.

YOU'RE CLOSING IN ON HIM

From the moment our children realize they are separate entities from us and realize that we will often stop them from doing what they want, they carefully study us to figure out how to get their way. That's why they can be so good at knowing how to wear us down or deceive us. We are up against experts.

When your son is close to being caught, there's almost nothing he won't do to get you off his back. Imagine this picture: You're the advancing army, and you have arrived at the castle walls. He's in the castle, and he's going to fight you to the death before he lets you see what he's been up to in that castle. As you begin your final attack, hot oil is dumped on you. Fireballs are next. Flying cows. Tar bombs. Whatever he can find. Nothing is considered off-limits to push you back, including his secret weapon—your love for him.

Here are three examples of brief exchanges between a son and his parent to show you how they do it.

BOY: Why don't you trust me?
PARENT: I do trust you.
BOY: Okay, good. *(End of conversation. Walks out of the room or puts headphones on.)*

BOY: Why don't you trust me?
PARENT: I mean, it's not that I don't trust you. I just want to know what was going on.
BOY: Now you do. *(Walks out of the room or puts headphones on.)*

BOY: Why would I still be trying to prove to you that I'm telling you the truth if I was lying?
PARENT: I don't understand why you're getting so angry.
BOY: I'm not angry. You're just being completely illogical. *(Takes out phone and texts.)*

When my mom is about to catch me in a lie, I yell and get in her face. Yes, I do it on purpose. I'm way bigger than her, and she backs down every time. —Drew, 16

Those exchanges don't usually happen with dads. If they're going to happen, it's typically with moms. If you recognize any of the dialogue above in your own life, this is a serious problem because it means one thing—your son doesn't respect your authority and he's learned that emotionally manipulating you works to get his way. He may love you, he may care about you, but he doesn't see you as an authority figure, and he doesn't take you seriously. Listen to the boys:

If my dad is questioning me, I never lie. But I do this with my mom because, to be honest, it works. I know it's wrong, but if it works, then I'm going to keep doing it. —Steve, 14

I think it is different when the dad questions you, at least for me, because I feel as if he has more authority, and I'm more "afraid" of him. Therefore, when he questions me, I am usually forced to tell the truth so that he finds out what he wants. With my mom, I tend to sometimes get her to back off, but it's nearly impossible to do that with my dad. —Alan, 16

I don't know what you guys are talking about. I'm scared of my mom. —Erik, 16

Of course, as Erik demonstrates, not all moms are emotional pushovers, and not all dads are truth serums. Plus, dads create their own challenges. Boys tell me that they commonly get this advice from their dads:

"Don't do something stupid."
"Don't get in trouble."
"If you do something stupid, don't get caught."

Think about what values are taught through this advice: Do whatever you want but don't get caught. Ethics don't matter if you don't get in trouble. This parenting advice teaches boys to have an inflated sense of their ability to get away with doing things they know are ethically wrong, including lying to their emotionally manipulated mothers.

It doesn't have to be like this. Throughout this book, I'm asking you to take real power back and exercise it ethically with your son. As a mom, realize right now that you can love your son and stand your ground. You can call him out for lying, being disrespectful or dismissive, and trying to manipulate you and still have a good relationship with him. Dads or moms, it's not okay to open loopholes by counseling him not to get caught. That advice makes life confusing for him, and if he follows it, he'll never be the man of honor you say you want him to be.

In addition, people are usually parenting with another person. Whether you're married or not, or parenting with someone who has a different approach to parenting, this is why you have to be a united front. You have to back each other up. It's these moments that lay the foundation for your son's moral framework, his relationships, and his sense of the world as an emotionally safe place where there are standards that he has to abide by.

YOU CAUGHT HIM—NOW WHAT?

Saving face is very important. If you confront your son in front of his friends, he'll be resentful and 100 percent focused on showing he has as much control as possible over you in the situation. You're not giving in or letting him get away with something if you wait until he's alone. In fact, waiting is a punishment unto itself. Remember when you got in trouble? Often the worst part was knowing you'd been caught and having to wait for the ax to fall.

If you have good reason not to trust him, tell him why. Describe the specific actions that led to your suspicions, explain how you feel and what you want, and let him know what he can do to gain back

your trust. Remember, your son may give you incremental information. Give him the space to do so—within a reasonable limit. I say
to boys that they have a day to "remember" anything that happened
that they "forgot" to tell me in our initial conversation. Anything
told to me within that twenty-four-hour period counts as telling the
truth and not withholding information. After the twenty-four-hour
period, it does count as withholding information. Whether he's in
trouble with you or he's had a bad experience that he wants to share
with you, he'll probably parcel out the story in chapters, if not sentences. If you've gotten to the place where you really don't trust him,
you need to say specifically why and then say:

*"I don't want to have the kind of relationship with you where I
doubt everything you say, but that's where we are. When you lie, you're
forcing me to be much more involved in your business than I'd otherwise
be, and I know that's the last thing you want. I want to trust you. I
want to respect your word. I need to know: what is so important to you
that you're willing to make this kind of sacrifice?"*

The only time when you can talk to him in public is if he lies to
you with his friends or if he's involved in a group effort to deceive.
Then walk out of the room with phone in hand so they can listen to
you call the other parents.

He may not cooperate that easily. You could do all these things
and he'll still try to distract you. If that happens, what I find most
helpful is to go back to the basics. I'll share with you a recent conversation I had with my older son, who *loves* to argue with me relentlessly when we catch him lying.

His dad forbade him from playing video games and had taken
the controllers and placed them in the closet. Not an hour later,
Elijah went into the closet, got the controllers, started playing, and
then lied about it. His punishment was not being able to play the
next weekend. (My kids aren't allowed to play during the week.)
The next Friday, Elijah came home with two friends talking a mile a
minute about the video game they were about to play. I heard it and
rushed out and reminded him that he couldn't play. Three minutes
later, he came into the kitchen ready to do battle with me.

ELIJAH: Mom . . . okay, listen to me . . . just hear me out.

ME: Did your father say you weren't allowed to play? Yes or no?

ELIJAH: Dad said I couldn't play "right now." "Right now" doesn't mean I can't play later. That's what I thought he meant.

ME: It's only a yes-or-no answer. Did your father tell you that you couldn't play and you played anyway and then you lied about it?

ELIJAH: Mom, we had guests over and I was just trying to be polite.

ME: Still not answering the question. Did you defy your father and then lie about it?

ELIJAH: Fine.

That was a small battle. But it's these little moments that dictate how the big moments go. If you stand your ground with lying about video games, he's going to know that lying to you about way bigger things isn't going to be as easy. Fight the small battles. And just because I "won" in this example doesn't mean there won't be other times when he gets the better of me.

SO YOU WANT TO GO OUT FOR A FEW HOURS . . .

Everyone knows that one situation where kids can run off the rails is when they're unsupervised in a house. But what if you want to go to a movie and dinner on a Saturday night and let your son stay in the house while you're gone? It's not like you're leaving town for the weekend. Some kids won't leap on a three-hour window of no parents in the house as an opportunity to go crazy. Some totally will.

Let's take a step back: What are you worried about? Your son having sex in your house? Allowing other kids to have sex in your house? Your son drinking in your house? Other kids drinking in your house and the possible consequences? Your son inviting someone over who steals or vandalizes? You have to ask yourself: Is it that

I'm afraid of what might happen in the house? Or am I afraid of letting my child be off the radar for a few hours?

There are a couple of ways you could handle it when you leave your older teen unsupervised (and I'm much more worried about older teens than younger ones). You could install cameras in the house so you could see what he's up to when you're not around. But there's no way you'd be able to cover every part of the house, so that's unreasonable, not to mention counterproductive because your kid will feel disrespected. You could say you'll be home around 11:30 and then come home at 10:00 and see what greets you when you get back. Or you could play mind games and say, "Bye, honey, we'll be home sometime after the movie." The beauty of this strategy is that you're not lying, but you're stoking the fires of your son's paranoia. Think about it—if he invites people over, he won't be able to enjoy himself because he'll be so worried that you're about to walk through the door.

Do you ever have probable cause to set him up? Depends. You could say he's a teen, so that's probable cause right there. But I don't think that's fair to him. However, there are some signs that would lead me to believe that he's more likely to invite people over when he's unsupervised. Here are a few: he's on a team with a coach who encourages or won't stop the "boys will be boys" mentality; he needs to prove his usefulness to his friends or teammates; he's changed friends and wants to please them; or he's in love or lust.

Remember, you are judge, jury, and executioner. Be fair and consistent, but don't be above playing the same mind games he may be playing with you.

SNEAKING OUT

Why do we sneak out? Because we've played [Call of Duty] for three hours. We've snorted cinnamon to see who chokes first. Then one of the guys gets a text from a girl to come over. Of course we're going.
—Sam, 16

What's the difference between lying and sneaking? Think of lying as untruthful words and sneaking as untruthful actions. Do boys sneak out of the house? Yes, of course they do. Hanging out with girls; throwing parties; going out to vandalize someone's house; getting food, alcohol, or drugs; craving the adrenaline rush of getting caught; that FOMO (Fear Of Missing Out) feeling that something better is going on "out there" and they need to find it—any and all of these are reason enough.

When your child reaches the age of twelve or thirteen, explicitly define for him what qualifies as sneaking out of the house and then have him say it back to you. There can be no room for misunderstanding. If you don't make this clear, when you do catch him, he's going to defend himself by accusing you of being unclear and making rules after the fact (even if he knows perfectly well that sneaking out is against the rules). Then he will succeed in getting you off the topic of what he did and onto the merits of your parenting.

Before Anything Happens...

"Hey, just in case it comes up, I want to be clear about something. When you're over at someone's house or you're here and tempted to leave, I want you to be clear in advance about the family rules. I'm not saying it'll definitely happen, but I don't want you to have any surprises. The moment you decide to sneak out of the house, I'll hold you responsible for anything that happens while you're out, even if you aren't directly involved. If someone you're with damages property or hurts someone in any way, I'll hold you accountable as well. Ultimately, this is your choice, but I want to make clear what the consequences will be."

Let's start with a classic example. Your son asks to sleep over at a friend's house. This plan may be true in the larger sense. His intention is to end the night at his friend's house. What's equally true is that the evening's plans include sneaking out of the friend's house to go hang out at a girl's house. From his point of view, you should be happy with his good judgment. He walks to the other house because he knows your rule about not getting into a car with other kids. He doesn't lie because he ends up exactly where he said he would. No harm no foul.

Pets make it hard. You know the dog is going to bark when you come back. —Rick, 15

There are also different kinds of sneaking out. There's sneaking out of his own house, sneaking out of someone else's house when he's spending the night there, and letting people who are sneaking out of their house into his house. You need to be very clear where you stand with your son for each of these situations. The last one—letting people into his house—is specifically about girls. If you come downstairs at 1:00 AM to find three girls "hanging out" with your son and his friends, it is extremely probable that those girls have snuck out of one of their houses to come hang out at yours. So no, these girls' parents aren't irresponsible. They're clueless—just as you would have been if the boys had left your house and gone over to theirs.

Here are some suggested guidelines to communicate with your son:

1. "If you tell me you're going to bed, or you wait for me to fall asleep and then leave, you're being sneaky, which I consider to be lying by your actions."
2. "If you tell me you're going someplace, this is in fact where you're going and nowhere else unless you clear it by me first."
3. "You may not use the excuse that you didn't call because you didn't want to wake me."
4. "If you allow other people into the house who have snuck out of their house, and/or I don't know they're here, that's also sneaking. If and when I find out about it, I'll call everyone's parents to tell them what has happened, and then we will drive each one of them home." (If that's impossible, you can ask the other parents to come get them.)

Some parents are fortunate enough to have a kid who learns his lesson from watching other people's mistakes or who learns after he's messed up once himself. One time is all it takes. If you have this child, count yourself very blessed. But other kids keep doing it. It's really hard as a parent to not get really angry or sink into despair. You're understandably worried sick, and it can get harder and harder to like your child—this person you love with all your heart—when he behaves this way. Your primary goal is to not allow this to become a battle of wills between you, because that's when kids get so defiant that they can put themselves in harm's way to prove that you have no control over them. I see this so often with girls, but it happens with boys too. So here's another approach you can try:

After You've Caught Him...

"I know you're sneaking out of the house. You and I both know that you ultimately control what you do and it's up to you to be honest with me. We both know that you're telling me things that aren't accurate. I feel like I have no choice but to second-guess what you're telling me, and I don't want to do this. I don't want to be tempted to go through all your texts [we will go over how to do this in chapter 9 on "Social Networking"] and call other parents the moment you walk out the door, but you aren't giving me a lot of options here. So you and I have to figure this out. What do you want to do?"

One thing's for sure: whatever strategy you use, there are going to be times when your son gets really angry with you. When that happens, you need to know how to deal with it because our response to boys' anger is one of the most critical dynamics of our relationships with them.

7

Rage Against the Machine

He just told me to go f—— myself. —Dan

I don't want there to be a fight. —Mary

I just don't want there to be a confrontation all the time. —Susan

I feel like he had one emotion. If he was sad, it came out angry. If he was upset, it came out angry. Everything came out angry. —Julie

Did your son ever throw a tantrum when he was little? Do you remember watching as he threw his toys across the room? Did you ever pick him up, arms and legs flailing, and leave him in a room to cool himself down and then come back a little while later to see him asleep on the floor? Later, when he woke up all sweaty and confused, you could give him a hug and it would be over (at least until the next tantrum).

As boys get older, confronting their anger gets a lot trickier and frankly scarier. The power dynamics change, and it's not in our favor. It's a lot different when that two-year-old now outweighs you or is staring at you with disdain, yelling in your face, and cussing you out, or you're trying to stop him from punching a wall.

We all bring our own baggage about how we express anger and how we react when people are angry with us. I believe that how anger plays out between sons and their mothers and between sons and their fathers is some of the heaviest baggage we carry. For women, how they were raised to express anger is often really loaded. Certainly women can rage and be emotionally abusive. Frankly, I had one such woman in my family. But many women are often silenced by their culture legacies. Down deep (and unfortunately not so deep for many women), their experiences with men's anger and violence silences them and prevents them from speaking their truth when they're angry themselves. They learn to suppress their feelings and try to get what they want indirectly. Another legacy is the belief shared by many women that acknowledging and then directly expressing their anger will end relationships. For both these reasons, they can be scared of the boys they love so much.

If you're a mom, or if you're female and you teach kids in any capacity, the best thing you can do for yourself and the children you care for is to develop the skills to articulate your anger while treating yourself and the other person with dignity and to claim your authority with calm confidence. Moms, I promise you that you can hold the line with your children and have a stronger emotional connection with them than if you're run over by them. It doesn't work to get angry, say what you really feel, and then, because you're so afraid to stand by your feelings, retract it by saying, "I'm just joking." I'm not writing this lightly. Loving someone unconditionally doesn't give that person permission to dismiss you or to not treat you with dignity.

LANDMINE!

While you're completely entitled to show your emotions, crying when you're angry at your children doesn't help you maintain your authority at all. They don't feel sorry for you. They think you're weak. They resent you because they think you're manipulating them. So after you stand your ground, go into your room, shut the door, and then cry there.

The anger baggage is just as complicated for dads. Of course, there's the dynamic of some boys becoming bigger and stronger than their fathers as they both age, and the conflicts they get into and the power dynamics will shift as a result. But these power shifts wouldn't be so dramatic without the unwritten rules of anger that govern interactions between dads and their sons. Many men who parent or teach boys today grew up with dads who were emotionally distant or emotionally abusive when they were angry. Many of these men intensely desire more loving and emotionally engaged relationships with their own sons. But just like mothers, if men don't reflect on how they learned (or, more often, didn't learn) to show anger—and specifically how to react to another person in a moment of conflict—they will fall back on what they grew up with.

THE RULES OF ANGER IN BOY WORLD

Think back to Batman. Batman expresses anger by saying nothing (sulking) or lashing out (i.e., exacting complete destruction and domination of the other person). But that doesn't work well for anyone in real life. You can't go around beating up your friends and family members when you're angry with them without serious consequences to everyone involved. This is how the ALMB allows boys (and many men) to express their anger:

1. Say nothing and suffer silently.
2. Tell yourself the problem doesn't matter and hope it magically disappears. It's not a big deal. Don't worry about it. I'm fine.
3. Laugh it off. Convince yourself that whatever is happening is funny so you don't have to do anything to stop it.
4. Give the person the silent treatment and refuse to admit you're angry.
5. Verbally humiliate the other person.
6. Get in the other person's face but know that you'll be held

back by your friends so you won't have to back up your words with action.

7. Lash out when the other person is someone who isn't going to put up a fight.
8. Drink and/or do drugs to numb feelings.
9. Bottle it up until you explode.

Here's what parents commonly say to boys when boys are angry:

"Get over it."
"You'll be fine."
"Better to be pissed off than pissed on."
"Boys will be boys."
"They were just playing."
"They don't know any better."
"Is it really that big of a deal?"

Or the opposite:

"How dare they? I'm going over there right now."

None of the ways described above allow a boy (or any of us) to express his anger in a way that makes him feel better or that truly addresses the problem. We need to give boys words that matter.

CHECK YOUR BAGGAGE

How does your son see you express your anger?

DOES ANYONE EVER LEAVE HIGH SCHOOL BEHIND?

This is a question that often comes up for women, as if they're the only ones who went to high school. But it's just as relevant for men and boys as it is for women and girls. Think about your typical guy (dad) and how he handles conflict now. To my mind, a sign of maturity, no matter how old you are, is being able to speak out when you don't like something and to do so while treating yourself and others with dignity. Have you noticed that most guys avoid conflict however they can, and that there are a few huge jerks everyone hates but no one stands up to? Have you had the experience of getting really angry and speaking out about it while your parenting partner says nothing, hides behind the plant in the corner, or gives a helpless shrug as though to indicate to the person you're speaking to that he thinks you're crazy too?

Why do guys do this? One of the common justifications given by the man hiding behind the plant is that "it's just not worth it" and "you never know how these things can end." Let's be honest: the chance of a conflict between adults resulting in a true threat to physical safety is not likely (and don't cite the one or two stories the media loves to report about some parent beating someone up). No matter what community you live in, you have to believe it's possible to resolve conflict without violence.

The real reason guys don't like to get involved is because they were raised in Boy World—where the only options when you're in conflict with someone is to ignore the conflict or physically dominate that person. Since you can't go around physically dominating people without getting into trouble (and it's scary), the only thing you can do is blow it off—with the added bonus, if you're parenting with a mom, that you can throw up your hands and tell her to handle it if it bothers her so much.

SEAL: CHANNELING HIS FEELINGS EFFECTIVELY

We all need help channeling our anger effectively. SEAL is the strategy I teach to repurpose the bad feelings we all have when we're in conflict or worried about someone. No matter how old you are, whether you're male or female, whether you're a parent dealing with a coach, teacher, principal, or your own child, or if you're a boy who's upset or angry, SEAL is a structure to put words to feelings and develop a strategy to approach another person.

When I ask guys to describe what it feels like when they're angry, they describe a feeling like there's a huge rock on their chest, or they want to explode, or they want to throw up.

All you can think of is, "Get me out of here." But you can't, so you fake it. You have to pretend that everything's okay until you get home. Then you just want to go up in your room and go to sleep. —Will, 15

No one wants to have these feelings. When you or your son has them, it's only natural that you want to get rid of them. The challenge is how. I'm going to show you a strategy to use when that feeling hits your stomach. I'm going to show you how to think through exactly what's bothering you, figure out how serious it is, decide how to approach the other person (or people) who's making you feel like this, and have the best chance of being taken seriously. This is a strategy you can use when facing conflicts with anyone, from friends to enemies. You can use it when you're angry, but also when you're worried. This is the strategy to use when you're upset or angry with your son, and it's also a tool, if he'll allow you to explain it to him, for helping him think through problems.

SEAL is a four-step process and stands for the following:

1. **STOP and SET it UP:** Breathe, look, listen, and think. Where should you confront this person? Do you confront him now, in public, or later, in private?

2. **EXPLAIN:** What happened that you don't like, want, or are worried about? What do you want instead? (Yes, the Explaining step may seem obvious, but it doesn't matter. The problem needs to be stated.)

3. **AFFIRM and ACKNOWLEDGE:** Affirm your right (or someone else's) to be treated with dignity and acknowledge anything you've done that may have contributed to the problem (anything from sitting on your feelings to doing something deliberately crappy to the other person).

4. **LOCK in (or lock out, or take a vacation):** If you're in a relationship or friendship with this person, decide whether you want to continue the relationship, and if so, on what terms.

Of course, using the SEAL strategy isn't going to be easy. I tell boys that they may start out feeling 100 percent miserable and stuck and nothing I say, including SEAL, is going to get them down to feeling 0 percent miserable instantaneously. But by going through this process, I'm confident that anyone can decrease their misery. Once you're down to anything less than 100 percent misery, it gets easier to think more clearly, things don't seem so desperate, and your confidence increases.

Part of the SEAL process is to always remember that people will probably react by getting defensive and trying to manipulate you into feeling bad, guilty, or regretful that you brought up the problem. This "push-back" is to be expected. When you use SEAL, you're always thinking about the possible push-back, how it could distract you, and how to prepare a response.

Success in SEAL isn't really about making other people agree with you or making them realize how wrong they are. SEAL is a way of putting into practice two things: (1) being socially competent and (2) doing so with a bedrock belief in treating yourself and other people with dignity (even when you think that's the last thing the other person deserves), with the ultimate goal of having the truest control possible over yourself and the situation. SEAL isn't about being nice or "using your words" or using "I" messages. It's a strategy that gives you the best chance of speaking your truth to someone you're in conflict with, in a way that you can be proud of, and of communicating your personal boundaries.

Do you remember Mark, the guy on page 82 who was really frustrated with his father? I met Mark after an evening parent presentation at his school. Earlier in the day, he had attended my student presentation and come back so he could ask me how to get his dad to listen to him. For the next twenty minutes, Mark, two other seniors, and I hung out and strategized how to SEAL it with his dad. The first step, Stopping and Setting it up, was critical, because trying to talk to his dad in the middle of an ongoing argument was futile. The Setup needed to be when his dad was relaxed. When I asked him when that would be, Mark suggested when his dad was watching TV. So I told Mark that the Stop and Setup could be muting the TV during advertisements, which would give Mark about three minutes to do the whole SEAL. Then we went through the possible push-backs from his dad that would set Mark off and derail his goal.

A few days later, Mark wrote me the following:

I had the talk with my dad just like you said I should and it worked out really well.

That one sentence made my week. I wish I could show you a picture of Mark, but suffice it to say he's a big guy and I'm guessing his dad is about his size. Clearly, any kid who waits for hours to ask an adult about how to get along with his dad cares deeply about that relationship. In spite of the power struggles they'd had in the past, Mark reflected on his own part in the conflict, strategized what he needed, and then took the risk to face his dad to speak his truth and listen.

In this context, I hope it's easy to see that if your child does any part of the SEAL strategy, he has used it successfully.

8

Your Parenting Profile

Parenting can make the sanest among us crazy. You catch yourself doing things you swore you'd never do (5:00 AM practices, anyone? Room parent for three years in a row?), but then you see other parents doing things that make absolutely no sense. I've written a lot about this in other books, but just as boys have the Act-Like-a-Man Box, moms and dads have their own boxes telling them what "good" parents do and what "bad" parents do.

Getting all these messages about what we should do as parents, we find it all too easy to lose our common sense in the process. It's as if we're constantly being torn between two forces. One is the overall culture telling us what to feel and do, and the other is what we actually feel and want to do. And sometimes it can be impossible to tell the difference. As a result, we've gotten so extreme and judgmental that we've become our own and each other's worst enemies. I believe that in the process of parenting we take positions that really stop us from giving ourselves and others a break, which ironically stops us from being the parents we aspire to.

You may be tempted to focus on all the other parents you know instead of yourself while reading this chapter. Don't get me wrong. When you're figuring out how to approach another parent with a problem, thinking about that person's parenting style can be really helpful. But also put yourself in front of the mirror.

As you read the following parenting profiles, keep in mind that people can fit into more than one profile depending on their life circumstances or their child. A parent can have one style with the oldest child and another with a middle or younger child. In almost every parenting profile, there are positives as well as negatives.

I also encourage you to ask your son to read these pages and give his opinion. Yes, this means giving him an opening to critique you as a parent. Yes, that power may go to his head and come out of his mouth in the form of snarky comments. If that happens, don't argue with him. Instead, let go of your discomfort and genuinely tell him, "You can't be rude, but if you really think that about me, I want to hear more." If you can do this, there's a good chance that your son will open up to you. This is the best way to transform your conversation with him into meaningful dialogue. Remember, you're reading this book because you want to get a better understanding of how your son sees his world. You must be ready to be changed by what you hear.

One last thing before you dive in. Please remember that no parent wakes up in the morning wanting to be enabling, micro-managing, in denial, or irresponsible. This is as true for you as it is for the craziest parents you know. It's hard enough to be a sane, clear-thinking parent when your child isn't having problems, the social waters are clear and calm, and no one is making him miserable or accusing him of some horrible deed. But of course, those aren't the moments when sanity is most called for. It may seem obvious, but it's critical to spell out why these situations can be so challenging for any parent regardless of their personal parenting style.

So here we go. The parenting profiles that follow reflect the personalities that boys told me they interact with most often—not just their own parents but the parents of their friends and other kids they know.

The Believer Parent

There's one best way to identify these parents: when they tell you something that happened to their son, they come across as if they were actually there when it happened. It doesn't matter if they were at work or at home miles away from where the incident occurred. I'm not suggesting that the child of "the Believer" isn't telling the truth. Every person has the right to his perspective, and that of the child is as valid as anyone else's. But if Believer parents don't consider the possibility that there are other sides to the story, three things can happen: (1) the Believers won't find out what's really going on; (2) when Believer parents find out that there's another side to the story, it's embarrassing because your child has just made them look like fools; (3) Believers' embarrassment turns into massive denial and defensiveness, and they become convinced that the other person is wrong and/or delusional.

> *It bugs me when parents defend their sons even if they shouldn't. I don't think they are doing it to support their son. I think they're in denial because they're being lazy parents. It's easier to do nothing than deal with the fact that your son is a bully or liar. —Michael, 14*

Believer parents...
- always let their kid talk his way out of trouble.
- try to blame their kid's problems on others.
- don't like to dig into any problems too deeply.

The Bear Parent

Being protective of your kid is the most natural feeling a parent has. But Mama and Papa Bears have a hard time picking their battles. They often have favorites with other parents, teachers, coaches, and administrators, but believe everyone else is either incompetent or out to get their kid. In situations that involve someone else disciplining their child, the claws come out fast and furious. Very few adults will call "the Bears" out on their behavior, rationalizing that it's not worth it because these parents won't change. Meanwhile, however, Bears are able to dictate policies that affect their children. Claiming their right to defend their cubs, they rush in without allowing their child to advocate for himself or be held responsible for his bad behavior. So Bears end up with either an incompetent child or a child who knows he can get away with treating people badly because his parent will always back him up.

Usually when the parent goes off like that, you just never want to be around her or her kid anymore. Guys hate it when parents step in on their problems, because no one wants to be known as a mama's boy.
—Andrew, 16

Bear parents...

- love to proclaim, "If you mess with my kid, you mess with me." They believe that even if their kid did something wrong, their kid was justified and therefore shouldn't be punished because the other person did something worse first.
- escalate conflicts by getting other people involved with things like petitions, boycotts, and alternative dances and parties.

The Dictator Parent

"The Dictators" believe that it's possible to control their sons' lives, that they're always owed respect (regardless of how they treat others), that effective parenting is based on establishing and maintaining authority over children, and that children who fight back are a reflection of what's wrong in today's more permissive "let's be friends with our kids" culture—a belief that couldn't be farther from the truth. This style of parenting has always had the same result, regardless of the generation—incredibly angry children who simultaneously want the Dictator's support and are desperate to be free of his or her tyranny. This parent believes that "just saying no" to drugs, alcohol, and sex will work. And because Dictators are so judgmental, their sons believe that they have no choice but to sneak behind their backs, hide things from them, and not ask for help when they're in trouble.

My friends that are the most out of control often have this parent.
They do the most drugs, drink the most, and hate their parents.
—Carson, 16

They take one look at a kid and think he's a druggie because he has
hair in his eyes. —Anthony, 15

Dictator parents...
- automatically do not trust their son's friends or their parents if they have a different background or look sketchy in any way.
- are known, in extreme cases, to investigate their son's friends and their families.
- trust people who share their background or look clean-cut.
- interrogate their son about what other people did or didn't do at social events in a judgmental tone that often results in the child feeling he has to lie.

The Boys Will Be Boys Parent

At first meeting, "Boys Will Be Boys" parents are fun and easy-going. They love hordes of boys hanging out at their house, and they're great to hang out with. But when their son (and his friends) has done something wrong, they won't take it seriously, because "boys will be boys." They cling to this rationalization, especially when all indications point to the boy's behavior being intentionally harmful and humiliating to another person.

Boys Will Be Boys parents can also hide behind the "let the kids work it out" philosophy. On the face of it, this makes perfect sense. Your son cannot become socially competent and develop authentic high self-esteem unless he learns how to think through and face difficult social situations like being teased or bullied. But there are big problems with this philosophy:

1. Boys Will Be Boys parents rarely maintain this attitude when their own kid is on the receiving end of problematic behavior.

2. These parents don't get involved at all except to protect their child from experiencing real consequences—which means that they provide no moral guidance and structure as their child navigates complex and difficult social dynamics.

"Involvement," to these parents, means micromanaging their child's life, and they're going to leave that to the helicopter parents they love to make fun of. But what all parents need to realize is that sane involvement means being behind the scenes, asking their child the right questions, and knowing enough of the details to hold their child accountable when necessary.

Boys Will Be Boys parents...

- don't punish their son in a way he takes seriously.
- always tell stories to their kids' friends about the dumb stuff their kid has done.
- talk in sports metaphors like, "Son, always bring your A game!"
- like to come across as more "realistic" than other parents.
- will support a bullying coach as long as he wins.
- tend to speak in slogans ("We all have to go through it," "What makes us stronger makes us better").
- love to talk about how other parents are helicopter parents.
- encourage their son to play in-the-box sports like football, hockey, and lacrosse.

The Pushover Parent

The only boys who don't wish they had a "Pushover" parent are the boys who actually do. Sons of Pushover parents are primarily left to make their own mistakes with little guidance or consequences. Although it can look like the children of these parents love the freedom they get, it's deeply unsettling to have a parent who doesn't stand his or her ground. Pushovers make it almost impossible for their sons to respect them, even when their sons desperately want to. These are the parents people refer to as wanting to be friends with their kids.

The stereotype of the Pushover is usually a mom who tries to hold her own against her son but is eventually worn down to the point where she caves in with a helpless shrug or laugh. But I want to expand what we think of as the Pushover. Dads can be Pushover parents too—think of the father who never puts his foot down because he wants to be the "fun parent." There's also the parent who isn't around a lot because of work travel or long work hours, or because a divorce doesn't allow him to have consistent time with his kids. His understandable feelings of guilt and frustration and desire to be the nice and understanding parent can make him look for ways to ingratiate himself, and his child isn't above using that to his advantage. This parent doesn't want his child to be angry with him because then the relationship will be messy. Since he can't or doesn't put in the time, he wants every moment with his kid to be pleasant, and one of the easiest ways to do that is to show your kid that you're on his side.

The Pushover can also want to do the right thing, but simply be too exhausted and distracted by work and other obligations to create the structured environment a son needs. This parent's biggest problem is inconsistency—initiating rules but then forgetting them because they're too distracted or tired to enforce discipline. When the son breaks a rule, he can take advantage of the parent's guilt and insecurity by changing the conversation from his own behavior to the parent's bad parenting.

Pushover parents . . .
- feel overwhelmed in the face of an angry son.
- feel guilty because they work long hours, travel, or aren't the primary parent.
- don't want to acknowledge that their own actions explain their son's lack of respect.
- rationalize that as long as everyone is reasonably healthy, that's good enough.

The No-Excuses Parent

"No-Excuses" parents have some wonderful qualities. Demanding the best from their child and holding him to a high standard of accountability and personal responsibility, they show their son through their own words and deeds that he should always get up no matter how many times he's pushed down. These parents usually raise boys who present well. Their sons are outwardly respectful to others and follow the rules. As good as this looks, there are significant challenges right below the surface.

No-Excuses parents tend to minimize any social challenges or anxiety their child feels. Their usual solution to any of that is, "You know the difference between right and wrong" or "You know how you were raised, so you know what to do." But neither of these answers is a real solution because neither says anything about how to concretely address the situation. Since the son has been taught that he should take care of whatever problem faces him, he can be reluctant to ask for help or even admit to himself when he feels anxious, like a failure, rejected, or sad. If he's in over his head, he can easily feel ashamed that he isn't strong enough to solve his problems on his own. Shame is a powerful feeling, and it can make boys feel so bad to have let down their mom or dad that they internalize their feelings and become self-destructive or disconnected from the family.

The message that No-Excuses parents communicate to their son is that other people may experience imperfection, fear, feelings of insecurity, depression, and helplessness, "but not us." So the boy can grow up afraid to reach out for help or not knowing how. When this parenting style is combined with the reluctance to ask for help characteristic of most boys, this person's son can feel so desperately unhappy that he can get into dangerous situations and his parent would never know because all they saw was the facade the boy showed.

That basically describes my life. If you make a mistake, it's hard to move on from that. —Ben, 18

My parents say, "How could you do that? I thought you were better than that." —Cole, 17

No-Excuses parents...
- can cause more stress than their kid already has.
- believe that family problems should stay within the family.
- are highly concerned about their place in their community and their reputation.
- can come from an insular community that sees itself as distinct from others.
- are surprised when their child messes up or has serious issues.

The No-Privacy Parent

On the other end of the spectrum, and more publicly embarrassing, is the "No-Privacy" parent. This parent believes that anyone, often unsuspecting strangers or unlucky dinner guests, should be privy to family matters, even if—or especially if—such revelations include embarrassing and humiliating information. Because teens are often horrified when their parents give random people any kind of personal information about them beyond their name, most parents could be innocently accused of this parenting style. There's a difference, however, between giving out factual information about your son and telling your new best friend about your son's recent devastating breakup with his girlfriend, latest sign of puberty, or embarrassing health issue. Since No-Privacy parents seem to believe that their son's life is a joke, he believes that they won't listen to him or know what to do if he has a serious problem.

No-Privacy parents...
- dismiss or laugh at their child's request to stop talking about the subject.
- dismiss their teenager's anger as oversensitivity and say things like "Just kidding!" or "Kids are so sensitive!" as a way of refusing to take responsibility for their own hurtful behavior.

- refuse to talk about their behavior later or admit that what they did was wrong.

The Don't Ask, Don't Tell Parent

Through an unspoken agreement, the son doesn't tell the "Don't Ask, Don't Tell" parent what's going on and the parent doesn't ask. Many parents who feel unprepared or don't have the support they need believe that ignorance is bliss. Since they haven't thought about or rehearsed certain scenarios in their mind, they aren't prepared to respond to them when they happen in real life. Some boys know this about their parents and use it to their advantage. So when their son walks into the house with his girlfriend and heads straight for his room, the Don't Ask, Don't Tell parent doesn't say anything. The boy uses the parents' reluctance to talk about anything real to get away with things they disapprove of. This makes for pleasant yet superficial conversations at the dinner table, but as the son gets older that is all the relationship with his parents is about.

Don't Ask, Don't Tell parents...
- don't see when their son is high.
- don't see when their son is drunk.
- don't see when their son is gay.
- don't check how their son is doing in school.
- are prone to making statements that reinforce their clueless image. For example, they make comments about how other kids are getting high and how glad they are that their son doesn't do that kind of thing.

The Glory-Seeker Parent

"Glory-Seeker" parents get too tied up in their son's athletic, academic, or extracurricular achievements. Of course, parental involvement in a son's schooling and interests isn't always bad. But the identifying factor with Glory-Seekers is that they come across as if their son's outward achievements are the chief reason they're proud of him. Other parents are extremely reluctant to confront this parent about his behavior but talk behind his back about what a horrible role model he is. The Glory-Seeker's son is embarrassed by his outbursts and often has to apologize for his behavior to his friends—who don't like the Glory-Seeker either but also feel sorry for their friend for having a parent like that.*

Many years ago, a father told me that as the assistant coach for his son's hockey team, he used to record the practices—with no sound. One day he forgot to mute the audio and was horrified when he heard himself screaming at the boys. Deeply ashamed, he promised himself he'd never coach the boys like that again. This story has always given me hope that if only these parents could see (or hear) themselves, they'd realize how painful and counterproductive their behavior is.

Glory-Seeker parents . . .

- justify their behavior as pushing their son to be his best.
- are capable of publicly humiliating their son and other children when they lose their temper.
- usually have a spouse who won't confront their behavior or, if pushed, will make excuses for it.
- have little, if any, ability to reflect on how their actions push their son to hate what he excels at or to feel that he's nothing without it.

ARE CERTAIN PARENTAL ROLES ASSOCIATED WITH ONLY ONE SEX?

According to the boys, yes. As uncomfortable as some of the preceding styles may be, the following ones make me more uncomfortable

---

*Glory-Seekers aren't just dads. If you've ever seen a Glory-Seeker mom screaming or being pushy on the sidelines of a soccer field, you know what I'm talking about.

because I don't like putting a gender label on parenting styles. But this is what the boys say . . .

Bro Dad

"Bro Dad" tries way too hard to be liked by his son and his son's friends. He loves to overhear his son and his friends' conversations and then interrupts with dirty jokes and makes comments about women (sometimes about the girls the boys know). When his son understandably asks him to stop or go away, Bro Dad dismisses his son's request to leave as a teen being overly sensitive—not a child who is correctly trying to maintain appropriate boundaries between child and parent. Bro Dad is also good for buying beer or looking the other way when his son sneaks in contraband. He justifies his own behavior by believing that if the kids are going to drink or get high, they might as well do so under his roof.

I've never seen a child who truly respects a Bro Dad. This parent is easily manipulated and disrespected by his children, especially in front of others. And forget discipline. Once you go down this road, it's almost impossible to set guidelines and rules that your son will take seriously. Your child wants and needs you to be a parent, not the friend with the ID. Your connection with him is profound and unique. You can revisit the best friends thing when he's an adult.

Bro Dad . . .
- uses slang terms that don't quite make sense or makes it look like he's trying too hard.
- tells his kid to have people over all the time.
- urges his kid to have a party and be social.
- tries to tell his kid what is cool and what isn't.

My dad will show off when my friends are over. One time we were hanging out in my basement talking about a girl. I guess my dad overheard us, so he comes in and says something about the girl like in a sexual way. That was totally crossing a boundary. —Michael, 15

The one I know tries to act ghetto to be funny. —Dylan, 16

My friend has an incredibly messed-up home life when he stays with his dad. We'll be hanging out on a Saturday night, and his dad will walk in, clearly drunk, talking about how he's going to get some "hot ass." Then he comes in at 3 AM and wants to tell us all about it. I feel really bad for the kid. —Hunter, 17

The Girlfriend

"The Girlfriend" is the counterpart to Bro Dad, but instead of making inappropriate sexual innuendos to the boys, she laughs when they're made in her presence.

By seventh grade, boys have designated some moms as "hot moms." They tease the boys who have these moms. By junior or senior year, when some of these boys look like young men, they can seriously flirt with these moms. And while it's gratifying to be "seen" as an attractive woman (especially as we age) by younger men, it's also appropriately uncomfortable, like a colleague of mine who chaperoned a spring-break trip and overheard her son's friends comparing her to the girls they were hooking up with.

Now don't get me wrong. I fully support moms taking care of themselves and wanting to look good. But there's a world of difference between wearing cute jeans that don't flatten your butt and showing up for your son's game wearing a miniskirt and a tight T-shirt with your son's team name or mascot on it. I've been to many games where I've had a hard time telling the difference between the moms and the girls. In contrast, girlfriend moms like the attention, can even seek it out, and there's no way they'll hold their own against these boys, whether the issue is alcohol or anything else.

The Girlfriend...

- can't be differentiated, from the back, from her son's female peers.

- laughs when a friend of her son's makes a joke about how hot she is.
- is very good at looking the other way when her son is doing something illegal.
- wants to be the best friend of her son's girlfriend.
- loves to go to her son's events as a way to gossip with other parents about the kids and other parents.

I dated this girl, and I liked her, but her mom totally freaked me out. She was always super-hot, and she was always making comments about my body and how she'd love to date me if she was a teen again. I broke up with the girl because I just didn't want to deal with that. —Riley, 18

I love flirting with the hot moms. —Trevor, 18

The Peace Vigilante

"Don't throw rocks!"
"Stop using that banana/pencil as a gun!"
"Don't ever point a stick at anyone!"
"Stuffed animals aren't to be used as soldiers!"

Wanting to throw and hit things and pretending to shoot or blow things up isn't criminal, violent behavior that should be stifled at every opportunity. Likewise, allowing a boy to play like this doesn't make it more likely that he'll grow up to be violent or sexist. But that is exactly what the Peace Vigilante parent seems to believe will happen if her son is allowed to indulge in his preferred style of play. Whenever the boy exhibits signs of characteristic male behavior, she deems it antisocial and unacceptable.

Think about it: what is the connection between a boy who likes to set up five hundred little green army men in his room and imagining mortar fire exploding all around him and that same boy growing up to say to a girl "make me a sandwich" when he wants her to stop talking? None. We have got to give boys some credit. If a mother allows her son to play with Nerf guns and talks to him and role-models respect for women, he gets it. What Peace Vigilante parent is blind to is that her constant judgment and negativity comes across as rejection, as a belief that who he is is inherently bad.

Unfortunately, this style of parenting sometimes expands to take over an entire school, which is just as counterproductive as the Boys Will Be Boys extreme found in other parents. Before I had boys, I never noticed how common this was among parents and educators who perceive themselves to be progressive. While I hate saying this, it's been my experience that these people are supportive and understanding when it comes to encouraging girls or "gentle, sensitive boys" but not so much when it comes to loud, "out there" boys. Instead, these boys are designated as troublemakers or as being deeply troubled. Naturally, these boys quickly grow to resent these adults and then actively work to undermine them. It's a totally predictable cycle.

The Rock

"The Rock" is the parent who can influence a son's actions even when not physically present because the boy hears the Rock's voice in his head. The Rock is the parent we should all aspire to be.

Of course, getting there is hard work. Maybe like asking boys to have Champion moments, it's more realistic to aspire to have "Rock" moments. The Rock's kids are still kids who make mistakes, but there's always a baseline of mutual respect. These parents know that their son may hide some things from them, but they don't take it as a personal insult or an indication that their relationship with their son is weak. They don't shy away from uncomfortable conversations. They own up to their mistakes and right the wrong, and they encourage their son to do the same. They love their son unconditionally but hold him accountable for decisions and behavior that go against the family's values and ethics. When they're told that their son may have done something wrong, they listen and don't blame other people for their son's behavior. At the same time, they don't make him feel ashamed of who he is.

Parents who are Rocks also realize, especially as their children get older, that they may want to confide in someone else about a problem. They realize that the most important goal is for their son to have someone reliable and sane to talk to—even if it's not them. Boys with these parents are less likely to do stupid things because they don't want to disappoint their parents; as an added bonus, they don't even want to think about how miserable their lives would be if their parents found out.

> *My parents were strict in the raising of me as a child, and then gradually became less strict as I proved to be more mature and understanding. My parents define success for me as just trying my hardest and having fun in whatever I do, whether that is an A or a C. —Andrew, 17*

Rock parents...

- are good at hanging out with their son without any pressure to make it a bonding experience.
- take their son, if he's done something wrong, over to the other person's house and watch him apologize.
- are good at coming up with effective punishments.
- don't gossip about their children while waiting in carpool lanes or watching athletic events.
- are affectionate with their son and have no problem with hugging him in public.
- are not afraid to admit when they feel overwhelmed or unsure about how to handle a difficult situation with their kids.
- know how and when to approach their son to talk.
- make certain that their son's friends respect the rules of the house.

> *He's been in my shoes, and he remembers how he felt in them.*
> *—Jake, 17*

What I like about this dad is when your father stops looking at you, at least momentarily, as his young childish son and sees the developing man that's coming forth. —Austin, 16

For any of this to work, you must practice what you preach. Nothing will undermine your authority more than hypocrisy. Don't lay down your values, expect your son to follow them, and then act differently yourself. If you talk badly about other people (especially other children he knows), it's only reasonable to assume that he won't do anything different. If you lie, expect him to do the same. If you make a mistake and don't own up to it, don't expect him to hold himself accountable. If you're defensive and refuse to apologize, he'll be self-righteous. Being a credible role model depends on you consistently demonstrating the core values you believe in and want him to practice. And if you're parenting today, that means you have to teach your son how to be an honorable person not only in real life but also in his complex, nuanced online life.

9

Social Networking

ecently, a middle school principal introduced me to his students. There I was, standing in front of hundreds of sixth-, seventh-, and eighth-graders, and this is what he said to warm up the audience. "Ladies and gentleman, we have a special speaker today who's going to talk to you about a very important issue. Bullying and all those things you do on your phones and computers. The problem with you all is that you abuuuse technology with all that texting and the Facebook. Adults uuuse technology. You abuuuse it. Do you know that? You abuuuse it."

You have no idea how much I wanted to push that guy off the stage.

If we're to have any hope of talking to our children about using technology responsibly, we have to recognize three weaknesses in our standard arguments. First, collectively, we're horrible role models, but we don't admit it. We text while driving, we look at embarrassing pictures of other people, we hide behind our screens and make anonymous snarky comments instead of confronting people face-to-face in civil ways, and we constantly check our emails and updates. Second, we forget that all this technology is incredibly cool and it can solve real problems. Third, either we completely give up using technology as a way to teach the social contract or we lay down laws that make no sense. It's not just parents. In school, cyberbullying assemblies often come across to students as irrelevant, unrelatable, and patronizing, which is ironic since most of the kids know way more on the subject than the person conducting the presentation.

In my work with kids, I constantly worry that I can't keep up with them and will be giving them outdated information—and, in turn, useless information to their parents. I've learned that to even have a chance of success it's imperative to be in constant dialogue with young people and admit to them what I don't know. But it's equally important that I consistently reevaluate my beliefs. In preparation for writing this chapter, I've done that and realized that my thinking has changed in fundamental ways in the last two years.

LAYING DOWN THE LAW

If you're raising kids today, your child's first interaction with technology happens through games when they're very young. It usually starts with letting them use your phone or another device when you're standing in line and you want to keep them distracted. By four, they've probably memorized your password to open your phone, and they can download a game app by themselves.*

Most boys don't really want or need email and won't until eighth grade—if they ever do at all.† But a lot of boys like to play games with their friends using video chat. They can see their friends, talk smack, and gossip about other people, all while still playing a game. In spite of all the jokes about boys not being able to multitask, that's exactly what they're doing.

At whatever age your child begins to socialize with other kids online, in whatever format, it's time to have the first conversation tying

---

*This is the exact reason why you must maintain the secrecy of your passwords. I change mine about every six weeks because somehow my boys eventually manage to get it out of me.

†While writing this book, I'd get long emails back from high school boys within five minutes of asking a question, I seriously struggled to get email responses back from my middle school editors. The only way I could do it was to talk to them in person, and then I couldn't get them to stop talking. I also used Edmodo, an online assignment program, with great success.

ethical standards to their online behavior. That talk needs to be age-appropriate and concrete. To begin with, go over the different kinds of teasing in chapter 11. This way you're immediately connecting his real life with his online life, which are completely interconnected in his mind anyway. Then say something like this (but in your own words—it needs to be natural):

"You're old enough now that you're talking to people through the Internet. There are a couple of rules you're going to have to follow to continue doing this. What do you think those should be?"

After your child responds, make sure you cover these important points: *"Great, here are some I'd like to add. You tell the truth about how old you are. You can joke around with people just like you do when you're face-to-face with someone, but you can't do the bad teasing we talked about. Like make fun of them to make them feel bad. If someone starts talking to you like that or using bad or scary words, go get an adult. If an adult isn't around right away, then write down what you heard."*

As your child gets older, you're going to change the message to be appropriate for his age and reflective of the things he's likely to experience:

"Now that you're getting older, I need to check in with you again about communicating with people online. Above all, the same rules are true today as they were when you were eight. You don't use these platforms to humiliate or embarrass other people. You don't misrepresent yourself. You don't use another person's passwords without the person's permission. You may not post any videos or pictures of anyone else without their consent. If you want to download music or movies, you do it legally. I'll be checking once in a while to see if you're honoring our agreement. I think you will, but just so there aren't any surprises, if you violate the terms of our agreement, I'll take your technology away until you earn the right to have it back."

Don't worry, we'll get to video games later.

MOBILE PHONES

There are very good reasons why parents give their children phones at early ages. Number one is safety. If I lived in a city where my child was taking public transportation, I'd give him a phone. Closely connected to safety is documentation. If they're on a school bus for extended times (and many rural kids are), I'd give them a phone because if some kid goes after your child or another kid and there isn't a competent adult around to stop it, it's good to have a record of what happened. Most phones today include video cameras and other ways to record conversations and browse the Internet. By the time I write an updated version of this book, we'll have forgotten there was ever a time when all phones didn't have these capabilities. I also like texting my kids. Beyond telling them I'm on my way to pick them up from somewhere, it's a way to tell them I'm thinking about them when I'm out of town. I don't do it ten times a day but I do it once in a while because it makes me feel connected to them—even if I only get a "Yup" in response to texting "I love you."

What's harder to remember are the social consequences of mobile phones. They're status symbols among kids and a prime way for them to become mindless, relentless consumers. (Think about how many times your child has begged you for the latest app, game, etc.) You don't necessarily know where your child is even if you can technically reach him. (Whether he picks up is another issue.) Phones are the engine behind our insta-share desire to spread gossip and other people's conflicts for our individual and collective entertainment. Lastly, they generate and sustain the celebrity culture we live in that drives us to do anything for attention.

When Should I Give My Son a Mobile Phone?

If your child isn't taking public transportation or a school bus, when should you give him a phone? In general, when your child starts middle school. That's when the school day varies depending on his after-school activities and also when he begins to spontaneously go over to friends' houses. That's when we handed out phones in my family, not only for the above reasons but because my sons like to go to a neighborhood bike park where there's a good chance of injury and I wanted them to call 911 and me (in that order) if that happened.

However, you don't just hand them a phone. This is a very special, rare moment in the parent-child relationship where you have all the power. Unless your child is smart and patient enough to save money and get himself a phone with a prepaid card, you're the access to the phone. Don't underestimate your leverage here. This is a great teachable moment about honoring agreements and understanding financial responsibility, and you don't want to miss it.

First, wait until you want to upgrade your phone, because the person who's getting the new phone is you. He's getting your old one. Then the two of you will go to the phone store. Have the salesperson explain how much it costs to add the phone to your plan and what limitations will be on your child's phone. Have the salesperson explain how much money it will cost if your child goes over the plan. Then turn to your child and explain that he'll be responsible for paying the cost of going over the plan.

Walk out of the store with your nice new phone. Before handing over your old phone—with his hands reaching for it like manna from heaven—have him repeat back to you what you said to him about the rules. Then ask him:

"Do you understand that you must obey these rules even if you think they're stupid? Do you understand that I'll be checking what you say and do online? If the phone breaks or you lose it, you'll pay for its replacement. These are my ironclad rules. There's no negotiation about these rules. This is the arrangement if you want the phone. Do you understand the terms?"

Then, hand him the phone, realizing the first thing he'll probably do is look up dirty jokes and share them with all his friends.

Terms of Service

Because kids begin using technology so young, by the time they're eleven to thirteen or fourteen (middle school), you're deep into the process of teaching your children and guiding them with incremental freedom. At this age, it's absolutely appropriate to monitor what your child is sending and receiving. That means you check his texts, you know his password to open his phone, you enforce the rule about no texting or phone calls during dinner (that includes you too), you charge his phone downstairs or in your room, and you make sure he shuts off his phone from 8:30 PM to 7:00 AM. If you do the automatic shutoff, then he can use the phone for an alarm clock. If you don't do the shutoff, give him an alarm clock.

Your child's phone should have a password to enable it. One of your rules should also be that your child will not share this password with his friends. This is very important, and not only because it teaches good security habits. There are so many reasons to enforce this rule, but here are the main two. First, a "friend" who knows the password will think it's really funny to go into your kid's backpack to get his phone, take a picture of his balls, and send it to a girl at school—whereby your son will get in trouble for sexually harassing that girl. Or the problem could be more mundane—maybe that kid texts someone something nasty and it looks like your kid sent it. Or your son shares his password with a girlfriend, they break up, and she "finds" the phone and goes to town doing all sorts of damage.

Here's how you can say it: *"I can't stop you from sharing your password with your friends. However, it's just a fact that sometimes friends take advantage of it. Think about it. Do any of your friends think it's really funny to embarrass you or other kids? If they know your password, they can use your phone to embarrass you or make you look like you did something that you didn't. This is your privacy and your property. Treat it as such."*

You may also want to make the following suggestion to your child: *"It's probably a good idea to tell your friends that I check your texts, etc. Because if I see them doing something crazy, rude, etc., I'll tell their parents."*

MANNERS

There's never an excuse for bad manners. I don't care if you're a teenager or an adult who's had a bad day. When you're around other people, especially if there's a reasonable expectation of social interaction, you need to show interest in their presence and be polite. This is not only the right thing to do, but people will like you more, which is exactly how I'd present it to your son. So . . . allowing boys to use or play handheld devices during meals or sitting in the corner of your cousin's wedding is enabling them to be rude and socially incompetent in the real world. We can't let our children off the hook for participating in social functions. Games in this context are a distraction, meant for mundane situations like waiting in line at the post office. Playing games is not a substitute for daily human interaction.

SHOULD YOU GET THAT SOFTWARE?

In the last few years, I've been inundated with requests to review new software that promises to monitor your child's online activities. Here are my issues with the entire concept. They certainly aren't a substitute for consistently teaching your child to use social networking ethically. If you do use a monitoring program, I'd tell your child beforehand. If they find out after the fact, they'll most likely perceive what you're doing as an attempt to control them, which they will naturally fight against. Then you all are caught up in a power struggle instead of focusing on the actual topic—using technology responsibly.

To show you how much my thinking has changed, a couple of years ago I advised parents to check the history and the cookies as a consistently good way to track their child's activities. Now that has become a ridiculous thing to advise, for the following reasons:

> *To hide what I do online, I usually delete the history of my websites. But if I'm doing something I really shouldn't be, or Googling something I don't want my parents to see, I'll do it on my iPhone and then delete its history, because there's no way my parents will be able to see what I search that way. —Brad, 13*

> *It's very easy to hide what I do online. I have my own laptop. —Dave, 15*

The only kids I've met who aren't confident they can hide their information are kids whose parents are computer programmers, security technicians, and teachers. I don't see how it's possible for a program to truly keep up with a young person who really wants to circumvent the rules. Even if your son doesn't know what he's doing, chances are he has a friend who does. The games begin. The system doesn't matter, whether it's the firewall at school or the monitoring program that parents buy. It's always a game of beating the system.

EARNING TRUST AND BUILDING SKILLS

Jack McArtney, the director of corporate and community responsibility at Verizon, was a pioneer in the design and development of the first cellular networks in the United States. He's also a dad. So I asked him: "How did you teach your children about using technology?"

> *We enabled their PCs' and Xboxes' access and were involved in establishing screen names, which IM to use, and "netiquette." They didn't like it a lot, but learned to deal with it. Occasionally I looked over their shoulder, questioned who their "friends" were (if I didn't know them). Also, I coached their softball/soccer/baseball teams, so*

I knew their true friends and their parents. I believe in setting limits, earning your way to responsibility, but even through all of this, I had to threaten to throw the machine in the trash more than once.

Our [Verizon] parental controls tell you who your kids text with and when, not the content. But it's about being engaged. I didn't like (nor do I now) 'N Sync, but my daughter and her friends did when they were teens, so I went to the concert. Ditto for my son. . . . I was never more personally frustrated with incompetence than my total lack of skill at Halo or EA FIFA Soccer on Xbox, but I played 'cause my son did, and I met his virtual friends and listened to them chat (I had to silently listen to cussing and violent comments longer than I wanted to, but if I listened in long enough, my son would cut them off), and he learned for himself his own personal filter the same way.

PRIVACY

Monitoring your child's online life is about teaching an ethical framework and in the process creating an environment in which, if something in your child's life does run off the rails, you'll have a better chance of knowing about it and working through it. Every child is different, but in general I now believe that if your child has conducted himself according to your rules, by the end of his freshman year of high school you can allow him to have a password of his own and you can stay out of his social networking—until and unless you see or become aware of something that makes you worry.

I've really changed my opinion about this in the last two years. My thinking has been greatly influenced by Danah Boyd, a senior researcher at Microsoft and a fellow at Harvard's Berkman Center (plus a lot of other things). She defines privacy as the combined ability to control a social situation and to have agency to assert control over that situation. Young people want that agency and power.

Why do we, as parents, want to control them? Even though it's illogical, we want to control them for the reasons we always do. We want to stop them from being hurt, getting in trouble, and doing things that'll make us look bad.

As a parent, it's easy to get even more reactive about this because our kids appear to not care what they post online as long as we (their teachers and parents) don't see it. Again, Danah made me think about this dynamic in a different way. It's not that young people want to be public everywhere—what they really want is to participate in a public place that's meaningful to them and their peers. Imagine living in a city where there are a lot of parks, and you know that one of the parks is the place where all your friends hang out. You want to be able to go there and be a part of that community, and you would want to have the ability to present yourself and participate in that community as you like. Your child's chosen social network (whether that happens to be Facebook, Instagram, Tumblr, Twitter, or whatever) is that park.

The park metaphor is a good one to explain one of the most bewildering aspects of teens' social networking. The majority of the interaction seems to be little more than, "Hi! How's it going?" To which the other person says, "Nothing . . . just hanging out." But isn't that what anyone would do if they took a stroll in a neighborhood park and ran into people they knew? Of course. It's the same conversation. Then keep in mind how busy and scheduled our children are. Going to the park (i.e., checking in with his friends on Twitter) is having unscheduled social time.

Young people are deliberate about how they present themselves and who they let see what. But the other insight I've learned from Danah is that young people assume that everything online is public and actively create structures to exclude certain kinds of information from being generally available. Contrary to the stereotype that kids don't value privacy online, they do. They value it so much that they'll come up with incredibly creative ways to hide in plain sight what they really feel. So even if you're a parent who checks their social networking posts, you may look at the images they're posting and have no idea of the meaning behind those images.

Really, teens have been doing this forever. How they choose to dress and what music they like are the most obvious ways they present themselves. But what's important to recognize is that the way your child chooses to present himself online is extraordinary meaningful to him.

LANDMINE!

Please don't say to your child, "You know that whatever you say or do online will stay online." While it's true, your child already knows this, and statements like that have become a signal to a young person to blow off the person who's talking.

What Happens If He's Harassed About Something He Posted?

If your son is harassed online, there are a couple of ways this will go down. But one thing is for certain: this isn't the time to say anything that remotely comes across as, "How could you have been so stupid?" He's going to feel humiliated, embarrassed, dumb, possibly defensive, hurt, and paranoid that everyone he's ever had contact with knows about what he did. On the other hand, don't say, "Everyone will forget about it tomorrow. Don't let it bother you." Just give him a hug and tell him how sorry you are. No matter what he did or what you feel about it, this is the time to tell him you will get through this as a family.

Everyone makes mistakes. Every one of us can have bad things happen to us that go public. It's how we conduct ourselves after messing up that shows what kind of person we are. Work on figuring out how your son is going to walk down the hallway at school the next day. This is exactly where SEAL can be so helpful. Tell him to take a deep breath, and if anyone gets in his face about it he can respond with, "I made a big mistake. Your bringing it up is just rubbing it in. I'm taking care of the situation as best I can. But I promise you that I'd never make you feel bad if you were in my situation, so I'm leaving now."

SEXTING

Our son was being sent photos by a girl in various stages of nudity— e.g., naked bum in the air with only a feather boa thingie round her nipples. It was sent with the [message] "You are special and no one else gets to see this." My son eventually discovered that it had been sent to all her "special" ones, numbering about a handful. We printed out all the photos and wrote a very concerned letter to her parents and posted it by recorded delivery. What we did was extreme. However, I was forced to ask myself, what I would do if this [girl] was my own child?

It's important to see this incident from teens' point of view because it also ties into how they define privacy and intimacy. When I asked my editors if they thought the parent had done the right thing, here are some of their responses. Most of the editors agreed that the boys' parents were in the right about notifying the girl's parents about the pictures. The only thing they disagreed with was the necessity of initially sending the pictures as proof.

If she had the audacity to send inappropriate pictures on her parents' bill and lie about being faithful to one guy, then letting her parents know was a good choice. Those kinds of pictures should be limited to boyfriends only. She shouldn't be sending false messages to everyone saying they're special, because soon every guy will think he's special. —Adrian, 17

There's a fine line between protecting kids from themselves and protecting kids from actual harm. Chances are the girl isn't a comfortably sexual human being. But she could be, and maybe her parents aren't comfortable with that and go into either ultra-slut-shaming mode or ultra-hide-your-kids-from-life mode. Sending the pictures rather than giving a friendly "Hey, you should talk to your daughter about this" would, I think, put them on red alert, regardless of how cool they are with their daughter's sexuality. I think the pictures can reasonably be sent if (a) the parents seem to dismiss the idea and/or (b) more naked pics start being sent. —Sofi, 17

What the mother did was right. I just wouldn't have attached the photos. No parent wants to see their child like that. It's hard enough to hear that your child sends those pictures, they don't need to see them. —Sam, 16

Crotch Shots vs. Kissy Lips

From the classic pouty kissy lips in a bra to full frontal nudity, why are girls sending guys these pictures and then being completely shocked when guys show them to other people? Doesn't a girl forfeit her right to be upset the second she presses Send? What did she expect to happen?

Some of the reasons why girls send these pictures may seem really foolish. But not so fast. Guys send inappropriate pictures of themselves a lot; they just don't go public the way girls' pictures do. Here are some common "hilarious" things guys do that are technically sexting: Sneaking a friend's phone out of his backpack, sticking it down his pants, taking a picture, and then sneaking it back into the friend's backpack so the friend sees his penis the next time he uses his phone. Or his friend takes a picture of his balls and asks another guy, "Do you want to see my brain?" When the other guy is stupid enough to say, "What?" he shows him the picture (and they both laugh their asses off).

The fact is, guys have a serious advantage over girls in the stupid inappropriate pictures department. Because it's almost always a close-up of some guy's genitals, it's much harder, shall we say, to confirm the identity of the guy attached to those genitals. Plus, if you get a picture of a guy's penis, his ALMB status isn't going up if you show the picture to every guy you know. Quite the contrary. When girls get a picture like this, their reaction is, "That's disgusting. Why is that immature jerk sending me this? And if I'm telling anyone, it's my parents, because I'm a little freaked out." For all these reasons, the public nature of guys sending sexually inappropriate pictures is limited. Not everyone in every school in the general vicinity plus your mother in Iowa will see those pictures.

But it's not the same for girls at all. Girls send inappropriate pictures for completely different reasons and have different consequences as a result. And frankly, taking the picture isn't always inappropriate. The problem is the tsunami of problems that happen to her when that picture goes viral. Sometimes girls really do know what they're doing. But after they get caught, it can be so embarrassing that they have to say they didn't know. They look like either a fool or a slut. Most girls would choose fool.

Why Girls Do It

Reason 1—Non-skanky flirting and courtship: Teens today have lived their lives online, so it only makes sense that they would flirt online. Many people in relationships do it as well. There's nothing wrong with that. Sometimes that flirting looks like sexy texts or pictures between people that aren't intended for public display. So your son may receive a sexy picture from a girl that's intended for his eyes only.

Reason 2—Getting attention: There are girls who are so insecure that getting attention for being sexy is like a quick drug fix. These girls will spontaneously send boys pictures that mimic the porn look I describe a little later in this chapter. This girl is a train wreck, but your responsibility is clear: make sure that your son doesn't take advantage of her insecurities. Some boys (Masterminds, Associates, Bouncers, and even some Entertainers and Flies) will argue that "those pictures give her exactly the attention she wants. That's not my fault." Your job is to challenge that line of reasoning, which is like justifying giving meth to a meth addict. Sure, they want it, but you're contributing to their sickness.

Reason 3—Wanting to please: When a guy asks a girl to send him a picture because she's so sexy and hot or to prove how much she loves him, and then he forwards it to all his friends, the whole school knows in two hours. Yes, she was stupid for doing it, but it wouldn't have happened unless some guy took advantage of her feelings for him.

Reason 4—Revenge: A girl could send a picture to a boyfriend that he kept private until they broke up. It's horrible to spread around old private pictures of your ex.

Reason 5—Blackmail: In rare circumstances, a guy tells a girl that she has to send him a picture or else he'll somehow make her life miserable. A guy can also use a picture to stop a girl from breaking up with him ("If we break up, I'm sending the pics to people"). In one school I worked in, a girl sent a topless picture to her boyfriend, who forwarded it to one of his friends. When the friend got it, he told her he'd share it with everyone unless she sent him another picture. Thankfully, she finally got over her embarrassment and told the principal, who handled it well. The girl had to meet with a counselor, the ex-boyfriend was suspended for the day for violating the school's tech policy, and the friend was expelled.

What Do I Do If My Son Gets These Pictures?

You can assume that your son at some point will get a picture like this. Here's what you can say to him before it happens:

"There's a chance you'll get a picture from a girl where she doesn't have a lot or any clothes on, or that someone will forward it to you. Obviously, I'm not going to be around if you get this kind of picture, and even if I was, you wouldn't want me to see it. But I still want you to know what I think you should do if that happens. Give yourself one minute to look at it and then delete it. Delete it because, if you don't do

it right away, you're going to forget you have it on your phone. When you forget, then there's some kind of weird universal magnetic pull that will make you leave your phone in your pants pocket and put your pants in the laundry. Then I'll take out the phone and see it."

LANDMINE!

Don't say, "Is this what your girlfriends are doing these days? Sending pictures of themselves to you? Is that why you're friends with these girls?"

Having your parents find a pic like this is the worst. Worse than if they find drugs and alcohol. If my mom found it, it'd be like a ten out of ten. If my dad found it, he'd say, "Get that off your phone," and then walk away, but it'd still be pretty bad. Like 8.5 out of ten.
—Will P., 20

You may also want to tell your son to delete pictures like this for the following reason:

This girl I'd recently broken up with decided to get drunk at her house and send pictures of herself topless. I deleted it, and then the worst thing possible happens. Her father looks at her phone and sees that she sent pictures. Instead of talking to his daughter, he decided to call my parents. My parents called me in a fury, and I told them I'd deleted the pictures. But her dad took it to the school and told them to kick me out for harassing his child. I was afraid I was going to lose my scholarship and get kicked out of school.
—Wesley, 16

If your son deletes an inappropriate picture, he can prove it on your phone records. The big issue with pics is fairness. I know "life isn't fair," but we don't have to make it worse by just accepting it.

We can do our part to make it better. A girl sending a topless picture to a guy she stupidly falls in love with and ending up humiliated in her entire community isn't something any of us should be okay with. We can take the time to verify what happened before we accuse a boy.

If Your Son Is Part of the Problem . . .

Make no mistake, forwarding pictures or embarrassing information isn't being an innocent bystander. Your son has made a choice to make the problem bigger. Here's how you can lay down the law:

"Look, we made an agreement about how you could use the Internet. I know it was a mistake, but I need you to take responsibility for your actions. You're going to pull it down wherever you posted it. You're also going to ask your friends if anyone forwarded it to any other social networking site, and you're going to do whatever you can to pull that down as well. You will lose your technology privileges for (X amount of time you think it'll take for him to realize you're serious). I really do get that this was a mistake and you didn't intend to do it, but you also have to understand that if it happens again I'll be forced to take away your phone/iPad/laptop because you're showing me you aren't mature enough to handle these things like I need you to be. But more than the punishment, I don't care what you think about this girl, it was wrong to do it and I want you to make it right."

If he participated in the creation of negative information or the forwarding of that information about someone else, he has to apologize to that person in person (see page 204 for apologies), and he has to send an email to all the people he knows it went to acknowledging what he did. It should look something like this:

To everyone in the ninth grade,

Last week I wrote stuff on my Facebook wall about Allison that wasn't true. I shouldn't have done it. I have apologized to Allison in person, but I also needed to write to you so you would know it wasn't true.

You will be standing over him and watching him press Send. He'll hate you for making him do it. Too bad. Someone has to take a stand about this stuff, and that someone is you.

PORN

This book isn't about how to have talks about sexuality with your son. It's about how you help your son navigate the culture we live in while developing his own standards of behavior. It's about helping you guide your son so he can have healthy relationships with girls. And these days, whether we want to admit it or not, porn is something he'll almost certainly encounter at some point if he spends any time at all online.

To be perfectly honest, this isn't a topic I have a lot of easy answers for. So I talked to boys about it—and they were beyond shocked that I wanted to discuss it with them.

> *Your email made me laugh, because it is a topic so right field that I never expected you to send me something like this. It's also funny because it's actually true. I've always thought of it as a "I can't get any so why not watch this" kinda thing. But now I realize how it skews the thoughts of people who watch, and like everything else, it's troubling and successfully doing its job. —Carl, 16*

According to Family Safe Media, the average age at which children are first exposed to pornography is eleven, earlier than most parents think they need to talk to their kids about sexual decision-making. Ninety percent of kids between eight and sixteen have seen pornography, usually while doing their homework. Meanwhile, my *Family Circle* editor told me about a survey the magazine had done with Planned Parenthood that found that while half of all parents are comfortable having the sex talk with their kids, only 18 percent of teens said they feel comfortable having the sex talk with their parents. My immediate thought was that those parents probably aren't thinking that their child has watched hard-core pornography. So while the parents are thinking they need to ease their child into the sex conversation, their kid is already way beyond them in what they've seen. Who would want to admit to their mother or father that they know what sexual intercourse looks like because they saw a close-up of it on their friend's phone yesterday after school?

As they should, children and teens have questions about sex. Because YouTube is one of their go-to websites for everything, it's perfectly natural for them to type "kissing" or "boobs" into You-Tube, and a few seconds later they're seeing soft porn with a website underneath it to direct them to the actual porn site. I know that boys regularly show each other favorite porn sites—like their dads did with *Playboy* and *Penthouse* a generation ago. Before you think, *Where are the parents?* or *Why don't those parents have filtering devices on their computers?* realize that both questions are irrelevant. Kids have regular access to devices that allow them to research and share topics they're curious about. And sex has always been and always will be a topic that kids are curious about.

If you're a parent and don't know any of this, you're going to approach the sex conversation from an entirely different context than your child. Imagine: you get over your discomfort and sit down with your child to impart your deeply held values about healthy sexual decisions—without realizing that there's a good possibility he's seen images of graphic, up-close sexual intercourse and oral sex.

Now look at this from the child's perspective. Your parent sits you down to have a meaningful conversation about sex. If you were that kid, would you want to tell your mom or dad that you know exactly what they're talking about because you saw it on a website last week? Of course kids don't want to tell us they've seen these images. What are they supposed to say? If they admit what they've seen, you're probably going to respond, in a very intense tone, "Who showed you those? Where were you? What exactly did you see?" Kids don't want to have that conversation with you. Plus, they think that, if they tell you, you'll react by taking away their phone or computer.

You can have all the filters on your computer you want, block the TV, and take away their phones—it won't matter. You can't take away every portal to the Internet in your child's life.

I have more to say about porn in *The Guide,* but to address the question here of what parents should say to their sons about it, I would say:

"I know that if you want to see those pictures, you're going to figure out how to do it. I could take away every computer in the house and every phone, and it wouldn't make a difference. Here's why I don't want you to watch porn. It brings you into a really complicated world where you're being exposed to really messed-up images and messages about how men and women interact sexually. It's also all fake. Porn is to sex like the WWE is to fighting. It's a performance where women are supposed to look a certain way and to always like whatever the guy wants to do and the guy never cares about the woman he's with. I think you deserve to have more accurate information than what you'd see there. You also have the right to have information about sex in a way that's accurate and appropriate for you. If you have questions about sex, I want you to ask me or another adult who we both think is a good person to answer your questions."

The previous paragraph was written a few months ago—before I'd had this conversation with my sons. Remember, as I write this my boys are twelve and ten. Well . . . five days ago I had to take Roane, my younger one, to a soccer game and left Elijah home with a friend. Later that night, we had friends over, and James, my husband, opened my laptop to show them something. All of a sudden James started to laugh and asked me if there was something I needed to tell him. He turned my laptop around and I was looking at a full-screen ad of naked women. We looked at the history and someone had deleted my cached history.

Later that night, I talked to Elijah privately—ready to use all the advice I'd written down. Which I did, but here are some things I learned in the process. It's good to be calm as you talk to your child, but it's also important to show you're upset (if you are). Not in the "Son, you're a degenerate pervert and I'm ashamed of you" way. But I think it's totally acceptable to say, "It really upset me to open my computer and see those pictures. I don't want to open my computer and see close-ups of people's genitals." I was too calm. But like I've said in this book before, parenting will always give you a chance for a "redo."

No joke, two days later, James was out of town and I took Elijah to basketball practice and left Roane home. When I got back about thirty minutes later, I opened my browser on my iPad. What were the recent searches? "Sex" and "Sex videos." So then I realized that it was possible that both of my kids were searching for porn, or maybe it was just Roane. My head was whirling as I thought, *Is it possible that Roane knows how or would even think to delete the browser history? Was Elijah covering for Roane out of brotherly loyalty? And damn it, they somehow got my passwords again!*

I summoned them both and showed them the iPad. Since this was my second go-around, I did way better, and this is what I said:

"Boys, I'm not going to ask you who was looking at naked pictures. But I need you to know three things. First, those sites are notorious for bringing viruses into computers. You know if that happens, our computers could stop working" (the implicit threat therefore that their Xbox would no longer function). *"It's also possible that they could have 'bots' that could search my emails and files to get our financial information. Then whoever the hacker is could take our money or use our identities to steal things."*

Judging from how big their eyes were, I had their full attention.

"Second, I totally understand if you're curious about sex. There's nothing wrong with that. But what you see in those ads is really disrespectful to women, and you know how your father and I feel about that. So if you have questions, ask me or your dad. Third, I have now changed all the passwords."

It upsets me that pornography gives our girls and boys unrealistic and often very unhealthy messages about sexuality that will influence them to some degree. It's more than annoying that as parents we have to deal with the fact that our children can have totally appropriate questions about sex, will naturally seek out the answers from these amazing tools we have, and then in two seconds are seeing things that they aren't mature enough to process. But this is our reality.

We're going to go to games next, but before I end this chapter I want to reiterate that as parents we have to take social networking seriously. We can't just throw up our hands and laugh about how our kid programs our phones. We can't sit there and marvel at our toddler's ability to use the iPad. We can't have knee-jerk reactions to how our children are operating in this world. If we're really clear with our sons about our ethical standards and how to treat people, then they will apply these standards to their online lives. If we celebrate this technology but don't give them license to think they're entitled to every new product that comes along, they're going to be fine. Sure, they'll make mistakes. They'll press Post before they should. They'll press Send and regret it the next moment. That will happen. But that's what you do when you're fifteen. You make mistakes and you learn from them—so you don't do the same thing as an adult and lose your job.

10

Video Killed the Radio Star

I was in the middle of a presentation to three hundred middle school boys when an arm shot straight up. This was the kind of hand-raising that only happens when a kid has something monumental to say. I stopped, midsentence.

ME: What's your question?
BOY: Are you Xbox or Playstation? *(I freeze, realizing the magnitude of the question. Three hundred boys look at me with bated breath.)*
ME: I refuse to answer that.
BOY: Why?
ME: Because it's like telling you who I'm going to vote for. If I tell you, you'll make an assessment of my character and intelligence. You'll have to guess.
BOY *(mulling over my response)*: Fair enough.

Video games. There are few things that are more valued and important in Boy World, and few things that cause so much anxiety and conflict in Parent World. Games share a spot with sports at the top of the food chain as the dominant enterprise in young male culture. They're arguably the most influential form of media, both culturally and economically, that exist right now. And in part because kids play them, debate them, and experience them together as soon as they hit a certain age, they have a tremendous impact on how boys are socialized.

But unlike sports, the world of gaming is ever-changing, endlessly multifaceted, and filled with an ever-multiplying stream of options. There are truly thousands of types of games. And unlike in other forms of media, the line between popular and obscure is heavily blurred and volatile. An independently developed, casual game for a mobile phone can have as much influence and financial success as a huge AAA title for an Xbox. The games your son plays can come from anywhere and everywhere and be totally antithetical to his other interests, even when we're only talking about the most popular (and therefore socially acceptable) choices. A kid who's a football player can be obsessed with games rooted in medieval and Renaissance history like *Assassin's Creed, Dante's Inferno,* or massive open-world interpretations like *The Elder Scrolls: Skyrim* (think *Lord of the Rings*). An eleven-year-old struggling in math class can spend hours balancing the budget in an urban planning simulation (the *Sim City* series) or building complex worlds in *Minecraft*. A game can challenge your child to face difficult and relevant moral choices.

Understanding these underlying and essential facts is rarely if ever part of our discussion about the influence of games on our children's lives. Instead, we talk about two things: limiting their screen time and debating the appropriateness of violent content. In effect, these conversations are no different than the dialogues we've had for generations surrounding movies, television, and music. But there's something about video games that makes parents react more viscerally. As a mom who has watched her sons fall in love with games like *Halo* and *Call of Duty* (*COD*), I think I know what it is. Our sons are pulling those triggers as opposed to watching someone else do it in a movie or television show. We don't like seeing them gleefully slaughter "people," and it seems only logical that virtually stabbing and shooting someone must make our children more violent in real life.

I don't agree with this logic. I believe there's another reason for the discomfort we feel watching our children play these games. We are forced to come face-to-face with our acceptance of violence as entertainment in other areas. Since many of us find that too hard to acknowledge, we point to video games as the problem. In our denial and ignorance, we miss a chance to lay down the law about things in gaming that truly matter.

Our kids aren't taking us seriously about games because (apart from parents who are gamers themselves) they know we're attempting to regulate something we know very little about. They also tend to ignore us because we're inconsistent in our perceptions of what constitutes violence in video games. It's all too easy to get nostalgic and look at a "peaceful" game from two decades ago, like *Super Mario Brothers,* and forget that, despite its primitive graphics and happy music, that game involved bludgeoning literally thousands of living beings to death with the feet of an Italian plumber.* In large historical strategy games like *Civilization,* often (rightly) viewed as educational and nonviolent, your child can brutally conquer and massacre an entire culture. (Likewise, I've never heard of a parent being upset with her son for not providing adequate health care or fire department funding or earthquake building codes in *Sim City,* even when the result is a virtual holocaust unseen in any game where shooting is involved.)

Parents are even worse when it comes to comparing video games to other media, including our culture's most important books. There is no video game in history that can approach the level or intensity of violence present in the Old Testament. Or to take it down a notch, even *Grimm's Fairy Tales,* for example, "are grim indeed."†

"Just because I like violent video games doesn't mean I'm going to

---

*This is really quite similar to our conversations about music. The S&M-themed lyrics of a modern artist like Rihanna are really no different from any number of Prince songs that many of us loved and happily sang along to when we were young. If you want to talk to your children about song lyrics, it's better to focus on the mindless consumerism and product placement.

†Justice Antonin Scalia, delivering the opinion of the Supreme Court in *Brown v. Entertainment Merchants Association et al.* (2011).

go out and start killing people. I know the difference between real life and a video game." Many boys have said this to their teachers and parents, and it often stops adults in their tracks. After all, these boys are proving their point just by standing there and not shooting someone. For the record, I don't think video games "cause" violence. But some video games can normalize humiliation, degradation, and senseless violence—as do a lot of things in our culture that we fully or tacitly accept. Some of our most popular and treasured music, movies, sports, political figures, and television and radio shows do it. If we don't admit that, we have no credibility when we talk to our kids about the violent games they're playing.

REASONS TO LET THEM PLAY

One reason to let boys play video games (and the reason they're most likely to care about) is that video games are part of the social fabric of boys' lives. That doesn't mean that we should let boys play video games all the time, but being able to play games and talk about them can be part of how boys relate to one another, and it's understandable why many boys wouldn't want to feel cut off from that any more than they'd want to be cut off from sports or popular music.

But there are some other good reasons for allowing boys to play games. Right now, there's a tremendous amount of research evaluating the impact of games on brain development, and much of it contradicts our popular assumptions and what is most regularly reported in the media. Daphne Bavelier is a brain scientist who examines how to make brains smarter and faster. Her research shows that gaming can have positive effects on the brain, even first-person shooter games.* For example, people who play those games between five and fifteen hours per week have better eyesight than people who don't play. Specifically, they see small details, distinguish between

---

*A first-person shooter video game is based on the player fighting with guns or other weapons from a first-person perspective.

different levels of gray, and track objects better than people who don't play.*

Jane McGonigal's influential book *Reality Is Broken* uses Bernard Suits's definition of a game as "the voluntary attempt to overcome unnecessary obstacles." McGonigal's book was the first one I read that backed up what boys say to me. I had played video games myself in sixth grade—it was my favorite thing to do after school. But I'd often wondered what it was about gaming that made people willing to devote so much of their lives to an activity that promises no tangible reward. McGonigal's premise is that a good game fulfills what human beings need for happiness: satisfying work, the hope of being successful, social connection, and meaning beyond oneself. When I read that, I literally stopped reading and realized how much better we'd all be if our educational systems were designed around these four concepts.

Games make you want to work, overcome obstacles, and think through things in a different way to achieve your goal. Ironically, the fact that games are entertaining is both the reason so many people dismiss their value and what makes them so compelling. For proof, you only have to look at the numbers. In the first month after *Call of Duty: Black Ops* was released, it had been played for more than 600 million hours, the equivalent of 68,000 years. But that's only one game. Many games, many of them vastly different from *COD*, are equally popular.

For those children who attend schools with burned-out teachers who teach to the test and don't explain the context for what students are learning in the first place, gaming is literally a graphic example of school's irrelevance.

---

*Daphne Bavelier, "Your Brain on Video Games," *Talks/TedX*, June 2012.

GAMING BASICS FOR THE UNINITIATED

Some games today (like the popular fantasy game *Skyrim*) are meant for a single player and often feature involved stories that can help the player feel as though he is starring in his very own movie. But many games are played with other people. These are called "multiplayer" games. Some multiplayer games can be played in split-screen mode, where the players sit on the couch next to each other, each with his own section of screen—for example, a lot of guys play first-person shooter or racing games with their friends all piled onto a couch together.

There are also multiplayer online games with anywhere from two to dozens of players sharing the same virtual environment and playing with or against each other. Some of these games (like *Call of Duty*) have a concrete beginning and end, although some systems allow players to accumulate points over time to buy rewards. In Xbox, for example, players have a "gamer tag" that is their online identity whether they're playing *COD* or *Just Dance,* and as they play games under that tag they can accumulate and unlock things they value. The popular MOBA (multiplayer online battle arena) genre, in which players engage in intense team battles, with each player controlling his character of choice to help destroy the other team's base, tends to follow this format.

Other games let players participate in an ongoing virtual world with no beginning and no end. They decide how they want to participate in that world. All of these games have complex social dynamics and rules. But what it always comes down to, whether the game is *Club Penguins* or *League of Legends,* is that all multiplayer games have the potential for their players to go after each other.

PWNED*

As you saw toward the beginning of this book, the ideals of the ALMB express themselves loudly in certain popular (usually first-person shooter) video games. These games pick up where the Batman toy left off, offering your son unfeeling, independent, self-reliant, detached enforcers to not only look up to, but to become. Not coincidentally, many of these competitive, mass-marketed titles—made to appeal to as large an audience as possible (*Halo, Call of Duty,* etc.)—could easily be described as "jock" games. Most of them have a single-player component that has the rough plot of an explosion-filled action movie and a multiplayer component centered on the experience of the "deathmatch"—i.e., free-for-all tag with bullets, lasers, and rocket launchers.

Let's talk about death in these games, because if you don't play them, it may really upset you when you see the screen turn red from someone "dying." It's natural to assume that dying in the game is traumatic, but it's not. Dying is so inconsequential that it doesn't even kick you out of the game. You can die twenty-five times and still win (though that would be a very long game). It's the point-scoring mechanism, like scoring a basket in basketball. As soon as you're killed you automatically regenerate or "respawn."

These virtual arenas, whether limited to four boys playing on a living room TV or sixteen scattered across a continent, are just like the playground at recess. By the time boys are age ten or eleven, these games have become a central feature of many boys' group dynamics. And all too often, unfortunately, their culture is one of brutal competition, degrading trash talk, cheating, and humiliation of opponents by any means necessary.

Imagine what you'd hear on the toughest street basketball court on the planet, and then multiply that by the fact that your virtual

---

*"PWND" is a corruption of the word "owned." It means to be dominated by an opponent or situation, especially by some godlike or computerlike force.

self fears no physical threat, that your raw insecurity can be covered by whatever bile you can summon from your mouth, and that if the going gets too tough or you are outmatched or embarrass yourself, you can instantly quit and vanish. There's no accountability.

This is one of the reasons why playing on the couch with friends is less hostile than being online. The group roles are still there. The Mastermind decides the teams, what game everyone is playing, and what scenario they'll play in the game. The Punching Bag is still relentlessly teased for choosing the worst scenario. All of that is still there, but there are limits to how much boys will trash each other while playing on the couch because there would be social consequences.

Another problem with online games is that players can enable the chat function. So say your ten-year-old figures out how to enable the chat in his World War II flight simulation game. He's worked really hard to be good enough to play against other players online, and his reward is that within a few moments a thirty-year-old guy is calling him a pussy or faggot. Or, on Xbox LIVE, a player can send your son a private message and viciously go after him. If your son is being continuously harassed, or the single message is bad enough, he can block the harasser (sometimes called an "Internet troll") from contacting him, but the harasser can always make another account and go after him again.

Unfortunately, we have to play games with terrible gender and racial politics because the industry has done next to nothing to create positive social norms while the players are blowing each other up. Gamers can be as bad as, if not worse than, the most sexist stereotypical jock. One of my favorite websites, fatuglyorslutty.com, chronicles the horrible things that guys say to girl gamers.* Many girls and women don't wear their mics while they're playing so the other players can't recognize that they're female. Some will only play with their mic if they're playing with friends.

---

*Notice that the website is cleverly named "fatugly *or* slutty," because all the comments call girls only one of two things: fat/ugly or slutty.

Recently two female executives from video-game developer 343 Industries—general manager Bonnie Ross and the executive producer of *Halo 4*, Kiki Wolfkill*—spoke out about the industry's responsibility to stop the gaming environment from being so hostile to girls. But while the industry figures out how to evolve, you need to put your foot down with your son's online behavior. You must explicitly articulate your expectation that he will not be a degenerate sexual harasser. Not only that, but you expect him to do his best to report to the server when some horrible guy starts attacking female players (even if he doesn't feel capable of standing up to the guy in the moment). For the same reasons that some gamers feel anonymity gives them a license to be sexist, many gamers will also indulge in a lot of racist or homophobic trash talk, and your son shouldn't feel that he has to turn a blind eye to that either, especially if he hears an actual person being degraded with such slurs through chat. Knowing how to report a problem will vary according to the platform your child uses, so it's worth educating yourself about your options whenever he gets a new console or computer game.

If there's anything your son shouldn't have thin skin about, it's this. He's getting trash-talked anyway, so this is the moment to empower him not to be the silent bystander. Worse comes to worst, he drops his gamer tag and creates a new one. From a nongamer perspective, that may not seem like a very big deal, but for your son it may be a harder decision. If he drops his gamer tag, he loses all of his accomplishments assigned to that name. I know that doesn't seem like much compared to helping someone out who's being harassed, but those accomplishments represent a lot of hard work. He still needs to do it, but just recognize that from his perspective dropping his gamer tag may be an incredibly selfless act. If the harasser is a real-life friend, then he's dealing with a problem in real life as well. (I address how to handle that problem in the "Friendly Fire" chapter.)

Whatever your justification, these are the moments when you need to apply your values concretely and relevantly in your son's

---

*Yes, this is her real name.

life—for the sake of the girls, the younger children who are inevitably playing, and your son's moral development. This is the moment literally for him to be the hero.

THE DIFFERENT KINDS OF GAMERS

A **casual gamer** limits his gaming and tends to play easy-to-use games.

A **mid-core gamer** is a player who loves playing different kinds of games but has a few favorites.

A **hard-core gamer** plays more involved games that require time to complete or master. He often participates in competitions, events, and conventions.

A **griefer** is a player who deliberately irritates and harasses other players within the game. He derives pleasure primarily or exclusively from annoying other players.

I'm giving you these definitions because it's critical for parents to understand what kind of gamer their child is. You may be freaking out that your son seems to be obsessed with playing video games. But what if his love of gaming motivates him to create his own games or learn computer programming, or graphic design, or storytelling? Wouldn't this be something you'd want to support? Learning by immersing yourself in something you love is a creative problem-solving experience. This is education at its best.

On the other hand, your son should know that being a griefer who intentionally sets out to ruin other people's fun isn't all that different from being a bully in real life (more on this in a bit). Like anything else, games can be a positive or a negative depending on how they're used—and you won't know what your son is getting out of gaming unless you take the time to pay attention.

WHEN SHOULD I LET HIM PLAY? WHAT SHOULD I LET HIM PLAY?

Whether or not your child should be able to see a certain movie or play a certain game depends on your beliefs as a parent and your child's interests, intellect, and emotional makeup. But honestly, all your vigilance will fly out the window if your son has older siblings. For example, when your oldest was five, you put on *Dora* and there was no possibility that another kid would come along and change the program. But then that five-year-old becomes twelve, and now he has eight- and five-year-old siblings. That five-year-old is probably hanging out with his older brother when he's playing some game that would have made you hit the ceiling if you'd walked in on it seven years before.

But say you've held to your standards no matter how old your kids are or how many kids you have. At some point, usually around third grade at the latest, your kids start hanging out at other friends' houses. Those families can have different rules and older kids in the house. Older kids mean older games. This means that you need to sit down with your six- to nine-year-old child and say something like:

"You're invited to another kid's house this afternoon. I don't know what you'll end up doing, but in case they want to play a game, some of the games or the way the games are played can be really stressful. As you get older I'm going to let you play different kinds of games at different levels, but for right now, if you go over to someone's house and they're playing a game that's making you uncomfortable, I want you to ask the kid to do something else. If they don't want to, you can tell the parent that you don't like it, if you feel comfortable doing that, and the parent can help you find something else to do. And if you feel really uncomfortable about the games or anything else, you can always call me to come get you and take you home."*

---

*This is a last option just to give the child an out if he's really feeling unsafe. You never know. This is also why it's so important to know another family before your child goes

BULLYING AND CONFLICT WITHIN THE GAME

We see a lot of in-game bullying, even between the best of friends. . . .
They'll destroy each other's stuff on Minecraft, *ban each other from*
their servers, kill each other on Modern Warfare, *even when they*
aren't playing against each other, etc. It's as if they all suddenly be-
come little Napoleons with these online personas, and some take it
very personally, but never do they act like this with each other in real
life. —Sandy

I'm going to use this parent's quote to talk about what's annoying,
aggressive, and bullying in Boy World related to video games.

These dynamics are exactly the same as in any other social networking or online venue. Destroying someone's work on a game
like *Minecraft* is a deliberately hostile act. This is exactly the same
as when a kid in kindergarten builds a castle out of blocks and
another kid deliberately knocks it over. If that happens repeatedly
online, that's "cyberbullying." Killing someone in *Modern Warfare*
could be somewhat aggressive or not at all aggressive. It entirely
depends on what kind of game is being played within the game. If
the players are messing around (i.e., the game has no stakes), that's
annoying. If they're directly competing in a deathmatch, killing is
no different from blocking a shot in basketball or tagging someone
out in baseball. If a player is targeting another player repeatedly to
kill him, that can be aggressive, but it still isn't as bad as destroying work.

Banning a player from servers isn't usually a hostile, aggressive
act. It's an appropriate response to a player who isn't behaving according to the prosocial norms of the game and the community of
gamers who play the game. If that's the case, this is a good reason to
ban someone and it gives him meaningful social consequences. This

---

to their house. Sometimes it's not always possible, but I know a lot of parents who don't
let their kids hang out with another family unless they've checked them out.

is exactly the same as the kid who's been mean to other kids in real life discovering that the other kids won't play with him anymore. Just like in real life, the over-aggressive player usually has to behave badly more than once to be banned.

If the player is banned because he's socially weak, then this is social exclusion. He isn't being granted access to the group. One of the ways this could happen most easily is if a boy is in charge of the server. If that's the case, then he has total control over who participates in the game. If he bans someone because he wants to exercise or demonstrate his power over the other kid, then that's obviously unethical. So if your child is in charge of a server, be clear with him about the responsibility that comes with that authority.

HOW MUCH IS TOO MUCH?

Bingeing on anything is never good for anyone. It's not good for a mom or dad to drink too much wine after their kids go to sleep, just like it's not good for their son to play his favorite game every day after school. With video games, it's not good for your son's physical health to sit in front of a screen all day and not get any exercise. It's also not good for his social health if he's predominantly socializing with people online, because interacting with people in real life can get increasingly weird for him.

I've read tons on how much "screen time" kids should get, and I've talked to boys about how much time they think they should have. Asking boys how much gaming they should do may seem absurd to you, but it's not as crazy as it seems. If they're not talking (i.e., arguing) with their parents about it when they're in the middle of an intense battle, they're pretty reasonable. And I tested things out on my own children. I'll now share with you one of the dumbest ideas I ever tried.

One Saturday when my children were eight and ten, I told them that there would be none of the usual limits on screen time. If they wanted to spend the entire day in front of the TV, they could. I assumed they'd eventually get sick of it. They still remember that day fondly. No exaggeration—eight hours later, they were still going strong when I called parent executive privilege and turned off the screens.

From that experience I had two epiphanies. First, assuming the installation of basic parental controls, the problem wasn't content. It was duration. Second, video games had become the biggest source of irritation, arguments, and family discord between us. I was regularly coming into the house to find them on the couch playing their fifteenth round of *Mario Kart*. At that point, I thought the only reasonable answer was to get rid of all the video games we had in the house, which I communicated to my boys by yelling at them as I stomped around the room grabbing the controllers out of their hands. Then I'd see the empty bag of chips, the crumbs all over the couch, and their smelly socks stuffed between the cushions, and I'd freak out all over again.

This was the moment I realized I was becoming the mom I hate. The one who makes ultimatums but doesn't carry them out. Why didn't I follow through? Because I liked playing *Just Dance 4,* and if I threw out the console I wouldn't be able to play. And even though I'd pulled the console out of the wall before for weeks at a time, that hadn't stopped them because they would play at their friends' houses. Plus, as soon as I brought the console back out, they went right back to their old behavior.

This is the real way video games cause violence—by making mothers want to kill their children. I had to find a better way. After I calmed down, I drew up a list of rules. It took me a few months to refine them to what you see below, but these rules have been successful in that there's been a decrease in my yelling and my kids' whining. I'm calling that a win.

VIDEO GAMES RULES FOR THE WISEMAN EDWARDS FAMILY

In the understanding that family harmony is of paramount important, we agree to the following:

Children

1. I realize I have no ability to accurately gauge how long I've played because I lose track of time. Therefore, when my mom or dad tell me time's up, I won't respond with, "What!? But I've only been on for a few minutes! I'm about to get to the next level! Let me just throw myself off this cliff! It'll only take one minute! I promise!"

2. I will keep track of how long I play by using a timer that my parents provide.

3. I won't constantly ask if I can play video games after my parent tells me no.

4. If told no by one parent, I won't go ask the other parent who doesn't know what the first parent said.

5. If told no, I will not respond with, "Why?"

6. I won't compare how long my sibling has played with how long I've played. For example, "But he has gotten so much more screen time than me" will result in an automatic reduction in play by ten minutes the next time I play.

7. If one person is playing and wants to concentrate on his game, the other person can't constantly bug him. As in, "You only have five minutes left and it's my turn. You never share!"

8. I'll pause the game within one minute after being told my time is up. If I don't comply with this rule, I understand that my parent will turn off the screen so that any unsaved progress I lose will be because of my actions, not because my mom turned off the screen.

9. The words "never" and "always" are not in my vocabulary. For example, "I never get to play what I want and he always gets to!" If I feel that way, I will record the amount of time each of us plays for two weeks, write it up in graph form, and present my evidence to the parental authorities.

10. I won't buy videos or apps without my parents' explicit permission. If I violate this rule, I understand that I'll be forbidden to play for the next week without exception and that the amount of

the charge will be deducted from my savings account or allowance.

11. I won't play games or visit websites that my parents have forbidden. If I do, I understand that I'm in breach of contract and my
parents can restrict my technology access until they believe I
have shown I can respect their terms.

12. When I'm playing multiplayer games, the family values apply.
Therefore, I can't use homophobic, racist, or sexist terms when
communicating with other players. If they do, I will immediately
tell them to stop, leave the game, complain to the server, or find
another game or group who's playing the game.

13. I understand that if my grades slip, my game time may be less-
ened or revoked to make way for more study. Reinstatement of
normal gaming will be based solely upon my parents' review of
my progress and/or effort in regard to my education.

14. Parents can and should dictate gore and explicit-content settings.

When I Can Play

1. I'm not allowed to play during the school week.
2. On weekends, I may play up to ninety minutes per day.
3. During vacations, I may play up to ninety minutes per day. If
necessary, to allow opportunity for others to play, this will be
done in thirty-minute segments. I must set the timer to keep
track of my time.
4. Total playing time includes the use of all gaming devices (iPad,
phone, Xbox, Wii, etc.).
5. The weekend is hereby defined as Friday (after school) through
Sunday night.
6. If by Saturday night homework/studying/projects for the upcom-
ing week have not progressed satisfactorily, all gaming rights for
Sunday may/will be put on hold.
7. On weekend mornings, I'm forbidden to wake up and immediately play. I must take care of my basic hygiene first, including
going to the bathroom, brushing my teeth, putting on some form

of clothes, eating something, and making sure any dependents are given the same care. That specifically means taking care of any pets, including but not limited to *walking* (not letting out) the dog. Violation of these rules will result in automatic suspension of play until the next day.

8. The one game with time immunity is when the family plays *Just Dance* together (or any other family game the mother chooses).

These rules may be changed by parental executive decision at any time.

Signed:

Child X_____ Child Y_____

Parent_____ Parent_____

PUTTING THE CONTROLLER IN YOUR OWN HANDS

Even though you're restricting your son's game time, you have to play his games, though it'll probably be unpleasant for a lot of reasons. For one thing, it will be a sensory overload. Second, you're probably going to be really bad at it and your child is going to kick your butt. You're going to be respawned or regenerated countless times. When my children first taught me, they loved bossing me around. They loved it too much. I couldn't understand all the simultaneous directions they were giving me. They also steered me right to where they knew a guy would come out and attack me.

Most video games have "gore" levels that the player can control and a training version that teaches you how to play. Take the course. Even if you hate it, you have to show that you took the time to learn about it. If you do play, this is actually a great bonding time with your kids. When my husband and I play *Halo* with our boys and one of us "kills" one of my boys, I think there's more than a little bit of cathartic release.

The other benefit of playing with your child is that you'll actually be able to see what he plays and how he plays it. Ask yourself what these games are telling you about your kid—does he want to play games where he works creatively? Does he work in common with people? Does he want to play so he can annihilate the opposition without genuine challenge? Does he want to win for the sake of winning regardless of how easy it is to win?

As kids get older, gaming will continue to be part of their lives, but a lot of the boys I work with don't play games as often as they did in middle school because their high school obligations won't allow it. They'll still play with their friends on a Saturday night before they go out, but their overall playing time decreases substantially. Other kids will pursue gaming as one of their primary creative and social outlets. And other kids will lose themselves in it to escape the real world.

> *There was a time where I would only practice the game and wouldn't hang out with my friends. My mom noticed that, and she told me, and at first I denied it, but then I realized it was true and took a break from gaming. So it's good to remember that there still needs to be social interaction, and in my case the weekends (especially Saturday) were when I did not play video games and only went out with my friends. Unless, of course, if you go to a friend's house to play video games, then it's okay, because you are socializing, but if you're doing that all the time, then it defeats the purpose because you can do that at home. —Milo, 16*

Remember in the beginning of the book I described how frustrating it is to be five and how great it is to run around in a Batman cape? Being a teen can often feel very similar. For many reasons, it's frustrating to be a teen. It's natural for teens to want to escape the limitations and frustrations they have in their real lives and feel powerful and useful in their virtual lives.

If your teen is spending a huge amount of time playing video games and isn't involved in other things in his life, it's time to ask yourself some hard questions about why he's so driven to find meaning and fulfillment in those games. It's time to educate yourself about the specific game or games he's most drawn to. Look them up in Wikipedia, Reddit, or Urban Dictionary. Look up what players are posting about the games or scenes from the games on YouTube. Don't take the advice of people who don't know the specific game but have very strong opinions about video games in general.

Games can also help kids get through incredibly difficult times in their lives. This blog submission from the website howgames savedmylife.com says it better than I ever could:

I entered my sophomore year of high school coming out of the aftermath of four years' worth of bullying that I was thankful I survived. I felt that sophomore year would give me an opportunity to turn over a new leaf and be a more positive person. About a month into the semester, I learned that I wasn't going to get that opportunity. I started to get bullied again by the students who had followed me through the years and hadn't yet grown out of the habit of picking on me, my parents put our house up for sale for fear of foreclosure, and my dad began nursing an increasingly serious drinking habit and an unhealthy fascination with the biblical end times that eventually got so bad I would skip meals and stay locked up in my room to avoid him and his ranting. Between bullies, school, my parents, and their palpable disappointment in me, I became quiet, lethargic, and withdrawn. I began experiencing the beginnings of suicidal thoughts.

So it's ironic that the game that saved me from this depression was Fallout 3, *a game that pretty much screams that the future doesn't look too good. I felt the joy of every victory, the sting of every tragedy, the thrill of every escapade, and the camaraderie between myself, the characters, and my companions. I know without a shadow of a doubt why* Fallout 3 *pulled me out of my depression. It wasn't because it helped me escape from my troubles, it was because it made me feel like I was worth a damn. That in this period of my life when I felt like a piece of decaying organic waste, I was still able to hope, still able to achieve, still able to do anything. That even when times were hard, I, as a person, was actually worth something, even in a future that was hopelessly deadlocked in a constant cycle of survival and conflict (which my dad feels could be the imminent future of today's society). I was saving people, changing lives, and vanquishing evil—I felt like someone worth living as, and this translated to my real life and gave me a more optimistic outlook on the future. I'm currently halfway through my junior year of high school and haven't touched Fallout 3 since beating it nearly a year ago (or maybe I didn't beat it . . . it kept freezing on me). I haven't been bullied in months, I'm closer to my parents, and I'm not the antisocial introvert I was last year. I credit Fallout 3 for helping me through this dark part of my life.*

I know it seems impossible to believe that a violent video game based on society's total destruction would make a guy feel more connected to other people and better about himself. If you look at the game he's referring to, you may *really* have a hard time believing it. But what we think doesn't matter. If boys are telling us that their real lives are so hard and they feel so worthless that escaping into a virtual world makes them feel better about themselves, that's their truth and it needs to be respected. For this blog writer, in the absence of support and guidance from the people in his real life, the people in his online life gave him support. So when you hear people, including parenting experts, decry the inability for today's youth to have meaningful, real-life relationships because they're constantly playing online, I think we're overlooking one really important possibility: maybe those children never had those relationships in their real lives in the first place. Maybe their online relationships give them support that they have never been able to get—and that they desperately need—from the adults and other kids in their lives.

11

Friendly Fire

We are confused about friendships. When girls whisper to each other, sit on each other's laps, or walk arm in arm, we believe we're seeing close friendships in action. When we see boys trade sarcastic put-downs, intensely argue over who cheated, and put each other in headlocks, it can be unclear if these boys hate each other or are best friends.

We value what we believe we see. And what we see most easily are girls and their social dynamics. The stereotypical appearance of girls' close friendships—the whispering, the huddling together, the sharing of earbuds while listening to a favorite song—is the standard against which we often judge boys' friendships. It's not a conscious decision on our part, but we often assume that girls not only have closer, better friendships with each other but also need them more than boys.

These assumptions are wrong. Behind boys' arguments and put-downs is a complicated social system in which friendships are deeply valued. And strangely enough, if you look and listen beyond the put-downs, yelling, and laughing, boys' friendship dynamics are just as complex and nuanced as those of girls.

Believe me, I understand if this is hard to believe. Listen to what Auguste said when I asked him to pull back the "boy curtain" for you:

I know it looks like we're insane and loud . . . okay, we're really loud.
And we can be really rude, and our parents don't even hear how we

usually talk to each other. But I'd do anything for my friends. I can't really explain the bond we have, but it's deep. And by the way, those girls Rosalind wrote about? The ones who are all over each other all the time? The truth is, most of the time those girls hate each other.
—Ted, 17

Ted is mostly right. I'd say that "some" of the time girls only look like they're best friends, not "most" of the time. But everything else he's saying I totally believe because I've repeatedly heard boys say, "I'd do anything for my friends."

Here are other boys describing their friendships:

I love the guy. We've stayed up all night walking around and talked the whole night. But we went through times when we hated each other and didn't talk for six months. But there's a bond there that isn't going to be broken . . . although he can be so stubborn when he thinks he's right. He's my hard-truth friend. Just calls it out. Doesn't moderate his approach. That's why I call him "the Mule." (The Mule, sitting next to him, smiles and nods in agreement.) *—Hunter, 17*

Good friends help you get through the long school day. What I mean by this is that if you do bad on a test or get bullied, they will comfort you and you'll do the same. —Preston, 12

Friends aren't there only when things are going well. They were there for me when my dog died, when my parents got divorced, and when my brother left for college. Because of them, things were bearable. —Matt, 16

But there's a big problem in male friendships that makes them fragile, no matter how strong an individual boy thinks those bonds are or wants them to be. It happens when the friendship that "you'd do anything for" requires you to face your friend and communicate anger, disappointment, frustration, or worry. Boys' friendships are fragile because somewhere along the way boys become afraid to tell the truth to each other. If they feel betrayed, they suffer and rage internally. When their friends go over the line, they force themselves to laugh along, convinced that their complaints will only result in more ridicule. If they're worried, they convince themselves there's no point in reaching out. In their discomfort and ignorance about what to do, boys will say nothing until the friendship dissolves and they're left silently mourning the loss.

Why does this happen? And what can we do to help boys have the friendships they want and deserve? That is what this chapter will explore. We'll build on the ALMB and the overall social structure and connect that to how boys' friendships and conflicts are structured. Then I'll show you how to reach out to a boy when he's going through a hard time but probably really doesn't want to tell you. As this chapter will show, it's far too easy for a boy to learn that it's more important to maintain a friendship than to take a stand on how he's treated within that friendship.

What do boys' conflicts look like? Here are some common answers from boys in elementary school:

My best friend and I fight a lot. The most frustrating conflicts start as just a little spark. Then the spark will catch on to something, and the boxing gloves will come out. I don't mean literally boxing gloves and throwing punches, though. I hate these little disagreements, because then my friend and I will blow up and then shun each other for days. Sometimes it really hurts, and I wish everything could just go back to normal. I usually don't talk to my family because I get tense talking about that stuff. —Owen, 11

My most frustrating conflicts are when people exclude you from things, and when they try to get away with stuff they're not supposed to. When we try to tell them, they get all angry and violent. —Harry, 10

I think that the most frustrating conflict with friends is when there is a problem and a bunch of kids agree with one person and another bunch agrees with the other. —Alan, 11

My most frustrating conflicts with friends are not-kept promises. We tell our parents, but they just say, "Talk it out," but we need advice on how to talk it out. —Felix, 11

My friends sometimes get mad at me and make fun of me because I like to protect my stuff. Then they say I sound like my sister. That really hurts my feelings. —Elijah, 10

Here's what it looks like when they get older:

My group of friends were not a nice group of people. I feel like it was a power struggle between everybody. Like if you were funny, that's good, or if you were friends with this certain person, that gave you good "rank" among us. I was trying to be too funny again, and it blew up. All my friends started calling me "not funny." By the middle of eighth grade, all the guys were calling me it. It got so bad that whenever I tried to speak, they would cut me off and just say, "You're not funny," and then they'd all laugh. That's the first point where I actually felt alone and isolated, because they pretended and said they were sorry when it was one-on-one with a friend, but the next day, when we were all in a group, they would join in on the "not funny" joke and even tell everyone whatever secrets or trusted things I'd told them. Of course, I exploded during eighth grade throughout the year, but that just gave them fuel to do it more. —Jack, 14

I have a friend who goes out of his way to make people miserable. But it's all a joke to him. I want to confront him, but no matter what I say, he'll just blow me off. You don't understand how he is. He doesn't listen to anyone. —Ethan, 17

I was hanging out with some of my junior friends by the lunch tables. I wasn't saying much, just hanging out, laughing at jokes, and this one kid named Drew said a funny joke. I laughed and said a smart-ass comment in reply, and he said to me, "Who let the niggas talk?" I almost fought him, but some of my (white) friends held me back and told me to calm down. I don't want to calm down. They have no idea what it feels like. —Wes, 17

HUMOR: THE INVISIBLE WEAPON FOR GOOD AND EVIL

Being funny always has been and always will be one of the most important skills to have in Boy World. It's the great equalizer against the ALMB. It diffuses tense social situations. It teaches guys to get through the everyday annoyances of life without taking themselves or other people too seriously. If a guy can mutter sarcastic, mocking comments under his breath through a cough, brag but not too much, and make fun of himself, his social status will always be solid. Moreover, doing humor well can be tremendously valuable in relationships with girls. Boys realize this at a very early age, even if they aren't capable of humor themselves.

The unwritten rules of humor in Boy World are incredibly nuanced. Here are some of the most important:

1. You must have quick comebacks.
2. You must put yourself down in a funny way that doesn't convey that failure, weakness, or vulnerability actually makes you feel bad.
3. You must never be passive when people put you down. You must respond according to the first two rules above. If you don't, you're opening yourself up to constant attack by everyone from your closest friends to the guys who'll go out of their way to make you miserable.
4. You must laugh as a way to shake off being embarrassed. Always.
5. You must never take anything seriously unless your masculinity is questioned. Even then, it's still better to keep your mouth shut unless you're willing to fight.

For all these reasons, it's hard to know when boys are playing with each other, teasing, or being really hurtful. Sometimes they don't know themselves, or even if they do, they insist that they don't care. Depending on the power dynamics (and there are always power dynamics) between a boy and the person who's teasing him, or vice versa, there could be a lot more going on than he can articulate to himself or his parents.

All boys will experience someone in their life taking advantage of these dynamics to humiliate someone. Many will also do it themselves. What it comes down to is that a lot of guys get away with being cruel because these unwritten rules stop the target or the bystander from ever complaining. If they do complain, the response is, "It's just a joke. Relax. I'm just messing around." That stops boys from saying anything else.

What all this means is that kids get away with a lot of bad behavior because a term like "teasing" can mean everything from people bonding with each other to one person relentlessly making another person miserable. We need to clarify the difference. Here's how:

Good Teasing

Good teasing is one of the cornerstones of great friendships. Friends who care about each other, know each other well, and are comfortable together can tease and joke around with each other—"with" (not "at") being the operative word. With good teasing, there's no intention to put the other person down, and everyone knows what's off-limits to tease about. The friend on the receiving end knows that he can ask his friend to stop and he actually will.

Guys can "good-tease" each other by saying incredibly rude things: comments about who farts the most and the loudest, their mothers, and how much sex they're getting (or not) and with whom. Think of it as a democracy of put-downs. If all the guys in a group can go after each other, then it's good. But the reality is that those roles of Mastermind, Bouncer, etc., within the group often dictate who gets teased and how low the attack can go.

Ignorant Teasing

It's always hard for guys to tell someone they like or have to have an ongoing relationship with that they're angry about something that other person said. But when the intent isn't malicious (which isn't to say it couldn't be insensitive), once the teaser understands the impact of his behavior, he'll get over his defensiveness and sincerely apologize because he recognizes that he went over the line.

Malicious Teasing

This so-called teasing is done to make the targeted person feel inferior. Malicious teasing highlights the difference between the target and everyone else, it's relentless, and it's public. If there's any resistance, the malicious teaser either claims ignorance, refuses to take responsibility for what he's doing ("Dude, I'm just messing with you," "What are you making such a big deal of this for?," "Don't be so gay/retarded," etc.), or makes the "complainer" feel so stupid or weak that he ends up apologizing for speaking up.

CHECK YOUR BAGGAGE

Were you ever teased when you were a child or teen? What was it about? How did you handle it?

Did you ever tease other kids? Siblings? Why did you do it?

How do you think that impacts your relationships now?

If you're an adult teasing a boy and there's even a chance it backfired, say, "Hey, sorry about that." If he says "Don't worry about it" or "That's okay," that doesn't necessarily mean he feels good about what you said. What are the signs that he doesn't like it? When he says "Um . . . okay" and avoids looking you in the face or looks down, make a mental note that whatever you were teasing him about is off-limits.

And parents, look back to the definition of teasing above. None of us are immune from hurting other people, including our kids when we say things like "I'm just joking" or "You're being too sensitive; you're being a moody teenager." If you just realized that you've been doing any of the above with a boy, it's never too late to address it. Be strategic about how you bring it up, and don't come across as if you think he's walking around devastated about it. Just say something like "Hey, sorry about teasing you sometimes. I've been thinking about it, and I've been over the line."

LANDMINE!

What do you tease your son about?
Does he like it?
How do you know?

USING SEAL WITH FRIENDS

When a boy is dealing with either an ignorant or a malicious teaser who's a friend of his, someone he associates with, there's a specific SEAL protocol that usually works. What I mean by "works" is a boy thinking that strategizing may solve the problem. It's a victory just to have him thinking through a solution and not dwelling on a problem that he thinks he can't address.

The Stop and Setup is always the same. The boy and the teaser should have the conversation one-on-one when they're playing a video game, walking back from practice, or just hanging out. The basic rule is that it's better to have intense, awkward conversations with this person while you're doing something else so you don't have to look at him. It doesn't mean it won't be weird, but it'll be less weird. Think of it as easing into the conversation and easing out. The whole thing shouldn't take more than two minutes.

Say your ten-year-old son is being teased for being short by his really good friend. You've overheard the kid tease him, and you're pretty sure your kid doesn't like it. The only problem is that he hasn't said anything to you about it and you don't want to bring it up because, if you're wrong, you'll be bringing attention to a problem that maybe didn't bother him until you brought it up. Here's what you do.

Keep what you say brief, and say it while you're doing something else, like bringing in the groceries (just like you want him to do talking to his friend while playing video games). Do not under any circumstances sit him down to have a talk about this, because that'll make him feel like a huge loser. This is what I'd say:

"Hey, now that you're getting older, it's common for guys to say obnoxious things to each other and say, 'Just joking.' We may not be able to stop the problem immediately, but if we work on it together, you'll have more control over the situation. You don't have to talk to me about this right away, I just wanted you to know I'm here. Can you get that last grocery bag for me in the back?"

Remember, don't expect your son to spill his guts right away. But if he does, or if he comes up to you a few hours later or even a few days later with something like, "You know, those guys are sort of bothering me," you're ready. You say something like: "I'm so sorry. Thanks for telling me. Can you tell me a little more about what you mean when you say they're bothering you?"

If he's on the younger side (not a teen) or he's more open in general, you can walk him through an ideal SEAL or have him write it down. Your job is to be involved in this situation by helping him put his feelings into words, articulate to himself what he wants stopped, think of any possible push-backs, and have a way to ease out of the conversation. Here's an example of an ideal SEAL. The Stop and Setup is walking back from practice across a field.

BOY *(explaining)*: Okay, sort of embarrassing to say this, but I need you to stop making comments about how short I am.

FRIEND *(pushing back)*: What?? You know I'm just joking. And you laugh when I say that stuff.

BOY *(explaining again)*: I'm laughing because I don't want to make a big deal of it, but I want you to stop.

FRIEND *(pushing back again)*: Sure, if it bothers you that much *(laughs)*.

BOY *(locking in while easing back into regular territory)*: Thanks. Did you see who we're playing Saturday?

I know it doesn't seem like it, but this is a successful SEAL. Your son has made his feelings clear to himself and his friend. He's thought about where and when to make the approach. He may not get a sincere apology, but that's an unrealistic expectation anyway. Instead, his goal is to communicate his message, not conduct some weird hour-long conversation. Plus, he stays in control of the conversation and then gets it back onto more normal ground. Mission accomplished. Remember, it's critical to tell your son that however much of this conversation he manages to have, it's been a success.

LANDMINE!

If you help your son plan a SEAL, don't ask him how it went the next time you know he's seen the kid. If he didn't talk to the kid, he doesn't want to talk about it with you because he'll feel like he's let you down or he's failed. Maybe later that evening or the next day you can ask him how it's going with the kid. You want to come across as curious, not intrusive.

Now let's go back to Jack, who I quoted in the beginning of this chapter. Jack is in eighth grade. His friends are deeply important to him. They give him a sense of belonging and identity.

Let's look again at what Jack had to say:

My group of friends were not a nice group of people. I feel like it was a power struggle between everybody. Like if you were funny, that's good, or if you were friends with this certain person, that gave you good "rank" among us. I was trying to be too funny again, and it blew up. All my friends started calling me "not funny." By the middle of eighth grade, all the guys were calling me it. It got so bad that whenever I tried to speak, they would cut me off and just say, "You're not funny," and then they'd all laugh. That's the first point where I actually felt alone and isolated, because they pretended and said they were sorry when it was one-on-one with a friend, but the next day, when we were all in a group, they would join in on the "not funny" joke and even tell everyone whatever secrets or trusted things I'd told them. Of course, I exploded during eighth grade throughout the year, but that just gave them fuel to do it more. —Jack, 14

From the outside, it can be easy to draw the wrong conclusion that Jack's large circle of friends = popularity = happiness. This isn't true. It's way better to have one good friend who you can truly be yourself around than be in a group with a Mastermind and his minions. But here's the big challenge for Jack's parents. It's likely that they have no idea that Jack's friends are doing this to him. What they're more likely to see are the consequences—overnight Jack may become anxious, rude, or aggressive toward his parents or his siblings. People don't act out "for no reason" or "out of the blue." There's always a good reason, and Jack's parents just don't know what it is yet. They don't know that Jack's "closest" friends are making him feel more isolated, just as happens in groups of girls.

Most kids don't talk about friends and their social lives [to this extent] with their parents, so this is probably something that Jack would keep bottled up inside that would make him either choose a new group of friends, become completely isolated, or do something really stupid. —Brian, 16

How do Jack's parents get him to talk to them? When they're preparing to talk to him, they need to remember that he's worried about them judging his friends or thinking he's stupid for wanting to hang out with them after they learned how mean they've been to him. First, they need to say something similar to what I suggested above: "It's common for guys to have problems with their friends, so if you want to talk about it we're here."

Second, if Jack's behavior becomes more aggressive, they need to ask him if there's something they should know that would explain why he's so angry. That's not to excuse his actions but to let him know they understand that he wouldn't be acting aggressively without a good reason. His good reason could be absolutely ridiculous to them, or his way of talking about it could come across as trivial, so if they come across as being judgmental, he'll be even more frustrated—at himself, his friends, and his parents.

Third, if they get him to tell them what's going on and they respond "What do you want to *do* about it?," as soon as they say that word "do" he's going to think doing something is a very bad idea. His parents can't force him to confront these boys and stand up for himself. As an example of what Jack may be dealing with, here's what another one of the fourteen-year-old editors admitted.

> *We love verbally abusing him. Everyone in the group does, but we still love the kid. He's our boy. But anytime he talks to a girl or makes a joke, we destroy him. Why? Because it's funny and embarrassing to him. He likes it secretly. Well, he probably secretly hates it, but he's not going to say anything. I know it sounds mean, but it's really not because he knows we love him. —Aiden, 14*

Honestly, it may take Jack being much more frustrated than he is now. When I'm trying to convince boys to say something, I present my argument like this:

"You have two choices, ignore it or face it. If you ignore it, you're sending the message to your friends that you're fine with how they're treating you. But you're not fine with it, so sooner or later you're going to explode about something small, and then they're going to make fun of you even more. If you're not fine with them controlling you like this, then sooner or later you're going to have to confront them."

Boys can be convinced to speak out if they understand that sooner or later they're going to have to say something . . . or they'll spend their entire lives letting people roll over them. How they can be convinced to speak is through SEAL.

Here's an ideal SEAL for Jack and his parents to think about. The Stop and Setup is Jack inviting the Mastermind over to his house to play their favorite video game.

JACK: Can you do something about the not-funny thing?
FRIEND: Why? It's funny.
JACK: Can you just help me out here? Just let me finish a sentence.
FRIEND: Why are you freaking out about this?
JACK: I'm not. I'm just asking you to ease up a little. You don't get it. If you were in my shoes, you'd get it.
FRIEND: I guess.

Notice that I'm not suggesting that Jack lock in (or lock out) out loud, because the other boy would laugh at him for doing it. But Jack should still go through the L step in his mind so that he can begin to think about what he's willing to put up with (or not) in the friendship.

LANDMINE!

Has your son ever told you that another boy in your extended family or a friend's child is mean and you responded by saying "But he's really a good kid; he's from such a nice family" or "You know he has had some problems"? Listen to your child. He's telling you what his experience is with that child. Yes, that child may have some problems, but you don't have to deal with this kid, your child does. Your son's experience with other boys is more important than yours. Think about it from your son's perspective: why would he tell you when someone is mean if you're going to excuse it?

HOW DO I MAKE MY REALLY SENSITIVE SON STRONGER?

For a lot of different reasons, boys have different thresholds for what bothers them—family dynamics (if his siblings are constantly going after him, for example), deficits in social skills that make him unable to read people's intentions well, or just being a person who feels things deeply. I go into these issues in more depth in chapter 14 on "No Man's Land," but here are the basics.

You never want to take away your child's emotional truth. If he's upset about the way someone treated him, then he's entitled to his feelings. No amount of telling him otherwise is going to change his mind. It's also true that if he gets more easily irritated or has a harder time letting things roll off his back or is intent on making the other kids follow the rules, he becomes an easier target, and other children will be less likely to want to defend him.

This is a tricky balance. You have to accept him for who he is while at the same time recognizing that he may need to be pushed to build his tolerance and reaction to other kids. You don't coddle him. You give him skills. You encourage him to think through his feelings, confront people using SEAL, and debrief with him about the things he did well. Often these kids feel so stuck, like they're trapped and can't breathe. Your job is to get him unstuck and let him breathe. Each increment of movement gives him confidence that he can handle these moments well.

How you talk to him about this is critical. Stay away from saying things like "You just need to make an effort" or "You're so great, you just need people to get to know you."

Instead, the boys think the following would work better: "I'm really sorry that happened. Do you think the person intentionally wanted to hurt your feelings? How can you tell?" Then, depending on his maturity level, either go over with him or have him read the three kinds of teasing and help him decide which one best describes his situation.

If you can see how he's contributing to the problem—like he's inflexible with other kids, gets angry when other kids don't follow the rules, and believes that he's "right" and everyone else is "wrong," then you need to ask him a few questions. Say your fourth-grade son gets really angry at the other kids when they play foursquare at recess. He's furious at the kids for calling "redos" as a way to cheat and deliberately make him angry. He could be right—because there are always kids like that. But it could be that the other kids genuinely are doing a redo as a way to ensure fairness in the game. Your job as the parent is to help him figure out which one is happening and then decide what he wants to do.

If the kids are in the first category, then ask him what the positives and negatives of playing with these kids are. If the positives outweigh the negatives, then he needs to use a SEAL strategy to address the problem. If the negatives outweigh the positives, then he should find another activity. If the other kids are in the second category (go back to the teasing definitions and the group breakdowns with him to help him decide), then he needs to ask himself what is more important to him, being "right" or getting along with the other kids. If he's really struggling to understand this choice, then I want you to read the "No Man's Land" chapter carefully and see if your son may need additional help to build his social skills.

BYSTANDERS

Adults love to talk about the importance of bystanders in stopping social cruelty. But bystanding is really complicated, and when we encourage our children to do it we rarely think about whether we're willing and able to do it ourselves. This is because it's hard. Speaking out is uncomfortable at best. That's why most of us will often do everything we can to convince ourselves that we shouldn't intervene. We ignore the problem or distract ourselves so that we'll look clueless. We "stay neutral," which looks like we're either intimidated or support the abuse. We laugh to convince ourselves that what's going on isn't serious. Or we join in the cruelty because it's safer to be on the side of the person with the most power.

Here are the simple facts your son should know when it comes to being a bystander:

1. At some point you will see someone doing something really messed up to another person.
2. No one wakes up in the morning looking forward to telling someone else that they don't like what they're doing. Doing that is always hard and uncomfortable. That doesn't mean it's okay to stay silent, but it does mean it's critical to acknowledge that it's a hard situation.
3. It's common to get involved based on your relationship to the individuals involved or the power each one of them has. If one of them is a friend or has high social power, you'll find his behavior easier to excuse. If one of them is annoying or doesn't have social power, then it will seem easier to make excuses for what happened or to blame him for somehow bringing it on himself. Ideally, all of that should be irrelevant. Getting involved should be based on facts, not on popularity or how much social power each person has.

When Your Son Is the Bystander

Let's imagine that you have a son named Mark, and he has a friend, let's call him Andy, who thinks it's funny to humiliate other kids. Your son has been friends with this kid since second grade and likes to hang out one-on-one. Now they're in middle school, and things are getting more intense. Mark tells you that a boy named Michael dropped his phone on the bus, and when he bent over to pick it up, Andy took a picture of his butt crack. By the time the boys got off the bus, Mark had forwarded the picture to everyone in their grade.

This is your initial response after Mark tells you something really general and vague about how annoying Andy is:

"What do you mean by annoying?"

Your son explains:

"You're right, that is annoying. Especially for that Michael kid. Thanks for telling me, because it's probably hard to tell me about a friend of yours, but I really respect the fact that you did. Now let's think about how you want to handle it."

Here's the ideal SEAL, with the Setup being (what else?) a video game.

MARK: Taking that picture of Michael was messed up.

ANDY: No, it wasn't! It was amazing!

MARK: You know he was really mad.

ANDY: No, I don't! If he was so freaked out, why didn't he say anything?

MARK: Because then you would make fun of him even more.

ANDY: I wouldn't mind if he did it to me. And wait a minute, you laughed just as much as I did.

MARK: I'm not proud of this, but I laughed because I was nervous. All I'm asking is that you lay off.

ANDY: Fine, I'll back off, but you do realize how gay you're being about this whole thing, right?

MARK: Right, I'm gay because I want you to stop making a kid miserable. Whatever. (They go back to the game.)

There are some important takeaways that you want to make sure Mark understands. One is making sure that Mark recognizes that when Andy says "You laughed just as much as I did," this is a strategy to make Mark feel that he has no right to say anything because his laughter makes him as guilty as Andy. It's critical for boys to realize that laughing doesn't mean they can't make it right later. "I wouldn't mind if he did it to me" is also a strategy to label the complaining kid as weak. Your job is to remind Mark that Andy doesn't have the right to decide how Michael takes his joke. Plus, it's way easier to say something doesn't bother you when in fact it hasn't happened *to* you. Last, be sure to point out how Andy uses the word "gay" to try to silence Mark. Again, it's critical to remind Mark that Andy isn't going to instantaneously agree with him. He can't. It's hard enough for Andy to hear what Mark's saying, let alone be mature enough to acknowledge that Mark is right. How many adults do this?

FIRE-STARTING

Fire-starting is when a guy creates or increases conflict between two other guys by backstabbing, gossiping, or lying to drive them further apart. You think this sounds like something only girls do? Wrong. Say two guys have been really good friends, but they get into a fight over something stupid and drift away from each other. It's not like they are officially not speaking to each other, but they're giving each other lots of space. Meanwhile, the fire-starter comes in and starts lying to each of them about what the other guy said or did. They'll react by just staying away from each other indefinitely and never directly confronting what happened in the relationship.

HONEY, SAY YOU'RE SORRY!

Have you ever seen a parent force their son to apologize and you know that kid doesn't mean a word he says? Then the parent shrugs and smiles because, after all, she just did the best she could, right?

Your son will apologize to you and to other people and not mean it. Boys are socialized to apologize insincerely. Not only because they see public figures insincerely apologizing, but because teachers and parents force kids to apologize without realizing how counterproductive it is and how clueless and incompetent they look.

If kids are going to apologize and mean it, they have to feel like it's absolutely the right thing to do. But it can take a while to admit to yourself that you were wrong. Also, the need to save face makes guys say "I was wrong" in such subtle ways that everyone else can miss it (except for the guys in the inner circle). From the outside, almost no one would ever perceive the emotional depths and clear communication that occur in these brief exchanges. For example, when a guy wants to tell another guy he forgives him, this is best done by doing things like sharing food or offering the other guy something he wants, like passing the ball to him or saying "Good job" at some point while he's playing. If he's a gamer, he invites the other guy to play a game.

> *When I need to apologize, the next time we're playing basketball I make a point of saying "Nice shot" or "Good game." I know I'm not actually saying, "I'm sorry," but my friend knows what I'm really saying.* —Rick, 13

> *We could be randomly walking in the hallway and I'll say, "My bad," and he'll know what I'm talking about.* —Al, 16

But sometimes boys won't apologize. And this is where you as the parent must clearly communicate what a genuine apology looks like and role-model how a person makes one.

True apologies have four characteristics: (1) recognition that every person has the right to their feelings and perspective, as in, no one has the right to tell anyone else that they're "overreacting"; (2) a genuine tone of voice that conveys sincere meaning; (3) an understanding of what hurt the other person and a willingness to admit responsibility; (4) a willingness to back up words with action. Examples of good apologies are "I'm deeply sorry I said those things" or "I was really out of line, and I didn't think about how what I did would embarrass you."

In contrast, a fake apology is a combination of arrogance, stupidity, and insincerity. Here's how you spot a fake apology: (1) an insincere tone of voice, often accompanied by sighing and eye-rolling; (2) an effort to make the other person feel weak for wanting the apology ("If you really feel that strongly about it, then fine, I'm sorry" or "I apologize if I offended you"); (3) manipulation of the person apologized to, usually in order to get something the apologizer wants ("I'm sorry, can you please just drop it?").

How your son deals with a fake apologizer really depends on how important that person is to him. If he gets a fake apology from someone he doesn't know well or care about, it'll be annoying, but he doesn't need to deal with it more than remembering that the person didn't mean what he said. It's a different story when he's dealing with a fake apologizer on an ongoing basis. If your son is in a relationship (friends or more) with someone who consistently does what he or she wants and then apologizes later as a way to wriggle out of it, then at some point your son needs to address it with that person. (And remember, being a good fake apologizer requires high social skills and intelligence, so he's probably dealing with a Mastermind or an Associate.)

If your son chooses to call out the fake apologizer, here's a strategy you can suggest:

FAKE APOLOGIZER: I didn't realize you were so sensitive!

BOY *(explaining)*: To be honest, the way you just apologized doesn't seem like you mean it. If I'm wrong, tell me.

FAKE APOLOGIZER *(in sarcastic tone)*: No, I totally mean it.

BOY *(affirming)*: I just want you to say what you mean. Otherwise, don't say it.

If your child is the one who needs to do the apologizing but refuses to, don't make him give a fake apology. That gets him off the hook, and he doesn't learn what an apology is. Here's how you show him. It can be in the moment immediately after he's done something bad, or it can be when you're discussing with him the possible outcomes of his situation. If it's in the moment and he won't apologize, go up to the other kid and say,

"On behalf of my son, I apologize for what he did to you. If you have additional problems, here's my phone number and feel free to call me."

If it's not immediate, you say,

"I'm disappointed that you won't apologize. I understand that you feel some things were done to you too. But that fact doesn't take away from the things you did that you need to apologize for. I don't want you to apologize and not mean it. So I am going to write an email to the parent and child (or go over to their house) and apologize for you."

Forgiveness

When someone apologizes, the best response is to say something like, "Thanks." Stay away from "Don't worry about it" or "It's okay," which can come across like you don't think it's important. You want to acknowledge the apology and move on. If the other person says, "Do you forgive me?" and you aren't ready to say yes, you can say, "I'm not there yet, but I really appreciate that you apologized." I strenuously object to anyone being forced to say they forgive someone else, because it's manipulative and ultimately unproductive.

Adults Making Amends

It's profoundly meaningful to boys when an adult acknowledges a mistake he or she has made, apologizes, and works hard to make it better. Yes, it's unlikely that you'll get an effusive "Thank you." Just remember, boys like to play hard to get, but they really do want mutually meaningful relationships. Sam, Andrew, and Evan lay it on the line.

> *Many times when my parents do something wrong and I get mad at them, I get mad at the fact that they can't admit they've made a mistake. They make themselves the omnipotent being in our lives— and it sucks. If they want to teach us to be honest about our actions, the best way we'll learn it is to see it firsthand with them. —Sam, 17*

> *Adults really disappoint me when they believe that they are always right. When I win the argument, they reply by saying that they are my*

authorities and that is the final answer. Adults need to realize they are not always right, even if they have had more experience than a teenager. That is contradicting for me to say because in thirty years I will always want to think I am right to kids, but hopefully I will be more considerate. —Andrew, 15

My parents never admit defeat. Just once I'd like my mom or dad or any adult to say, "I was wrong. I'm sorry." Instead, they always say things like, "I'm only human. People make mistakes." Just once I want to hear them own what they did. —Evan, 14

If you want to apologize to your son but also think there are some things he needs to acknowledge as well, say something like, "I'm asking you to acknowledge that I'm not in this relationship alone. We both have contributed to the problem. Are you willing to meet me halfway here?"

UNINVITED

I really didn't want to invite this kid to my birthday party because he's a huge pain and he just ruins everything. I told my mom that he couldn't come. But that was stupid because my mom talked to his mom and now I'm in trouble. My mom is making me invite him. —Jacob, 12

Elementary schools frequently request that parents be as inclusive as possible with parties. But as Jacob points out, that's so easy for us to say. Do you remember how excited you were when it was your birthday? Do you remember how much you looked forward to any kind of birthday party? And then an adult told you that you had to invite someone you didn't like? Someone you were absolutely sure was going to ruin your party?

On the other hand, for the child who isn't invited to parties, it can feel terrible. He may not realize how fully annoying he's been to the birthday boy. If you're the parent, you may not know how annoying your child is either. Even if you do, it's still going to bother you. And maybe your kid hasn't been annoying. Maybe their friendship has drifted apart, or maybe the birthday boy is being obnoxious.

For financial and logistical reasons, inviting everyone in the grade often isn't possible. Ideally, party invitations would be issued by group, like your kid's sports team, neighborhood, or class.

But what's uncool is inviting everyone in a group except one or two kids. This happens a lot, and I often wonder if the parents knew what they were doing. Let's assume most parents get caught in the situation I describe above: their child tricks them into thinking the kid can't come.

> You: I know we're inviting everyone in the group, and there're some kids who you like more than others. Do you want to talk about that?
>
> Your child: Mom, I *don't* want him to come!!!!!! You can't make me.

You need to remind your son that he can't exclude one person when he's inviting the group. And while he doesn't have to be this kid's best friend during the party, he can't be mean. You can also talk to your son about your expectations for his behavior (for example, he won't exclude the kid, and he won't talk to his friends about "having" to invite him).

If you're the parent of the uninvited child, please know that getting him an invitation doesn't mean everything is now going to be great. The birthday boy could be so resentful that he feels justified in being mean to your kid, and at best he may ignore him. If your son is really upset about not getting invited, take him out (hiking, to a movie, fishing, etc.) the day of the party, and build in some time when you go to give him the opportunity to talk about it.

WHEN YOUR SON IS THE MEAN BOY

We had sixth-grade mini-mafia that met early each morning before school started. The "godfather" of the group would literally hold court to decide who would be the target of the day. All members of the group had to prove their loyalty by following orders. If they wavered in their commitment, they were removed from the group and alienated.

What do you do if you get a call from the principal, and he tells you that your son is the Mastermind behind this scenario?

When you get a call like this, you may find it very hard to believe. So let's be fair to all of ourselves. There are understandable reasons why we have a hard time believing people when they tell us that our children have done something crappy:

1. We love our children, and we don't like thinking badly of people we love.
2. Our children's bad behavior is embarrassing. When children are mean, rude, or obnoxious, even the best parents can have moments when they rationalize the child's bad behavior. From being "overtired" and "oversugared" when our child hits other kids on the playground to "his hormones are taking over" or "that's just the way boys are" when he's a teen, we often miss opportunities to parent them responsibly when it matters most.
3. We feel powerless to stop our child because either there's a larger problem with him that we feel unable to address or at some point we've stopped being a credible authority figure.
4. Everything our kids do is a reflection of our parenting. Our ego is so fragile that our children's mistakes become a threat to our sense of self. This is one of the most common reasons why parents react so strongly and fight so hard against other parents, educators, and coaches when there's a conflict.

When we're in denial, it's not only our own kids who know it, it's all the other kids too. Kids talk about parents. By the time they're in eighth grade, they know which parents are in denial.* They see us, and this is what they think.

I think parents like this are the worst. One thing is standing up to your kid when he's right. However, when he's wrong, you have to educate him so he won't repeat whatever he did. —Miguel, 15

I think that parents really need to understand that their kid isn't perfect, no matter what they think, because if you keep telling your kid that they've done nothing wrong, then they will start to think they are perfect too. The kids that have these kinds of parents end up being the kids that don't know the difference between right and wrong. —Stanley, 16

So when you get the call or the email, remember that this is one moment, not a lifetime. Don't make excuses. Tell the person on the other side that you'll talk to your child and get back to them.

With paper in hand to write down his responses, and with no siblings around, say, "An incident was reported to me." Tell him what you were told and then ask, "Is this accurate? Is any of it accurate?" If he says even one percent is accurate, then you need to remind him that everyone has the right to his perspective (i.e., the other kid).

But chances are good that he's not going to own to any of it right away. Coming clean is a process. In the first moments of finding out he's been caught, your son's primary objective is to figure out how much you know. Second, he's going to try to control how much you're going to punish him and get involved. The higher the stakes the more motivated he'll be to convince you of his innocence. That motivation can come across as sincerity and honesty. Your goal is to

---

*This is exactly the information another child needs to know so that he can party at your house.

help your child internalize why he should come forward and admit the truth. After you've talked with him and listened to his side of the story, tell him he has a four-hour window of time (or let him sleep on it and tell you the next morning) to remember anything else about this situation that would help you understand it better. Let him leave to walk around or toss and turn in bed as he weighs the pros and cons of speaking the truth. This is tricky because he could decide instead to coordinate with any other culprits to strengthen their story. But at a certain point you must take the leap of faith that in the uncertainty of a messy situation, if your son is given the freedom and confidence to come clean with you, he'll rise to the occasion.

If your son is good at distracting and confusing you or you easily forget details, write down what your son says as he's saying it, because then you'll notice any contradictions in his story. You'll also have a record so that he can't deny that you said something you're sure you said, or vice versa. If your son accuses you of not trusting him and you don't, it's okay to admit it. Or at the least, don't lie and tell him you do when you don't. When he's done explaining his perspective, tell him you're going to read back to him what you wrote. After you do that, ask him one more time if what you've written down is an accurate description of what happened and then thank him for his time.

If your son is lying to you, he'll hate this entire process. Well, he'll hate the entire process no matter what, but his hatred will be more intense if he's lying. Be ready for distraction tactics, like getting angry with you or scapegoating someone who isn't in the room and therefore can't put up a defense. Keep focused and you'll be fine.

Here's your ideal SEAL:

STOP: As soon as you hear what a troll your son has been, go somewhere quiet and breathe. Remember, your child isn't the worst child in the world and you aren't the worst parent. He has made a big mistake, and it's up to you to make this an opportunity to see your values in action. Do not think about how much more or less guilty the other boys are. Your son was involved—that's all you need to know.

STRATEGIZE: Where can you talk to him where you have the best chance of him listening to you? If at all possible, both parents will be present, but no one else.

PARENT: It has come to my attention that you have created a club where you decide the rules of the club and which boys can be in it. Is that accurate?

BOY *(pushing back)*: It's not really a club. We just hang out before school. It's not a big deal.

PARENT: I need you to answer this question with a yes or no.

BOY: Am I in trouble?

PARENT: You're not answering the question. Yes or no?

BOY: It's not just me.

PARENT: Are you in any way responsible for the club and who is in and who is out?

BOY: Maybe, but it's not just me.

PARENT: I'm not saying you can't hang out with your friends. But you can't use a club as a way to exclude kids.

BOY: Who told you? Did David complain? Because he freaks out every day over nothing.

PARENT: Not only does it not matter who told me, but if David's life becomes more difficult because of this conversation, then that will result in additional consequences for you. *(Boy is silent for a while, then . . .)*

BOY: This is totally unfair. Why am I the only one getting in trouble?

PARENT: I have no idea what's happening with the other boys. But you have been identified as the leader. You are also my child, so what you do is my responsibility. To be clear, you may not have an exclusive club. You may not exclude people and go out of your way to make them feel miserable. You have

the right to choose your friends, but you don't have the right
to make people feel bad. Am I being clear?

BOY: Fine.

PARENT: Good. So that tomorrow everyone is on the same page,
you and I will meet with the principal so you can tell him in
person what he can expect from now on.

IT'S NOT ALL THE RAINBOW COALITION

*My son used the N-word against an African American student. I told
the principal it wasn't possible because we're Jewish. My grand-
father lived through the Holocaust. I refused to believe he could do
this, and then he admitted it. Of course I made him apologize to the
boy and his mother, but she just looked at us like we were animals.
Who could blame her? What do I do? He never heard racial slurs in
our house. This boy used to be his friend. He won't tell me what happened, and I'm so mad I can't talk to him rationally. —Bill*

Most white parents don't explicitly talk to their children about racism beyond giving them books when they're little and speaking in
generalities about treating people equally regardless of their race or
ethnicity. White parents assume their boys would never use racial
slurs if they didn't hear them in their home. Most minority parents
talk to their children about race and prepare them for living in their
particular community, especially if they're really in the minority in
their community. But these parents can also have a hard time believing their children would use racial slurs.

Until I worked with boys for this book, I didn't realize how regularly racial slurs come out of their mouths. Some of these boys
are great kids who come from decent homes and have wonderful
teachers, but that doesn't stop them from saying racist things or saying nothing when it happens around them. And to be blunt—the
wealthier and more sheltered the school, the more of a problem this

is. Honestly, it's been a consistently surreal experience for me to be talking with wealthy white parents who adamantly deny the possibility that their kids would say "nigger" or other really bad racial slurs. Not that other schools don't struggle with racism, but they do admit it's a problem.

Why is this happening? I think it's because lots of parents don't talk about race, class, and other differences beyond generalities. Even though we live in an increasingly multiracial world, adults are still uncomfortable talking to their children about it. And let's admit it: lots of parents are prejudiced against other races.

This is one of the main reasons why kids can get away with claiming, "(Offensive word adults are telling me to stop saying) doesn't mean anything. It's just what we say." The only people who say this are the people who are in the majority and who aren't on the receiving end of these jokes and comments. You'll never hear a black, Hispanic, Jewish, or Muslim kid say, "Please make racist stereotypical comments at my expense. It just makes me feel so comfortable when you do it."

The rationalization that the offensive word "doesn't mean anything" is what I hear all the time in upper-middle-class suburban schools and private schools. Again, kids in other schools may be saying these things too, as well as segregating themselves at lunch and going after each other, but at least they acknowledge the situation. Here's what I hear most often in schools throughout the country:

Muslims and Sikhs (whose religions are completely different) are constantly referred to as terrorists.

Jews are confronted with boys throwing money at them and making jokes about ashes and ovens.

Asians are said to have small penises, to not need calculators, and to have parents who drive them 24/7 and beat them if they don't become music or math prodigies.

Hispanics are the butt of jokes about being deported, uneducated, and lazy. White kids in private schools commonly joke about their Hispanic friends having gotten into their school or getting a scholarship only because the school needed to increase its diversity.

Black guys are greeted with forced, wannabe black slang or the use of the N-word.

There are also a lot of white guys who think an excellent way to bond with a black friend is to greet him with some stereotypical urban black comment. Sometimes their intention is good (they're trying to connect), but the problem is that they're using racist stereotypes. If your son does this, his black friends may never tell him how they feel. Why? Because when you're a minority, it's hard enough to feel comfortable in your environment without calling out people every time they say something stupid to you about you. If it happens with your friends, the pressure to not say anything is even more intense because those friends are the key to making you feel like you belong at all.

Let's also tackle the N-word problem—white kids saying "nigga." If they do slip and say it in front of their parents, they assure their parents that it isn't a problem because saying "nigga" is completely different from saying "nigger." And then their parents take their word for it. For the record, if your child says this to you, he is wrong.

Being a minority doesn't guarantee that a boy will apply that awareness to other minorities. In school, it's not like black kids can't make ignorant remarks to Jewish kids about how much money they have, or Jewish kids won't do the "Wattup" to their black friends or make comments about being a maid or being illegal to their Mexican friends. Everyone can be ignorant.

This isn't about being multiracial, black, Latino, Jewish, etc. It's about being singled out, stereotyped, and degraded and then feeling like you can't say anything about it. If your son is going to a school where only a few people look like him, it can take only one person to make him feel uncomfortable. It doesn't matter what race or ethnicity he is. He could be one of the few white students and run into similar problems.

LANDMINE!

If you're thinking that there's no way your son could make racist comments, ask yourself, "How do I know this?" Talking to your son about treating everyone as equals isn't going to cut it. What's required are ongoing conversations in which you talk to your son in specifics.

Any parent of a minority son can make it clear that it's okay for him to be offended and that it's okay to pick some battles. It's also okay for boys to be offended when they're in the majority. Admitting your feelings takes strength. Oliver shared his experience:

I'm not any minority, but I have a large nose and curly hair, so some of my friends call me a Jew. Sometimes I shrug it off like it's no big deal, but some people come up to me and say, "'Sup, Jew?" People call me a Jew and not my first name. They say I'm cheap, and some have even thrown pennies and coins at me. I don't really know what to say. I would hate being treated this way. I can't imagine how some actual Jewish kids deal with it. It actually opened my eyes on how some people are treated for just being different, and I try not to be racist or discriminate against others now because of it. —Oliver, 15

Will Your Son Become Part of the Problem?

Here's what you can say to your son so he knows where you stand:

"You know I have confidence that you know what I expect of you when you're with your friends. But I can't predict when and where you'll have experiences where these expectations will be put to the test. So if you're ever in a situation where someone is being singled out to be embarrassed or humiliated for any reason, that's exactly the moment when I hope you'll make me proud by upholding the dignity of the person being targeted. But just so you're clear, if I find out you participated in any way to humiliate someone, either in real life or online, not only would I be deeply disappointed in your actions, but you'll make amends

by standing in front of them and apologizing to that person and his family, and I will be standing next to you when you do it. I take these situations very seriously, and so should you."

THE RULES OF BROTHERHOOD

Some of the most painful conversations I ever have with parents are when they ask for advice on stopping their sons from fighting with each other. I can see the look of failure and helplessness in their eyes. Others will flat-out tell me that one of their children is bullying their sibling, and again there's this look of defeat that stops me cold.

Let's be clear. If you have a kid who is bullying his siblings, he's not only bullying them, he's bullying you too. Regardless of the reasons for his behavior, it profoundly affects your family's emotional and physical safety now and in the future. In fact, you can count on one thing if it doesn't get addressed. Your other children won't want to spend time with you as adults and they may very well carry with them the belief that you didn't protect them. I'm not saying this to make you feel guilty. I'm saying it because I've seen so many parents in this situation who don't want to admit how high the stakes are and therefore never face their fears and get the support they need.

These family dynamics are usually complicated. That's why any parent needs help. There's no reason to be ashamed. But for the sake of all the children (including the bully) you have to take a stand and say "No more," and mean it. If it's too hard to do on your own, you have to see a family therapist who can help you build these skills.

As you can imagine, this issue was a big one for many of my editors. In the *The Guide,* we have a list of "Blood Brother Rules" that I have adapted for parents. However you choose to present them, these are the critical points you should be conveying to your son about how to behave with his brothers (or sisters).

- Don't destroy anything your sibling makes or builds.
- Don't let your sibling take the fall for something you did.

- Never tattle on your sibling, except when he's doing something to hurt himself or someone else. But even then, be upfront with him, and give him twenty-four hours to come clean (unless it's such an emergency that it requires immediate action).

- Back up your siblings when they're bullied or teased. As in, do not join in, and don't stay silent when other people do it—including your friends. If your sibling starts the fight, you don't have to back him up but you do have to get him out unless he's determined to be in the fight.

- You can tease your sibling, but you can't humiliate him. If you went over the line, don't make excuses or blame it on someone else. Apologize and mean it. And don't make your mother deal with it if you can resolve it yourself.

- If your sibling does well in anything, don't minimize it or put him down. Getting a compliment, no matter how small, from a brother is huge. Likewise, put-downs are really deflating. If you feel awkward complimenting them, try wrapping it in humor. For example, "Hey I saw you aced that calc test . . . so when you're a rich CEO down the line, it's cool if I just mooch off you, right?" or "Dude, Kobe called. He wants his jumpshot back."

- Go to your sibling's game or performance. You don't have to go to every one and you don't have to tell him how great he was (although once in a while never hurts), but just showing up occasionally means a lot.

- If you don't get along with your sibling (either you never have or you think he's becoming a lazy, egotistical, self-obsessed, jocky, asshole-ish guy, as one of our editors described), you can tell him once that he's over the line but that's it. Your actions here are much more powerful than your words. Constantly pointing out his flaws doesn't work when your parents do it, so it's not going to work when you do it either.

- Don't flirt with someone your brother likes or liked in the past. Not cool. Which means everything beyond flirting is off-limits too.

- The world is hard enough without having your brother beat up on you. Some guys may think it's their job to be tough on their sibling. But as Dion, one of our editors, said, "When you do that he just builds his anger. And then he'll just turn around and take it out on someone else. You need to find a better way to teach."

12

Frontal Assault

Last Saturday night I went to a party with a friend. The party was located in a condominium building, so you had to go up these zig-zagging stairs to get to the main floor. When we left, there was a group of approximately ten people, who were drunk and sitting at the end of one side of the zigzags. They called us "China in Box" several times (which is a Chinese food chain where I live), and they threw cigarette ashes, spat on us, and cursed at us. They were all about the age of eighteen to twenty, and we recognized one of them was a senior in our school (who played varsity soccer) and one was a recent graduate. They only stood and watched. We were two against ten, and we couldn't say anything or else we would've got beaten. My friend and I were bursting with anger. We sat outside of the building and after five minutes they went down as well. It was like twenty minutes of stress, disgust, and somehow torture since we couldn't do anything. —Victor, 16

No matter where you're raising your family, your son will run into some guys who'll be a serious problem. In this chapter, I've laid out some tough situations that your son may encounter because other guys are either threatening to hurt him or skipping the threats and going right for the attack.

For your son, no matter how tough he is or how tough his neighborhood is, these situations revolve around feeling scared and trapped. The response is the crux of the issue. Boys feel that they have to respond. And they're right. They do. The problem is that they rarely have the tools they need to respond or someone with whom they can process what that response should be. So they stew in their feelings, usually bouncing back and forth between rage, fear, and helplessness. As the parent or an important adult in a boy's life, you can't save the day, but you can help him. First that means understanding how brutal these situations can feel to him. Then you need to give him a moral and strategic framework for making smart decisions.

THE RIGHT TO FIGHT

Since I'm a teacher and someone who works to prevent violence, it'd be fair to assume that I believe physical fighting is "never the answer." But that's not true. I don't feel that way personally, and I don't feel that way as a teacher. I've been hesitant to talk about my real feelings about this issue because it's so messy. By which I mean that many people will think it's irresponsible for me to say what I just did.

The truth is, boys are getting mixed messages from us. On the one hand, they're told over and over again by some combination of educators, coaches, and parents that fighting is wrong. On the other hand, they're getting the opposite message from some other combination of parents, educators, and coaches. Think back to Batman. Batman is about kicking ass and showing extreme anger. Boys are told, "Use your words," in situations where they'd really prefer to react like Batman. Moreover, the culture constantly tells boys to fight as a way to settle differences and demand respect.

Here's the way I look at it. I believe everyone has the fundamental right not to be attacked, as do the people you care about and anyone else. That means, under specific circumstances, each of us has the right to fight. But when your son actually faces the possibility of fighting, he has to answer two critical questions for himself: How willing is he to hurt another person? And no matter how righteous his position, is he prepared to accept the consequences from the institutions he's a part of, like school or the justice system?

There are also ironclad rules. He can't start the fight by his words or his actions. He must always match the level of his response to the level of the threat. He needs to stop the behavior, not the person. He doesn't have the right to humiliate the person. Having said all that, if getting into a fight is a realistic possibility, he should keep these things front and center in his mind:

1. It will hurt, no matter how tough he is (or thinks he is) or how many martial arts classes he has gone to or black belts he has.

2. The experience of fighting will go both slower and faster than he anticipates.

3. There will always be something about the fight that he regrets.

4. He can physically lose the fight but win the battle of public opinion (because people will respect the fact that he faced his opponent).

5. He can physically win but lose the battle of public opinion (if he acts like an aggressive jerk who likes to pick fights and go after people out of the blue).

6. Even if the fight doesn't happen at school, where it can easily be recorded by school cameras, it's likely that the fight will be recorded and become public anyway. If that happens, adult involvement becomes likely, and the consequences of the fight last longer.

7. He can always walk away. He may be angry with himself, but walking away in itself is a difficult decision, and he should give himself credit for it.

8. From the beginning, he should always have an exit strategy. He should be going toward safety (an exit, a car, a group of friends), not away from the danger.

If your son chooses to fight, he's made a choice to accept the consequences of his actions. The decision he needs to make is how he defines the threat and what his best reaction should be. His goal when faced with any kind of situation like this is to minimize his potential for injury and the appearance of mental weakness and maximize his ability to come across as physically and mentally powerful.

CHECK YOUR BAGGAGE

If you grew up around fighting, how does that influence what you want your son to do in a similar situation? Did you get into fights? What do you remember about the lead-up to the fight? During the fight? What you felt after the fight? Sharing your experiences with your son will mean a lot to him, especially if you're able to put it into the larger context of your life now.

If fighting makes you uncomfortable, have you expressed your feelings to your son in a way that is respectful of and acknowledges the situation he finds himself in?

STANDING HIS GROUND

It's always good for boys to learn how to stand their ground. I think it's great for boys to take a few martial arts classes or make it a regular part of their life. If you do enroll your son in a class, just make sure that he's not taking lessons from someone who brags about how good he is or how many black belts he has. The best fighters are humble and don't talk about how great they are. Regardless if they're male or female, they have the ALMB qualities that reflect internal personal strength. These people are great role models for boys anyway, even if they never have to physically defend themselves.

TRUCES

If done right, truces are powerful things. The success of a truce depends on the person brokering it. When a boy who is respected by the other boys brings the warring parties together to make peace, the truce has a pretty good chance of being successful—i.e., even if the boys continue to dislike each other, they leave each other alone.

An adult can broker the truce, but the boys have to look up to this person and believe he or she is a credible person to be talking about fighting. If the adult comes across as nice, kind, and wanting the boys to be friends, the truce will be a failure. That's why school "peace summits" and contracts so often don't work. The boys will say they agree with the adult, but what they really want is for the meaningless exercise to end. The only way these peace summits are successful is if the boys walk out of the meeting bonding over how stupid it was.

Nevertheless, authentic truces are so transformative in Boy World that their value shouldn't be overlooked. The boys could get a credible adult who walks in and says something like, "Gentlemen, we are here because you all aren't getting along. If you want to talk about that now, let's do it. But let me be clear about my agenda. I'm not here to make you be friends or get along. I'm here to broker a truce so that the hostility between you ends. But I only want you doing this if you're going to mean it. So if there's something I need to know that will make that impossible for you, let's talk about it and see if we can address that problem. Are you willing to try?"

GOING FROM DEFENSE TO OFFENSE

Dre's a smart, tall, big freshman who looks older than he is. He plays football at his large public school in Virginia and loves to trick teachers into thinking he's not as smart as he actually is. Two weeks before school was over for the summer, Dre was walking down the hallway talking to a female friend when the girl's boyfriend jumped him from behind. The school cameras recorded the whole thing. In the moment after Dre was knocked down, he had to evaluate and measure the various risks that confronted him. The possibility of getting suspended, having the fight on his college transcript, getting into trouble with his parents for fighting, getting into trouble with his parents for not fighting, and not letting his peers think he was weak had to go up against the need to defend himself now so he wouldn't have to fight later (which is a crapshoot because fighting hard can also escalate the intensity of future fights). All of these factors had to be weighed in the instant before he had to make his decision.

Dre threw the guy against the wall and appropriately defended himself. So far so good—Dre wasn't getting into trouble with the principal. Then Dre took off his backpack and went after the guy again. The boyfriend got a five-day suspension, and Dre got a two-day suspension. The principal didn't want to suspend Dre—she understood that Dre needed to defend himself—but the moment he went from defense to offense was the moment she had to discipline him.

It was the first suspension Dre had gotten all year—with only two more weeks of school to go. For Dre's dad, the suspension was unfair because his son didn't start the fight. He believed that Dre should have gotten immunity because he didn't initiate the fight, he responded to an attack. But that's not the way to see it. We have to teach our children to match the level of the attack and make difficult moral decisions in high-stress moments.

What happened in Dre's fight is typical—there's usually an initial exchange of punches, and then there's a lull. It's in that lull that boys have a decision to make. Do they reengage in the fight or do they stop? If they reengage, they'll probably get into trouble with adults. What kind of trouble really depends on what kind of school the boy goes to, which is unfair but true. If he goes to a private school, the boy will probably get suspended, and maybe it'll go in his file for a college admissions person to see. If he goes to a public school with a police officer assigned to it, not only will he get suspended and have the fight recorded in his school records, but he's more likely to interact with the juvenile justice system in some form. So yes, private school kids can do the same "bad" things as public school kids but get off way easier. (Not only with fighting, by the way, but with drugs as well.) Like I said, it's unfair but true.

If your son had been in Dre's situation, he might think it would have been worth getting suspended and whatever else happened to him. Dre believed he had to go after the guy full force to convince him to never go after him again. Using that line of reasoning, defense wasn't enough. From Dre's perspective, his offense was part of his defense—for the future. And that's the crux of Dre's problem. Dre understandably wants the future respect (meaning fear) of the guy who attacked him, so that he'll be left alone. But that desire for future respect among his peers right now messes up his overall future, because if he has a history of fighting, adults won't trust him. He becomes the problem. His future of doing well in school, going to college, having adults who can explain the fight to other adults, becomes much less likely. To gain the respect of his peers in the present, Dre is truly risking his future.

This is the way I want guys in Dre's position to think about it— knowing that it's *way* easier to say this when you're not the person who has to do it. I think of the guy who jumped Dre as literally trying to stop him from having the future that Dre wants and deserves. Dre is academically and socially intelligent. He has what it takes to be successful. What will stop him is being brought down by other people because they're dictating his behavior. Sometimes there are crossroads in life where you really have to make decisions that impact the rest of your life. This is Dre's crossroads: will he take off his backpack the next time someone comes for him?

WHAT IF MY SON HAS NO POWER?

I'm a freshman, and a junior calls me "piglet," referring to the fact that I go to school where everyone is uber-fit and I'm sensitive about my weight. I've asked him to stop, but he insists on continuing calling me "piglet." Knowing that he would not stop by me just asking, I attacked him and called him "geometry," because he's in geometry as a junior, which is really behind compared to the rest of the school. It doesn't seem to stop him, and tonight he hit me in the stomach, knocking the wind out of me. I'm afraid he's still going to call me "piglet," and if I talk back he might get more violent next time. —Andrew, 14

Andrew doesn't need to fight the junior. A more intelligent strategy is to use the social hierarchy of the school. He should use the same social hierarchy that the junior uses to justify why he has the right to put Andrew in his place because he has to pay his dues (i.e., be treated badly and keep his mouth shut) as a freshman. There are always a few juniors and seniors in any high school who believe the argument, "We showed proper respect when we were freshmen, and we put up with it." Almost every senior class complains that the freshmen don't show the seniors the respect they deserve, while the vast majority of freshmen are completely intimidated.

But for someone in Andrew's shoes, all of this is hard to see because it seems like he has only one choice: to let the junior keep harassing him. By definition, however, this is no choice at all, because he feels that there is no other option. But there is. Andrew needs to find a junior or senior guy who has enough influence over the junior that he can tell him to lay off. It could be a friend or teammate, but most importantly, it'll be someone everyone respects. (A Mastermind, Associate, or Entertainer would be the best guy to go to here.)

If your son is in a similar situation, if he has a sibling, family friend, or any kind of connection to a well-respected junior or senior, he should enlist his help. If he doesn't have these connections, this means he'll need to talk to a guy who is intimidating in his own right and to whom he has no connection beyond seeing him on campus. But if your son balances the one moment of awkwardness against weeks, months, or two years of enduring the bullying, it's worth it.

To make a good choice, he should take a few days to consider who he thinks would be best to enlist. Then he should prepare what he wants to say to this other kid by using SEAL. He should wait until he sees the guy walking across campus or when he's by himself and catch up to him. I'd suggest saying something like this:

"Hey, I know you don't know me (or you only know me because I'm Katie's brother), but I want to ask your advice. You know Todd, the junior? He's been going after me, and yesterday he punched me in the stomach. There's really nothing I can do about this but take it, so I was wondering if there's any possible way you could tell him to lay off?"

The reason this strategy works well is because it's a power play. The target of the bullying is demonstrating his understanding of the power this kid has (some would call it kissing up, but whatever) and his belief that he's the only one who can stop the junior. Even coming from a lowly freshman, it makes guys feel good to be recognized like this and to be asked to play the hero.* Then think of it from the junior's perspective. If a well-respected junior or senior tells him to back off, he has to. If he doesn't, he's now disrespecting someone who has equal or more power than he does. Then it becomes a problem between the two of them, which the junior wants to avoid. The junior now has the incentive to back off, not because it's the right thing to do but because his life will get more uncomfortable if he doesn't.

If you find out your son is having this kind of problem and offer him this option, he probably will not have thought of it. But it solves

---

*Remember the champion moments I talked about in the beginning of the book? Here's what I'm talking about. It's not saving the world, but to this ninth-grader it is.

the problem because he directs the situation in a realistic way that reflects his position relative to the other guys.

THE B-WORD

Almost all guys I work with think "bullying" is an overused term that doesn't apply to their lives. Or, if it does apply, they don't like it because it makes them appear weak and it triggers adult involvement. However, occasionally it's a useful, appropriate word to use. And one I'll use now. The official definition of bullying is using power and strength to make someone else feel worthless. Bullying is also usually defined as one-way and repeated—the bully apparently believing that humiliating the target is entertaining, that it's a normal rite of passage, or that his target deserves to be bullied for something he's done. If the target defends himself, the bully threatens (with or without words, it doesn't matter) to end the target's relationship or association with the person or group (a group of friends, a team, a gang, a college frat, a band, etc.).

I know I said that the behavior is repeated, but there are plenty of things that can happen once to a target that would qualify as bullying. Like having all his clothes taken out of the gym locker so he has nothing to wear but the tiny shorts the gym teacher finds in the lost-and-found. Or someone setting up a Twitter account in his name and tweeting racist, sexist, homophobic comments about other kids from it. Or a teacher making one joke about him and the other kids running with it. All of these are about an abuse of power.

Kids aren't the only ones who don't like to use the word "bullying" or are confused about when it applies. Many teachers feel like, with the attention placed on bullying, every conflict between kids is now labeled "bullying." It can also feel like we're coddling kids if we don't let them handle their own problems. Here's the way I see it. As I said in the first chapter, conflicts are inevitable, and so is abuse of power. Instead of teaching bullying prevention, let's call it "teaching social competence when someone is undermining you." Instead of coddling, teaching those skills is actually preparing children with necessary survival skills. And for the most part, you as the adult don't want to rush in and fix the problem. You want to be behind the scenes guiding the boy through the process.

This issue goes right to the heart of why boys are conditioned not to complain when they are being bullied or when they see someone being bullied. I have asked many boys, "What would it take for you to intervene if someone was getting bullied?" Invariably, their response is "They'd have to really hurt," "Like someone was going to die," or "Something would have to happen like what you see on TV." The reality is that some people are simply determined to assert their power and any resistance to that power has to be put down with an even greater display of power. All resistance must be crushed. Which is plenty of motivation to not stand up to the bully.

So what can we do? How can we counteract boys' belief that the threshold for coming forward is only when someone is at risk for assault?

It Doesn't Matter What You Call It

Any of the situations described above could be defined as bullying. But does it really matter what we call it? What counts is the fact that almost every boy on earth will experience an imbalance of power where he feels trapped. All boys who find themselves in this situation have to interact with the individual who started the conflict and with the guys who watched it happen and chose to do nothing. This would weigh on anyone. If a boy is worrying a lot, dreading interaction with the perpetrator, and beginning to suffer in his performance at school, in sports, or in other activities, then the problem has become too big for him to solve on his own and he needs to get help.

LANDMINE!

If you get a call from the school or a message from anyone that your son is being bullied, please, please, please don't text him right away with anything like, "You're being bullied!!!!!!" Or, don't pounce on him as soon as he walks through the door.

If I'm Not Aware of Any Bullying Going On, Should I Talk to My Child Anyway?

If you haven't heard of any problem with kids bullying each other in your son's school or social circle, yes, you should talk to him, but stay sane about it. Constantly telling your child to be on the lookout for mean kids will either make him an anxious mess or make him blow you off because you're so paranoid. But don't wait until things are in crisis mode either. Your goal is to communicate what you stand for and prepare your child to handle a problem when it comes up. Here's what you can say:

"I don't know if bullying or being mean is a problem for you (at school, in your youth group, on your athletic team), but I want you to know what I think. When people humiliate or put someone down by their words or actions, it's against everything I stand for. I stand for treating people with dignity. Everyone has worth. They don't have to earn it. They just get it. If you know someone is being consistently targeted, even someone you don't know well or don't even like, I want you to address it. That could mean backing up the target by saying it's wrong. It could mean communicating in any meaningful way to the bully that you don't support what he's doing. It could mean telling me or another adult. If you do tell me, don't worry that I'm going to freak out and randomly start calling people. But we will bring it to the attention of the right people so the target can get help."

The Problem Gets Bigger

For bullying that has happened on school grounds (or at any institution your child is involved with), your first meeting should be with the adult who has the most direct experience with your son. If he's in elementary school, that means his teacher. If he's in middle school, that means either a teacher or a vice principal or guidance counselor.

Before the meeting, use SEAL to prepare your kid to say exactly what's happening, why it's impossible for him to concentrate in the classroom, and specifically what he needs from the school. Your role is to literally sit behind your child, offering emotional support. Tell him ahead of time that if he gets too uncomfortable (in part because he may have to repeat words he's not used to saying to adults), he should give a little signal, like saying "Mom?" or a code word, that conveys he wants you to pick up where he left off. Focus on the behavior you and your son want to see go away, not on the other child's punishment. (Legally, the school can't discuss other students with you anyway.) At the end of the meeting, set a deadline for action by saying, "If two or three days from now this behavior isn't changing, what are we going to do?" If the behavior doesn't improve, then you can seek help from someone with more authority. In that meeting, explain everything you, your child, and the teacher have done so far and conclude with, "I need your help so my son can feel safe and be a participating member of this community."

Bringing in the Police

If there's an inescapable pattern of harassment or stalking (in or out of school) or your child feels physically threatened, it's time to report what's happening to the police. At this stage, it's really important that you have written documentation of all the efforts you and your child have made, so take careful notes from the time you first learn of a problem. But remember, while police can be incredibly helpful at stopping the harassment, there are parents who have felt very blown-off by law enforcement and the justice system when trying to protect their child. So just like you need to document the specific harassment your child is experiencing, you also need to document the treatment you receive from the police. That way, if you feel like you're getting dismissed you have a record to bring a complaint.

What If the Teacher Is the Bully or Is Blowing My Son Off?

If your son tells you he's having a problem in class with his teacher or a kid is harassing him and the teacher is ignoring that behavior, you need to meet with the teacher. This is completely different from your son complaining to you that he's getting a bad grade or that he wasn't given enough time to prepare for a test. When that's the problem, your son needs to use SEAL and meet with the teacher himself. The goal in that situation is for your son to learn how to advocate his position, not necessarily get the grade changed.* But when your son's problem with the teacher revolves around how he's treated in class, you need to take a more visible role. Here's a possible SEAL; the Stop and Setup is an email to the teacher requesting a meeting.

> You *(explaining at the meeting)*: Hi, Mr. Thompson. Thanks for meeting with me. I wanted to check in with you because Danny came home reporting that you said (X) to him. Is that accurate?
> *(Watch the teacher's body language and tone of voice. Meeting with parents can be very stressful, and even the best of teachers can get defensive. Even if they're initially defensive, however, most teachers will quickly communicate their concerns about your child and want to address the problem. But if you get push-back, follow up with this.)*
> You: Mr. Thompson, it's important that my son learn to respect his teachers. But I expect for you to treat him with respect as

---

*This is the same strategy you can use when having a problem with a coach about your son's playing time.

well. I'm asking you to stop making those comments. Danny didn't want me to come in here because he was worried about you being angry with him, but I felt like you'd want to know. What do you think the next steps should be so that Danny feels more comfortable in class? Thank you for the meeting.

If your meeting with the teacher is about the behavior of other kids, you'll start off like this:

You *(explaining)*: Thanks for meeting with me. In the last few weeks, Danny has been reporting that he can't concentrate in class because the kids are being so mean.

Teacher *(pushing back)*: Really? I've never seen the kids be anything but nice to him. I mean, they joke around, but nothing out of the ordinary.

You: Well, Danny has been trying to ignore it, but that's not working. Here are some examples Danny has shared with me . . .

Teacher: Okay then, who is it?

You: David and Karl seem to be doing it the most.*

Teacher: I'm not seeing it. But I'll talk to them about it.

You: Could you be a little more specific? Danny is really worried that he'll get in trouble with the boys for telling you what's going on.

Teacher: I'll tell the boys to stop. There's really nothing else I can do.

You: I believe there are other things you can do beyond telling them to stop. I'm not telling you what those things are, because you're the teacher and these are your students, but I'd hope you'd tell them that if Danny is treated worse because he told you what was happening that you would take additional steps to address the problem.

---

*Yes, you have to tell the teacher the names of the kids.

What If an Administrator Is Incompetent?

Sorry, our hands are tied. It didn't happen on school property, and they didn't use their school email, so we can't do anything.

If no one saw it, then we can't do anything about it.

I'm still hearing this way too often. More importantly, kids and parents are hearing it way too often. Meanwhile, this attitude allows the perpetrators to know that they are in control of the school. When administrators ignore these situations, the result can be teens and children who hate going to school, believe that the educators who are supposed to keep them safe are incompetent at best, and conclude that there is no point to standing up to bullying and harassment because it's so prevalent. The adults don't get it, so why in the world would kids take the chance to fight this battle when the grown-ups won't? In kids' minds, all the adults do about bullying is have assemblies or put a KINDNESS banner at the entrance of the school.

But instead of framing this in terms of what people do badly, I'm going to tell you what to specifically look for when an administrator is handling bullying the right way. In my experience, those people can be counted on in the following ways:

- They understand that what happens in the school affects what happens outside the school and vice versa. Many of the schools I work with use language that gets this basic concept across. Bullying often occurs outside of the school's physical grounds, yet these actions impact the safety of students as though they occurred on school grounds. Any bullying behavior demonstrated at school or outside of school that affects the school community is addressed by the school.

- They don't let their initial reactions guide their decision-making. They take the time to figure out as best they can the possible motivations, the social dynamics at play, and the most effective disciplinary strategy for each student involved.

- They listen to parents, accommodate where they can, but don't back down from making students accountable in an appropriate way, even if that's counter to what the parents want. Doing that, however, takes a great deal of skill and finesse because while they're uncovering who has done what, they're dealing with angry parents, defensive and embarrassed kids, and kids who are trying to hide what they've done.

- They understand the power of the public space. They don't just display trophies and pictures of the championship sports teams. Next to the sports pictures and trophies are pictures just as prominently placed of the theater kids and the debate team. They realize that if they glorify one group of students, students who have a conflict with someone in that group will never come forward because they'll believe that they won't be listened to or protected.

- They understand the balance between transparency and confidentiality. The people in a position of leadership in the school share enough information with their community so that people feel informed about how bullying issues will be handled, but they also make it clear that the names of the people involved in specific incidents and any disciplinary actions taken against them will be confidential to respect their privacy.

- They don't say, "We have a zero tolerance bullying policy." As if saying that means bullying doesn't happen in their school. Actually, I get worried anytime a school administrator, teacher, coach, or anyone who works with kids says they know with absolute certainty about any specific thing their kids are or aren't doing. I don't care if it's bullying, hazing, drinking, drug use, or anything else. Good educators know that at any moment they will be made aware of something their kids are doing that they knew nothing about.

13

Redemption and Reconciliation

Y ou pick up the phone. You open the email. You say hello, expecting a brief, pleasant exchange. The next moment you can feel your pulse beating, your stomach clenching, and your eyes closing as you try to process the information you've just been given. You have just found out that your son has done something really bad. Not just a little bit bad. Really bad.

Sometimes your son will mess up, and it can feel that life changes in an instant. Overnight you can feel that you and your son aren't welcome in a place that was your home away from home just the day before. For your son, the life he had before seems to have been snatched away, and he has no idea how to get it back.

When your child gets in trouble that becomes public—that is, he's done something bad that other people know about or that will be officially recorded on his school transcript—there are two reasons why he could be in this situation. One, he did something incredibly stupid but didn't realize it at the time. Or two, he knew exactly what he was doing, and his cover-up failed. The latter includes the possibility that he has developed a pattern of "bad" behavior and isn't getting how serious you or the school is about changing his behavior.

For him, the benefit of the first reason—of being ignorant until the ax comes down—is that he spends no time dreading getting caught. The drawback is that he'll probably have at least one but probably several very unpleasant conversations with adults who'll say, "What were you thinking?!!!!" (which isn't really a question), and he'll have no idea what to say except to miserably respond, "I don't know," fully comprehending how stupid he sounds.

When he knows full well that what he did was wrong, there's no period of blissful ignorance. He'll be such an anxious mess that his performance in all aspects of his life will suffer, he won't sleep well, and the most innocent comment by anyone will throw him into a panic. It's truly a horrible way to live. That's a good thing. If he isn't wracked with worry, that's a way bigger problem because that would mean that the adults in his life have given him the message that he's entitled to be above the law (either the law of the land or the law of his school or family).

DON'T KILL HIM

Just like when you've found out about a smaller mistake your son made, even though this is bigger, it's still a moment in time. Your son isn't doomed to be a failure or a terrible person. All of the reasons you love him are still right there alongside whatever else made him do this thing you're now dealing with. Just like you, his feelings could be so jumbled together that it's hard for him to sort them all out: embarrassment, anger that he got caught, fury at someone else for somehow getting him involved or selling him out, shame, denial, and paranoia that everyone is talking behind his back or that this one mistake will forever damage his future. These are all understandable feelings to have.

Ignorant or not, the moment he finds out he's in trouble he's probably going to go into cover-his-butt mode. Specifically that means he has to figure out what you know and just as importantly what you don't. Then he's going to attempt damage control. That's why, when you first speak with him, you should try to convey this point:

"The most important thing to remember for both of us is that the way we respond will determine if and when people regain their respect for you. If you refuse to take responsibility for your actions, if you blame other people, or if either of us makes a point of telling other people how

stupid the punishment is or minimizes what you did, that won't be any help. If you try to take revenge on the person you believe reported you, you'll be acting like an immature, vindictive bully."

If he does admit what he did and how it hurt people around him, he'll regain the good reputation he once had or build a better reputation than he had previously. Before I go any further, I'll own up to an assumption I'm making here, and it's a big one. I'm referring here to mistakes your son might make that hurt other people. Obviously, there are other things that can get boys into trouble. For example, if your son cheats on a test because he's overwhelmed, he's breaking a rule, but his feeling of desperation also needs to be addressed. If he gets caught violating a technology or alcohol or drug policy, he (and even you) may think the rules are stupid or unfairly applied, but he agreed to those rules by becoming a participating member of the community.* That means that if he violates those rules, he accepts the punishment and doesn't try to get you to get him off. By the way, if a kid shows up to school high or drunk or carrying drugs or alcohol, he has bigger problems then getting suspended.

THE GRAY AREA

Whether we like it or not, there are situations where the "right" answer isn't going to cut it, where moral dilemmas can lead to serious consequences. It's critical that our children know that we have a strong moral framework that guides how we parent. But it's just as critical that we acknowledge to them that sometimes applying these morals is difficult. Are we sending mixed messages if we admit the

---

*As much as we may hate to admit it, it is also important to acknowledge that the system can appear coercive to the boy—even though from an adult perspective that may make sense. In order to participate in many activities, you must sign a pledge that controls other aspects of your life that are seemingly unrelated to that activity. It's a difficult situation for a teen because it's developmentally appropriate for him to explore new and possibly dangerous aspects of life, but at the same time he's being told he can participate in activities only if he gives up other things that he values and that he sees others do around him all the time.

gray areas? Are we being hypocritical? Because the reality is that the institutions our kids are a part of (school, athletic teams, our communities' laws) are often governed by inflexible rules and policies.

Let's take the most common example: teen drinking. Imagine that your fifteen-year-old son tells you his friends were drinking at a party. If you respond with the standard line "Drinking is illegal and dangerous," you aren't admitting the complexity of the situation. As a result, he's going to think you can't or won't give him the information he needs. On the other hand, what can you say to him that doesn't come across as endorsing teen drinking?

Ideally, as with so many situations, we have to start earlier than when our kids are actually faced with the situation. We need to have a clear conversation about drinking, such as:

"Now that you're thirteen (or look like a teen), you can get into situations where people are drinking and/or doing drugs. [If so:] We have people in our family who have addiction problems, so you're going to need to be mindful about that as you get older. I also need you to know that if you do it and the police or the school gets involved, I won't be able to protect you from the consequences. I'll support you, but I won't bail you out."

The long-term approach is encouraging him to develop a passion for something—something that would be jeopardized by drinking or doing drugs. And that loss has to matter to him, not necessarily to you. For example, Elijah loves to play basketball. So when I talk to him about drinking, smoking, or taking drugs, it's about how these things impair his athletic ability and compromise his team loyalty. (If his performance suffers or he gets kicked off the team, I want him to view it as letting down his teammates). Our children will make these decisions when we aren't around. So if we want them doing the right thing, we have to explain the wrong choice in terms that truly matter to them.

As they get older, those concrete rules become the backdrop for the more complicated situations they get into. Let's go back to the fifteen-year-old. I'd say to him, *Thanks for telling me. I don't want to assume anything, so can you tell me what bothers you the most about it?*

What bothers most teens about their friends' drinking is how their behavior changes when they're drunk, like being fake, untrustworthy, and belligerent. It's one of those times when teens realize that doing more "adult" things can make people act in unpredictable ways that they don't like. That's the critical conversation to have with your child because it allows him to step back and assess what he needs to do and in the process develop personal boundaries. And you can still remind him about consequences. As I said above, if he signs a no-drinking contract to participate in a school activity, he has promised to act according to the spirit and letter of that agreement or accept the consequences of breaking his word.

Cheating is another common problem that seems like there's a simple "right" answer. But again, like drinking, the reality of cheating is more complicated. Our kids shouldn't copy or use other people's work and take credit for it. They shouldn't use their phones to hide information that they can use during a test. But most kids I work with believe most kids cheat. They think most adults cheat and get rewarded for it.

Most of the cheating I've seen is motivated by one of three things: desperation, entitlement, or a reasonable strategy to deal with a ton of busywork a teacher assigns that the child has no hope of finishing without splitting up the work with other students and then sharing their work. Those are completely different motivations, and they need to be responded to as such if you're going to effectively reach your child.

One of the best ways I've found to talk to younger kids about cheating is about recess. Have they ever seen someone change the rules or refuse to follow the rules? Demand a do-over instead of accept a loss? What do they think about that? Does that person deserve the win if they win under these circumstances?

If your child is older and they like playing video games, I bet they've experienced someone hacking the game and giving themselves infinite powers, making it impossible for other players to have a chance of success. That's the crux of the issue right there. Is it fair for some people to literally game the system in their favor? Is it fair for others to rig the system so they have an unfair advantage? That's what we should be talking to our kids about.

ENCOURAGING HIM TO COME CLEAN

When he gets home and you see him for the first time, leave him alone for a little while. Let him go to his room, listen to music, and have a chance to feel everything he's been keeping inside. It can be excruciatingly uncomfortable to admit to himself, let alone anyone else, that he's done something really wrong.

Remember that different situations require different responses. If your son has lied to you about a problem he's struggling with (such as his performance in school) or because he's worried you'll reject him if he tells you the truth about something important to him, then tell him you're sorry he felt like he couldn't come to you earlier, thank him for coming to you now, and use the steps I outlined in the previous chapter to help him think through his situation. Above all, it's critical to acknowledge your understanding of his motivation and clearly convey how much you respect him for coming forward.

If, however, he has done something that goes against your stated rules or values—such as doing something mean (or contributing to someone else being mean), being deceitful, or putting someone (including himself) in harm's way and then lying about it—your response should be focused on communicating that his actions are contrary to your values, his right to entertain himself or do whatever he wants is not more important than treating others with dignity, and you'll hold him accountable for his actions. But that's not all. Just as important is communicating to him that coming clean and taking responsibility for his lies is the course of action that will make you proud of him.

Do not underestimate how much boys want your respect or a clear path to regaining it when they have disappointed you. How you do that is a delicate balance of playing hardball and appealing to his aspiration, ultimately, to do right. Now it's time to make amends. The faster he publicly holds himself accountable, the faster he'll feel better. This is what he needs to understand:

1. He's really sorry for what he did wrong.
2. He recognizes what he did that was wrong and he's not making excuses for it.
3. He realizes that his future actions have to reflect his words now.

What If He Doesn't Seem to Be Getting It?

Saying sorry isn't enough. Getting an empty apology isn't enough. Have him explain to you why he's sorry. If you get a fake apology, use my suggestions in the "Friendly Fire" chapter to apologize on his behalf until he gets his act together. Jeff Lippman, the head of the middle school of the American School in São Paulo, often asks these questions of students:

> *What is the difference between what you do and who you are? If you repeat certain types of disrespectful or dishonest actions, at what point do you become a disrespectful or dishonest person?*

Lippman points out that "this kind of questioning is often very powerful with kids because they're so intensely involved in their own identity involvement." I agree because it gives the boy the power to define his destiny and what kind of man he wants to be.

DISCIPLINE

The word "discipline" comes from the Latin word *disciplina,* meaning "instruction or knowledge." The dictionary defines "discipline" as "to train someone to obey a code of behavior or rules." The purpose of punishment should always be the greater goal of learning. Unfortunately, this is often not the case. When adults run off the rails and impose counterproductive discipline, it is because they're angry, feel disrespected, or are imposing punishments according to a rulebook that doesn't make sense for the child and the situation.

This is important because boys have a strong response to authority figures who discipline them fairly, even if they hate the punishment. People in positions of authority are important to boys. Boys accord an adult great respect if they believe in the person's honor. They burn with resentment when they are under the control of an adult who abuses his or her authority, and they then take these experiences and often assume other adults will act the same way.

My general strategy in disciplining children (either my own or my students) is to frame my response in this way:

1. Tell them exactly what they did that was a problem.
2. Tell them why the specific actions they did are against what I believe in (as their mom or teacher).
3. Tell them specifically what privilege will be taken away and for how long (which requires that you know the child well enough to know which privilege means the most to them).
4. Give them a "way back"—i.e., a way to make amends that will make them and me proud.

Finally, if your son laughs or is disrespectful, tell him: *"You clearly don't respect me as an authority figure, and I don't want to have a relationship with my son where he doesn't treat me with dignity. It's your choice if you want to contribute to changing this relationship for the better, but the punishment/rules/expectations I have laid out still apply. If you choose to disregard them, then we have a different level of a problem. That's not a threat. It's just what I have to do to effectively address the situation."*

The Least and Most Effective Punishments
According to Boys Themselves

I've asked boys to give me examples of punishments not only from their parents but from their schools.

The least effective punishment is grounding them plain and simple, without taking any sort of electronic device, such as laptop, computer, cell phone, iPod, etc., because they still have the basic social freedoms and can still have contact with their friends, but can't go out and see them. In my opinion, it still gives kids the social freedoms they want, and they can still get by and not even feel remorse or understand what they did to get grounded was wrong in the first place. —Stan, 16

The most pointless thing is when they ground you. When my mom sends me to my room, I don't really care. I'm a musician, so I can always find something else to do. The most effective punishment for parents is when they take everything away from you. My mom once took my phone, my Internet, Xbox, guitars, pretty much everything. She did that so I would do this list of chores she had. It worked. —Landon, 15

I got into huge trouble recently, and my parents grounded me for three months, but after a month they stopped. It's like . . . I can't trust them. Is that weird? But that's what it feels like. Like I can't trust them because they didn't follow through. —Tom, 17

The thing is that most parents don't really talk about why they're doing this stuff. It makes it seem that the parent likes punishing their kid. If parents just talked, it would be so much easier. —Damion, 15

What's the worst punishment—that is, the most effective punishment? Time and time again, boys say the same thing. The worst punishment is losing their parents' respect and disappointing them and having their ability to communicate with their peers taken away.

No matter what, don't hand down a punishment and then change your mind or fail to enforce it—unless you want to lose all credibility as his parent.

LANDMINE!

None of these responses are helpful:

"I have failed as a parent."

"I can't believe my child would do something like this. I'd totally understand if Susan's kids did this, but not you."

"I knew it."

"You're just like your father."

Even if this is what you feel, don't say it. The way the boy hears these statements is that this one thing he did cancels out every good thing he has ever done. He feels not only rejected but angry with you for being so dramatic.

For any parent, it's really hard to discipline effectively because embarrassment, anger, and anxiety can overwhelm calmer, more strategic thinking. Fundamentally, you probably feel really worried and confused about your son. It's also possible that he has been giving you pretty obvious signs that things were running off the rails, but you didn't see them. So when you do have to face the problem, you're not only dealing with what's happening right now but with all the factors that led up to it—like your own denial. You also could be angry that he isn't representing the family well. This is not necessarily a superficial concern, since it might be masking your distress that he didn't act according to your shared values.

Without excusing the really bad and ineffective things that parents can do, it's important to recognize why this situation is so painful for them and for their son. In a nutshell, when a son gets into serious trouble, it can make his parents feel like they've been bad parents, make them worry about what people will think about their family, and make them worry that they don't know him as well as they thought they did.

Making Public Amends

Here's a sample letter your son can use as a starting point for writing his own letter to the school administrator, but he has to make it his own to mean anything to the people he's addressing.

> *I'm really sorry for [screwing up in a huge way]. I can imagine it's hard for you to believe that I couldn't figure out it was wrong before I did it, but for some reason that I don't understand right now, I didn't. I know the rules of the school, but I also know what the school stands for and what I did was against that. I know it's not just about what I say but about what I do from now on. I'd like to take responsibility for my actions by apologizing to the class. I hope to gain your trust back one day, but I know it will take time.*
> *Sincerely,*

HAS HE RUINED HIS FUTURE?

Schools can understandably struggle with the decision to include a student's disciplinary record in their school transcript. Sometimes they don't have a choice, as with suspensions or expulsions. But there are situations where they do have the choice, and young people sometimes should be able to make a mistake without it following them on their school record. For example, a student may be disciplined for cheating one time because he was overwhelmed, or was too ashamed to ask for help, and now the "fact" that he cheated is included in his school transcript and therefore his college application. Or a boy went camping over the weekend, put his pocketknife with a 3¼" blade in his backpack but forgot to take it out when he went to school on Monday morning and then got suspended for three days because he brought a weapon to school. I don't think it's right to include either of these incidents in a student's file.

On the other hand, is it fair for a student to repeatedly cheat because he'd rather not do the work, thereby doing better than the other students who worked honestly, and not have that reported? If he's getting away with it in high school, it's a reasonable expectation that he'd continue the same pattern in college. Or what if a student is involved in bullying, hazing, sexual harassment, or assault? I'm not suggesting that it be included in the university application as an effective disincentive. The very nature of the behavior reflects an underlying assumption in the right to act in this manner without consequence. But not only does this child need to be appropriately disciplined, it's more than fair to include a record of his actions in his file to serve as a caution to his next school.

I've had countless conversations with school administrators, and it always comes down to one thing. If your son takes responsibility for his actions, then teachers, administrators, and coaches will explain to college admissions officers what happened by noting the positive actions he took and what he learned after the event.

I know that, in the moment, it's hard not to fight as hard as you can to minimize the public nature of the discipline. But as hard as it is, you can't let your anxiety blind you to seeing the bigger picture. Maybe this was the wake-up call your son needed. Sometimes colleges will defer acceptance until a student has had a chance to prove that he's learned from the experience, and sometimes colleges will withdraw an acceptance. If that happens, it can feel like he's failed. I promise you that he's better off taking a step back, figuring out the best course of action for him right now, and trying to be readmitted to the school once he's had an opportunity to think and get himself together. Yes, I know this is easy to say when you're not in the middle of all your friends talking about their children's future plans, but if you and he don't stop and figure out how he got into this situation, he's doomed to repeat it, and each time the stakes get higher.

I'm not referring to the college he gets into. I am talking about his emotional, physical, and spiritual well-being.

These experiences are hard, even excruciating, and can truly be among the most challenging moments of parenting. But one thing I know for certain. The moment your son decides to face what he did and make amends is the moment he begins to regain his sense of honor and hope for the future.

14

No Man's Land

The complaining started as soon as my sons opened the door.

"Mom, there's this kid in our group who's so annoying! He's so bad at everything! He thinks he's one of the smartest people in the world. Right before you got here, we were on the basketball court and he missed a basket, so I gave him the ball and he freaked out that I touched the ball. I'm not going near that kid again."

Then my older son started in.

"Yeah, Mom, there's this other kid in my group . . . there's something wrong with him. He's constantly pulling on his shirt, he hums to himself, and he does some of the things Roane's talking about. He's obsessed with *Star Wars*. Obsessed. I mean, I like *Star Wars*, but this kid is on a whole different level."

This was one of those moments when my parenting and teaching intersected. Up until that point, I'd talked to my sons and students about how important it is for all of us to feel a sense of belonging to a larger group. I'd also talked about how hard it can be to join groups and make friends. But what my boys described was a different problem. They were talking about kids whose behavior was so strange and off-putting that my boys wanted nothing to do with them. In that moment, I realized that I have a responsibility to teach my sons and students how to understand and interact with kids like this, to do more than say, "Be nice to kids who act strangely."

There have always been weird kids. There have always been shy kids, nervous kids, and kids who can't sit still. This isn't a bad thing or a good thing. It's how some people are. I also work with a lot of guys who have depression, social anxiety, learning disabilities, panic attacks, and eating disorders. There are a lot of guys who convince everyone that they're fine and then have to excuse themselves to go hyperventilate in the bathroom. In the last twenty years, many children have been diagnosed with learning and social disabilities like autism spectrum disorder (ASD), obsessive-compulsive disorder (OCD), or attention deficit/hyperactivity disorder (ADHD). There's a huge span of severity with these disabilities, and they often aren't visible. You can't look at one of these kids and know that his brain is wired differently. They aren't in wheelchairs. They can see and hear.

I know there are huge debates about why so many people are now diagnosed with these conditions, about the implications of children (especially boys) being given medication as a quick fix to stop their natural rowdiness, and about the appropriate cures for these conditions. OCD and ADHD have become words to describe our everyday behavior. But as we argue about these issues, I believe we have lost sight of a much more important problem in the daily lives of all our children. Children and teens with social disabilities are more likely to be mistreated, manipulated, ignored, or identified as bullies and troublemakers. Let me give you a couple of examples that are typical for kids with autism and ADHD.

You're a sixteen-year-old guy. You go to a regular school, and you just seem odd and nerdy to the other students. In science class you're paired up with a girl. She's very nice to you because you do all the work. This goes on for a week. The homecoming dance is coming up, and you decide to ask her. When you ask her, she says maybe. On Facebook that night, you ask her again and tell her your plans for having a great time at the dance. Two hours later, you post a message on her FB page asking if she saw your earlier posts. You send that message three more times that night. You friend-request all her friends. The next day her parents file a complaint against you for stalking their daughter and you're told to stay away from her. You're completely confused. You thought this girl liked you.

You're a fifteen-year-old kid with high-functioning autism. Your history teacher can't control the class, so you frequently feel like you have to monitor the other children's behavior and tell on them to the teacher. The other students are always talking. You hate it. You can't think. The noise physically hurts you. You cover your ears even though your parents tell you not to do that when you're in public. A kid walks by your desk and knocks the papers off your desk. Last year another kid did that to you on purpose all the time. You assume this kid must be doing it on purpose too. You jump up, knock over your chair, and yell at the kid who knocked off your papers. The other students laugh. You yell at the other students to follow the rules. You're sent to the principal's office for being disruptive.

You're in ninth grade, you have ADHD, and it's sixth period. You just had lunch. Everyone in class is messing around because the teacher hasn't shown up for class yet. All of a sudden the other kids are in their seats, but you just can't settle down. You have to tell this joke to your friend. The teacher walks in to hear you say, "Pussy." The teacher asks you to repeat what you just said. All the kids laugh. You can't help yourself. "Pussy," you say again. She gives you Friday detention. Twenty minutes later, you can't keep your eyes open. You fall asleep at your desk. You wake up to the teacher making fun of you.

Even though our goal is to raise decent, socially competent children, there's something that people in education and in bullying prevention programs don't like to address. Children and teens with social disabilities are often "provocative targets." In the eyes of their neurotypical peers,* they look like they're asking to be mistreated or rejected because they miss obvious social cues and can be aggressive.

Occasionally, this aggression can turn into bullying, especially in children who have a combination of ASD and ADHD, because they're substantially more likely to be aggressive, impulsive, and unable to see the consequences of their actions.† That combination also means that they're "bad" at bullying, meaning that they're the ones who get caught while other kids with more sophisticated social skills appear to be innocent in the eyes of adults. It's part of the reason why I always say to teachers in my professional development trainings, "You always see the second hit, but you rarely see the first."

Here's a recent example. This fall, I was sent an email from a young woman who had heard me speak. She was upset about a video that was circulating in her community and asked me to watch it. I thanked the woman for her email and clicked on the YouTube link she'd attached. On it, a pretty high school girl is recording herself encouraging a male student with severe social disabilities to yell graphic sexual comments to other boys in the room. While he is delighted with her attention, the other boys (big guys, wearing football jackets) are not amused. As I watched this boy desperately trying to please this girl, I was disgusted by the girl's callous use of him for her own entertainment and worried for the boy's safety the moment she left the room. That wasn't the only video she posted. One depicted the girl encouraging the same boy to headlock younger boys, "pretend-stab" them with pencils, and say obscene things to them as well. All of the videos took place at school, three of them in a teacher's direct sight.

---

*The term "neurotypical" (or NT) was coined in the autistic community as a label for people who are not on the autism spectrum. Specifically, neurotypical people experience neurological development and states that are consistent with what most people would perceive as normal, particularly with respect to their ability to process linguistic information and social cues.

†Guillermo Montes and Jill Halterman report in "Bullying Among Children with Autism and the Influence of Comorbidity with ADHD" (*Ambulatory Pediatrics* 7, no. 3 [May-June 2007]: 253–57) that adolescents with both ASD and ADHD are five times more likely to bully than neurotypical adolescents.

As soon as I watched all of the videos, I called the principal of the school. Within twenty-four hours the videos were down, the parents were notified, and the teacher was held accountable. But here's the reality. I saw them because an adult in the community cared enough to contact me. The principal handled it correctly. But usually that's not what happens. Usually, the adults never find out. If they do, it's because the "problem" explodes into the adult world. Like when those football guys beat the crap out of that boy.

Imagine you're one of the football guys' parents and you hear that a boy had yelled, in public, that he wanted to rape your son. If you didn't know the context of how this happened, you'd think, at the very least, that anyone who threatens to rape your son started the conflict. If you'd heard that this kid was doing the same thing to younger children, you might think he deserved to be beat up. Now, imagine that the school administrator didn't understand the context and didn't have the common sense to wonder why in the world a boy would be stupid enough to say those things to those football guys. What usually happens in these kinds of situations is that the administrator gives the football guys a short suspension, tells them to stay away from that kid (which they won't do), blames the boy because he's a violent, sexual deviant, and disciplines him ineffectively. Meanwhile, the girl is never held accountable.

I'd like to think that I'd have known that kid was severely impaired even before I took the time to educate myself. But I don't know for sure. Even though I work with these kids all the time, I've never been trained. You know who else isn't trained? Most of the school administrators, teachers, and coaches I know. The only related training most of them get is in restraining techniques. As Kirk Dolson, vice principal at Potomac Falls High School, told me, "I work with these kids every day. But the only training I've ever received is for restraining techniques and holds." Yet this is a school administrator who regularly interacts with students with social disabilities because they're so much more likely to get in trouble at school.

Restraining techniques should be the last thing you learn as an educator, not the first, and certainly not the only thing you learn when working with children who have social disabilities and can be even more sensitive than other people to touch. As Dolson shared with me:

> Charlie is an eleventh-grader at our school and was recently sus-
> pended for pulling the fire alarm. (That's a mandatory evacuation
> of all 1,500 students.) When I called his mom, I explained what had
> occurred, and she came to pick him up immediately. I followed up
> with her later that week, and she said he wasn't doing well. I needed
> to speak with them both about the disciplinary action I was taking.
> She was really worried that if he came back to school to meet with
> me, he'd get out of control. I know school is a trigger for him. So I
> told her I'd come to them. The mom couldn't believe I'd do that, but
> those are the things administrators should do. When I got there, he
> was on the couch refusing to talk. Another teacher told me about his
> vinyl [record] collection, so I asked him about it. In a few minutes, he
> was cleaning an old REM record for me and giving me his favorite
> headphones so I could listen to a song.

The truth is that every day educators are working with kids who are likely to get into trouble for behavior directly tied to their disability, and most educators lack the proper training to recognize the disability and determine the best course of action. Dolson did a good job because he cares deeply about his students and he thinks carefully about how to reach them based on their individual situations, but unfortunately families can't count on school administrators—private or public—being like this.

We have to fix this. These children and their families are part of our communities. They deserve to be treated with dignity. It's in the best interests of all of us to handle the challenges they present effectively, because their challenges affect not just them but everyone around them. And educators in particular need to understand how these dynamics impact the daily interactions of their schools, because otherwise they can't be effective and do right by all the kids in their care.

As I've said, I'm not an expert on disabilities, so I went to people who are: the Association for Community Living in Boulder, Colorado, and Cincinnati Children's Hospital Medical Center Division of Developmental and Behavioral Pediatrics. What you'll read was vetted by both of these organizations' extraordinary doctors, therapists, psychologists, and parents of the children they treat. I asked them to demystify these children's behavior and then collaborate with me to give you some commonsense strategies that you and your child can use so that you both feel better equipped to interact with children with social disabilities.

EXACTLY WHAT KIND OF ISSUES ARE WE TALKING ABOUT?

When you read these descriptions, you may recognize some of the characteristics I'm describing in yourself or in people you know. That doesn't mean you or anyone else actually has ADHD, OCD, or ASD. Lots of us have a few traits associated with these conditions. And even if you do know people with these diagnoses, they're a lot more than their labels. We all are, no matter what label we've been given.

Autism affects the brain's normal development of social and communication skills. The latest statistics indicate that some form of autism is diagnosed in 1 out of 88 children. Because autism is a complex diagnosis, the term autism spectrum disorder (ASD) is used to accommodate the range of moderate to severe impairment in those diagnosed. For example, a person with autism can have high sensory input that makes it harder to tolerate being physically close to other people and also makes normal noises painful. Meanwhile, another person with autism will have low sensory input and as a result will stand way too close to other people and not hear something that is obvious to others.

Asperger's syndrome is often defined as a higher-functioning form of autism. People with Asperger's or higher-functioning autism may want to interact with others, but the way they do often alienates them from other people.

A person with *obsessive-compulsive disorder* (*OCD*), an anxiety disorder, has unwanted and repeated thoughts, feelings, ideas, sensations, or behavior that make him feel driven to act in certain ways. He knows that his behavior is different from that of his peers, and he feels really self-conscious about it. For guys who like to make others miserable, a child with OCD is the easiest target. One in 200 people are diagnosed with OCD.

Those with *attention deficit/hyperactivity disorder* (*ADHD*) are unable to regulate their activity level or manage impulses in multiple environments in developmentally appropriate ways. It's completely appropriate for ten-year-olds to have a hard time sitting in their seat at school for an hour, but the child with ADHD struggles to focus wherever he is, whether it's school, home, or an after-school activity. One in 10 are diagnosed with ADHD.

Usually these disabilities occur separately, but some people have a combination.

There's an important difference between kids with autism and those with other social disabilities and mental health issues. Kids with ADHD, for example, have an easier time seeing the impact of their behavior. They know that what they're doing is hard for other people, but ADHD makes it very hard for them to control and change their behavior. Someone with autism, on the other hand, struggles to see and understand the problem with his behavior. One of the great ironies of autism is that the more severe the impairment, the less aware the person is of being rejected. Even if he is aware and human connection is important to him, he's less likely to feel the pain of the experience.

Those with higher-functioning autism are likely to seek out or be put in social situations (like being mainstreamed in a school). Listen to Donna Murray, codirector of the Kelly O'Leary Center for Autism Spectrum Disorders at Cincinnati Children's:

> With autism, our kids are trying their best to get it all right. They don't know what they're doing wrong, but they want to keep trying. They feel the rejection, but they don't know why. Some of them are desperate for friends, and some don't care. If you ask them how they define a friend, some kids with autism will say, someone who isn't mean to me. Others will say, someone who sits next to me in class or someone who shares my interests.

Social anxiety is the extreme fear of being scrutinized and judged by others in social or performance situations. This disorder is not about being very shy. People with social anxiety recognize that their fear is excessive and unreasonable, but feel powerless against it. They are terrified they will humiliate or embarrass themselves.

Learning disabilities affect the brain's ability to receive and process information. In his excellent book *It's So Much Work to Be Your Friend*, Richard Lavoie describes why there can be a connection between social and learning disabilities:

> If your child is struggling in his academic subjects, he is probably experiencing difficulty in his social life too. . . . According to a recent government study, only 16% of children with learning problems reported that they had "normal social relationships." This is understandable because learning disorders influence the way a person perceives, interprets, processes, and explains his world. It's logical to assume that this pervasive disorder would have an impact as significantly on the child's sixteen-hour "social world" as it does his eight-hour "classroom world."

While it may be easy to assume that a struggling child looks insecure, nervous, and awkward, what I usually experience is that kids who struggle academically will be socially aggressive as a way to gain power and sense of self.

WHAT DOES AUTISM LOOK LIKE?

Because autism spectrum disorder is particularly challenging in social situations, I'm going to break down the signs of it in more detail. As you read, you'll see why kids with autism need our understanding. Part of normal teen social development is figuring out when you can get away with not following the rules, pretending that you're following the rules, and realizing when you actually have to follow the rules. People with autism literally can't do the first two and feel way more comfortable doing the third. If there were a recipe for not getting along with other kids and teens and making school as difficult as possible, this list would be it.

Obsessively talking about subjects that others have no interest in: Since a boy with autism can't read the social cues that the other person is bored or irritated, he keeps right on talking.

Interrupting others: Neurotypical kids talk over and interrupt each other all the time, but there's an art to it. Unless you're good at observing the specific details of how that happens, it'll be easy to miss these social rules, and that's precisely the skill these kids lack.

Little ability to compromise: There has to be a clear winner and loser. A person on the ASD believes that he knows the rules better than anyone else, so it's wrong to him when one kid insists on having a do-over and all the other kids let him. The kid with autism studied the rules and played by the rules, and now someone just won by cheating.

Taking everything literally: Sarcasm, double entendres, and the difference between little lies, lies people tell to be polite, and real lies are often lost. For example, if a child with autism invites another child over to his house ten times in a row and every time the other child says, "Maybe," the child with autism doesn't realize that he's getting blown-off. In his mind, it makes perfect sense to keep asking until the person says yes.

Poor physical agility: These kids can have difficulties riding a bicycle, catching a ball, or climbing, and that puts them at an immediate disadvantage when playing with other children. Imagine what recess or playing with the neighborhood kids is like for them.*

Repeated body movements: They can rock, flap hands, or do other body movements that can be very distracting for others. But don't think all people on the ASD are like Dustin Hoffman in *Rain Man.* Sometimes these movements can be pretty subtle. Either way, have you ever seen a guy bounce his leg up and down really fast? Have you ever bitten your nails? Seen a girl twirl her hair? That's what's going on here, only more so. This child is anxious, and he's relieving his anxiety. I once taught a class where an autistic boy put his leg behind his neck (you read that right) as he described why girls confused him.

Stilted speech patterns: A child with autism struggles or can't learn and mimic teen slang. Even if he is highly verbal and receives social skills training, he still has a tendency to sound stilted, robotic, or even "too polite."

Can't "code-switch": People on the ASD don't change what they say depending on who's around them. For example, boys use foul language all the time around each other, but know better than to speak like that around teachers and parents. Children with autism don't know to switch their behavior, so they get into trouble with their teachers.

Inflexible thinking: Eugenia Brady, from the Association for Community Living in Colorado, describes it this way: "Think of yourself as a car and a child with autism as a train. If you're driving and come up to a closed street, you can easily find another street so you can continue where you're going. Now think of a train on a

---

*Some kids on the ASD, however, have extraordinary athletic skill, like surfer Clay Marzo.

track and there's an obstacle on the track. You're the train. You can't turn around. You can stop or you can blow through the obstacle."

Snitching: Remember the scenario I described in the room where the kid flipped out because the teacher wasn't controlling the class and he reported how the other students were misbehaving? How much do you want to bet there was another boy in the class who'd deliberately do things to set this kid off? And really, what's worse in Boy World than acting like the teacher and snitching? If you were a student in that class, would you come to this kid's defense? You may not actively go after him, but you probably are going to struggle to empathize with or defend him.

Immature interests: Remember Pokémon? A lot of these boys still like them in high school.

His mom is his social adviser: Since kids with autism usually don't have a lot of friends, they talk to their parents, especially their moms, for advice on how to get along with other kids. Think about that. What if you had to depend on your mother to teach you the subtle social rules that exist among the kids you know?

HOW TO DO RIGHT BY EVERYONE

There are lots of answers to this, but I want to share with you one positive story and then focus on what we, people with neurotypical children, and educators can do.

Andrew is a mainstreamed junior in Cincinnati with autism and learning disabilities. He's also an incredible photographer and the manager of his varsity basketball team. In ninth grade, Andrew wrote an email to Steve Przywara, the ninth-grade basketball coach at his high school, asking if he could help out. Andrew barely knew the game.

I didn't know Andrew when he emailed me a very formal request if he could be our team manager. I asked around and found out he was on the spectrum. I still wanted him to do it, but my biggest concern was Andrew being around freshman basketball players. I was worried about the locker room and the language the boys use. I was worried that they wouldn't have patience with Andrew after a loss. I was worried about bullying.

I met with Andrew and his parents, and we set up ground rules and specific responsibilities for him. Although I decided not to have Andrew in the locker room, he came to all the team meetings and games. I also met with the other kids at the beginning of the season and said any mistreatment of Andrew wouldn't be tolerated. We also had a few really good leaders, and it projected through the team.

During games, Andrew was our cheerleader and completely invested in the success of the team, and that was really helpful because we were losing a lot. He set up a Facebook group so he could be in charge of sending messages to the players about practices and schedule changes. At games I gave him statistics to track, like rebounds and turnovers. When I first started coaching, a kid like Andrew was not who I thought of as far as my impact, but it's been really satisfying.

Two years later, Andrew moved up with the players and is now the manager for the varsity team. David Moss is the varsity coach, and this is how he describes Andrew's role now:

In the last year, Andrew took a lot of ownership of what we do. He always does the huddle break. He sets up the clock and gets the balls out. Andrew is allowed in the locker room, and when the players forget and say something, they immediately apologize to him. I've learned a lot from Andrew. Last year we lost in a tournament, and I was in a pretty bad mood. A few days later, I was still in a really bad mood when we had another game. Out of the tunnel, Andrew runs out with his pencil and clipboard and a big smile, ten feet ahead of the team. He runs under the basket and pretends he's starting the tip drill. That's the greatest thing I've ever seen. It got me out of my funk because I realized, What's wrong with me? What am I doing here? He's excited to be here. At the end of the day isn't that what it's about?

The goal for Andrew, and any person in a similar situation, isn't to be the team mascot but to contribute in significant and valued ways. This is tricky territory because a child's limitations need to be respected while pushing him to expand his abilities. In Andrew's case, he wasn't ever going to play on the basketball team, but he absolutely could be part of the team. Heather Johnson, a psychologist, counsels families on how to involve their kids in social situations in positive ways:

> *We want these parents to give their children social exposure and be in situations to develop their social skills. But by doing that you're putting them into situations where they will very possibly fail or look bad in the eyes of others. If the child with autism plays on a soccer team and repeatedly misses the ball or has a meltdown, his teammates are going to get angry at him. For all these reasons, I think it's better for these kids to not be on teams but participate in individualized sports like swimming or karate. It's sports and social exposure, but no one will get mad at you when you fail.*

This isn't to say that we should constantly force these kids to socially integrate the way Andrew has. They may want friends, but working in a group or on a team requires a set of social skills that the individual may not have. It can already be difficult enough for this child to try to make one friend. It's a delicate balance to push him to increase his skills while recognizing where he is now and what works for him.

Eugenia Brady from the ACL advises:

> *We advocate for the right of the students to work independently (e.g., when the teachers say "work group assignment") because of the anxiety that that puts on the student, not to mention bullying, etc. Many of the students and adults in the spectrum would tell you*

they would prefer to work by themselves instead of in a group. They are not always able to work independently at school, and I have heard enough people in the spectrum talking about how hard it was (and still is) to be in the group when you are socially awkward.

BEING A PARENT

Imagine what it feels like to know that your child starts with a specific deficit that makes him more vulnerable to being ignored or rejected by his peers, if not outright targeted or bullied. The stress of this impacts the whole family, your marriage, and your other children. You need support. All of this is to say that when you are interacting with a parent of a kid with disabilities, realize that this person is probably operating on a much higher level of anxiety than you. Amy Johnson, an occupational therapist, describes the common reactions these parents feel:

> *When we see a three-year-old, we often don't know what the child's future will be. Parents ask us, "Will he ever be able to speak? Have friends?" As they get older, and even if they see improvements, every day the parent worries, "Will today be a good day or a bad day?" And the questions keep coming. "Will we ever be able to have him stay alone without a babysitter? Will he be able to get his driver's license? Go to college? Will he be able to live independently?" When their child doesn't reach a milestone, they grieve over and over again. It's an ambiguous loss, and you don't know what that loss is going to look like until you see it. You get angry and anxious all over.*

What's really unfair to all parents, but especially the parents of kids with these disorders, are the assumptions and blame we put on them for being bad parents who raise spoiled kids. First, if you're a parent, I guarantee that at some point your child has acted so horribly in public that you were embarrassed. When you've seen a child acting out or having a meltdown (for some reason it's usually in the grocery store, isn't it?), your first reaction shouldn't be to think, *That kid is a spoiled brat*. Your first reaction should be to realize that you have no idea what's going on with that child or that parent. If you knew the reason, you'd probably be a lot more understanding. So if you ever see this situation, either walk by with a compassionate expression on your face or ask the parent, "If there's anything I can do to help you, let me know."

WHAT DO WE SAY TO OUR CHILDREN?

Children notice at very early ages that people are different, and most adults refuse to acknowledge it. Think about when a young child says, "Mom, the black repairman is at the door!" and we say, "Don't say that!" as if (a) the man isn't black, (b) he doesn't know he's black, and (c) we don't want the man to know that we know he's black. That well-intentioned, race-guilt scolding is one of the first ways children learn that there's something bad about being black—or else why would your parents tell you to not mention it?

As with race, you could be the most nonjudgmental, kind person in the world and still raise kids who are mean to a child with disabilities. And as with race, this will happen if you don't explicitly communicate your beliefs and your children see you acting on those beliefs. To my mind those beliefs are: All people are different. There's nothing wrong with recognizing that. There's nothing wrong with being curious about people who are different and respectfully asking them questions. Even though there are people who do believe some people are better than others, in this family we don't believe that. Everyone, no matter what, is always treated with dignity.

LANDMINE!

Just like you shouldn't assume that all black people can dance or that all gay men like musicals, don't assume that kids with autism are all math geniuses.

So . . . do you remember the last time you were forced to talk to an adult who was really awkward and annoying? What did you do? Did you stay and try to understand him better? Most of us run away at the first opportunity, and no one is going to accuse us of being mean or rude to that person.

This is a difficult balance. It's not good to coddle kids with ASD. They need to learn how to interact with neurotypical kids. That's what they want, and that's what their parents want. But neurotypical kids have a right to feel safe, and sometimes children with ASD can be aggressive or even frightening. In addition, teens with autism can be sexually inappropriate. Here are my suggestions for what to discuss with neurotypical kids:

In general, acknowledge your child's experience. Admit that kids on the spectrum can be hard to be around, but remind your child that they're being difficult unintentionally. Your child also doesn't need to know exactly what's going on with the other child. It's enough to know that the child isn't picking up on obvious social cues or that your child doesn't feel comfortable around them.

Recently, we had a family over to my house for dinner, and their child demonstrated many of the signs I've listed above. We didn't know these people very well, we'd never met their child, and they didn't tell us anything about their child. Part of me wished they had told me, but I also understood why they didn't. Nevertheless, here's why I believe telling is better than not telling.

The primary reason I think parents of kids with social disabilities should tell neurotypical parents is that, if you don't, all the responsibility for the playdate going well is on the child with the disability. That's a huge amount of pressure on that child in an already difficult situation. Not telling also assumes that the other children will be nice and accommodating. That's unrealistic. Neurotypical parents also need the opportunity to set expectations for their own child's behavior. Again, it isn't necessary to go into detail about the child's condition, but it's helpful to say something like, "My child can have a hard time with loud noises." For me as a mother of two very loud boys who like to run around playing air-soft in their backyard with full camo and black goggles on, that's great to know because then I can tell my kids that they aren't going to be playing air-soft that afternoon. (I don't think that's coddling. I see it as being considerate to guests. I can barely tolerate the noise and energy myself.)

In my case, as soon as I recognized something was up, I excused myself and briefly talked to my sons in my room. This is what I said—well sort of said. I made it a lot better after our editors reviewed it.

"There's an eight-year-old girl downstairs who I believe has some kind of disability. The family will be here for about two hours, and while they're here I'll need you both to be patient with her and slow down a little. If she does things that seem odd to you, unless it's hurting something or someone, let it slide. If you play any kind of game with her and she gets upset, don't take it personally. Be flexible. If she gets very upset, ask her, 'Is there anything I can do to help?' If she doesn't respond or gets more upset, then tell me and I'll tell her parents."

I'd adapt this for younger children—say, between the ages of six and nine:

"There's an eight-year-old girl downstairs who I believe may act and talk a little differently than you're used to. The family will be here for about two hours, and while they're here I don't want you to yell. Just slow it down a little. If you play any kind of game with her and she gets so upset that you feel uncomfortable, tell me and I'll tell her parents."

After speaking with our experts, I discovered another reason why the parents didn't tell me. It's possible that the parents didn't tell me because they didn't know. I know that sounds implausible, but the combination of fear, anxiety, and love often blinds parents. We rationalize. We convince ourselves of reasonable explanations. But here's what our experts said that shocked me. Some teachers are reluctant to tell parents what their concerns are. Some are prohibited by their supervisors from even saying to parents, "Here are the things that I'm concerned about. Here are your child's strengths and weaknesses. Here are the things maybe you should talk to your pediatrician about." Perhaps one of the reasons why this is happening is that teachers aren't trained. But that's ridiculous. A teacher who sees something physically wrong with a child would tell the parents. That teacher isn't giving a diagnosis, but just advising the parent to talk to the child's doctor. Why can't the same be done for children who might be on the spectrum?

WHAT IF A CHILD ON THE ASD LATCHES ONTO YOUR CHILD?

There's this really weird kid at my school who follows me around. I feel bad for him, so sometimes when he shows up at lunch I let him sit with me. But it's a no-win situation. If I'm nice to him, he follows me around more. It got to the point where I had to tell him to back off. I felt bad about it, but what else am I supposed to do? —Ethan, 17

Many parents have asked me how to deal with this situation. It can happen in elementary, middle, or high school. The follower doesn't have to have a social disability like autism—the child could just lack good social skills. Either way, whether it's a playdate, a sleepover, or the school cafeteria, as in the example above, you're striving for a balance between maintaining each person's dignity and respecting individual boundaries.

What does that mean when a child has repeatedly invited your child to spend time together? If it's from first to fifth grade and you don't know the child well, invite the child over to your house or meet the child at a park for a specified time (obviously this is for younger children). That way you can tell your child that there will be a finite beginning and end to the time spent together.

If it's the lunch issue, here's a strategy. If your son feels like the other kid is smothering him, have him read this chapter and ask him if the descriptions match his experience. Then clearly state to your son that he has the right to have some freedom away from this kid. A compromise that your son can try is to tell the other kid, "Mondays are a good day for me. How about we have lunch on Mondays together?" The only caveat here is that your child needs to follow through because this date may not be a big deal to him, but it's probably a really big deal to the other kid.

HELPING YOUR CHILD INTERACT WITH ALL SOCIALLY AWKWARD KIDS

Kyle, a socially awkward kid, shows up to play at your house. You think everything is fine until Kyle shows up in your kitchen and asks you where all the other kids are. "I don't know," you say, "let's go find them." As you look through the house, you start thinking to yourself, *There's no way my child ran out the back door to run away from this kid . . .* but by the time you look out the backyard, you're sure. Oh yes he did. At this moment you probably have many thoughts and feelings. One is what you're going to do to your child when you catch him. But the overwhelming feeling you'll have is awkwardness as you turn to Kyle and try to think of what to say that won't make him feel worse.

First thing you do is put aside all the ways you're going to punish your kid. Focus on who needs you now. Turn to Kyle and say, "Wow, I'm not sure where they are. Let me see if I can find out." If your child has a phone, text him: "Return home immediately. No arguments. Don't even think of disobeying this. Please confirm receipt of this text ASAP."*

If Kyle hasn't caught on to what's happening, say, "I'm not sure what happened. But are you hungry or would you like a cup of hot chocolate?" Continue small talk with him, which may help you understand why the other kids left him behind. When your son walks back into the house, don't call him and his friends out, because that will make the social dynamics between the kids worse. After about ten minutes, say, "Honey, I need your help with something. Can you come here for a minute?"

---

*See . . . mobile phones can help you sometimes.

When you can speak in private, say to your child:

"I know you left Kyle behind, and I don't want to discuss how and why that happened right now. He will be here for the next hour. What needs to happen now is that you and your other friends stop excluding him. That means you'll include him in what you're doing, and you won't make him feel stupid for being here. If any of the other guys are treating Kyle badly, I expect for you to say something fast and clear like, 'Quit it.' If you continue to be mean, I'll call all the other parents and explain what happened. At this moment, I don't care how annoying he is. As long as he is here, he will be welcomed. After he leaves, I will hear your perspective. Are we clear? You're excused."

If there's another child at your house who's in on the exclusion, ask him for his "help" as well. Say something like, "You know when you're under my roof, you're my kid. That means I hold you to the same standards as my own. I understand that it's harder to get along with some people than others, but that doesn't justify all of you being mean to Kyle. So when you go back into the room I want you including him in what you're doing. Feel free to tell your parents about this."

If the kids change their behavior, then you don't need to tell the other parents. If they don't improve, then you do talk to the other parents (obviously after Kyle has left or isn't within hearing distance). This is what you could say:

"Our boys were having a hard time being decent with Kyle. I talked to them and explained my expectations. Unfortunately, it still didn't go very well, which is why I'm telling you. It's hard because Kyle struggles socially, but it's not intentional. Our kids don't have to be friends with him, but that doesn't justify being mean to him."

Do You Tell the Parent of the Socially Awkward Kid When Things Go Badly?

If it's clear that things aren't going well, then I think it's wise to tell Kyle's parent. When his mother picks him up, you can say:

"I'm really sorry to tell you this, but my child didn't treat your kid

very well. I have spoken to him about it, and we'll be handling it over here, but I am really sorry that my child behaved this way today."

If the mother asks you what Kyle struggled with, you can tell her. But also tell her one thing that Kyle did well, because the parents of kids like Kyle often feel very beat-up.

LANDMINE!

One of the most common statements I hear from ASD parents is: "If the other kids just got to know my child, they'd realize what a loyal good friend he is." As hard as this is to hear, to most children and teens that isn't the incentive that works. Because ASD kids are often on the Outer Perimeter and come across as intrusive or odd, their loyalty and kindness doesn't matter to neurotypical kids. Integrating them into social groups is more effective. When Andrew was included on the basketball team, the guys on the team saw Andrew as one of them. Other kids knew that as well, so being on the team gave Andrew some measure of protection.

These kids can have successful, happy lives. We need to help these kids and give them the skills to manage themselves now as much as they can with what they have, but in a way that is helpful. That means seeing where they are now. —Eugenia

With a little bit of knowledge, patience, and work, we can help kids with these disabilities and benefit all kids. It's not about "let's all be friends." It's not about feeling sorry for disabled kids. They have a lot to offer us. They can make us remember and value things that we often gloss over. Like Benjamin Tarasewicz, a high school senior with autism, who told me he wanted to take bell choir because he loves the sound as the bell rings through the church. "It makes me wish I could grow wings like a bird and fly deeper into the music," he said. When he said that, it stopped me. I could picture exactly what he described and not many seventeen-year-old boys I know would allow themselves to feel that joy—let alone admit it.

Recognizing people's differences really is the way we see the world in a richer way. And teaching compassion isn't being soft. It's in the moment when it's demanded that it's often difficult. Your children need visible examples of what it means for every person to have the right to participate. Through the connection they have with a child with social disabilities, they'll be more likely to empathize with others and learn to see beyond themselves.

15

Field of Play

By the time you realize that you've lost your freedom, it's too late. You've been sucked in and you can't get out. Your work and social lives revolve around it. Date nights with your spouse and weekends without carpooling to strange foreign lands are but a distant memory. Using endless tanks of gas to sit on back-breaking bleachers in the heat or cold (with possibly something else in your "water" bottle) is your everyday reality.

Sports. Can you imagine telling a new parent as they hold their infant son in their arms how much time they'll spend worrying about whether they were in charge of the orange slices? But before we get into how to manage ourselves as we sit on the sidelines, we have to go back to where it all begins: freeze tag.

In first grade, most elementary schools let us drop off our kids early so they can play on the playground before the school day begins. Obviously, this is a great idea because they get their energy out. But as I wrote in the introduction, this is also when kids really learn what school is about. Play, as it should be, is filled with messy social dynamics, power struggles, and conflicts. Play reveals who is a gifted athlete, the rule-enforcer, or the peace-maker. Play is often when the Mastermind, Associate, Punching Bag, and all the other roles begin to reveal themselves.

Play at school is also about interacting with older kids. Like when you're in third grade and the fifth-graders are playing soccer or sharks-and-minnows with you. Even the nicest kids can be intimidating, and some of them aren't so nice. They say bad words, and they tell you you're stupid and you suck at the game. They deliberately try to hit you in the head with the dodgeball, right in front of a teacher. If you complain, the kids lie and say they didn't mean to hit you in the head, and the teacher says it was an accident. Then the pattern repeats itself throughout the day at recess, lunch, and after school.

LANDMINE!

Don't stalk the playground! If they see you, they're going to be mad that you're invading their space and babying them. Instead, watch to see if your son runs to the game or chooses another spot to play when you drop him off or pick him up.

CHOOSING TEAMS

The most frustrating conflicts with friends are arguing about who's on whose team. No, I don't talk to them about it, because I'm afraid that they might yell at me and not be my friend anymore. —Jackson, 11

Starting in elementary school, some kids excel at athletics. The reason why boys allow the best athletes to pick the teams is because they need to be split up. This isn't something the boys articulate to themselves, it's just one of those unwritten boy rules that makes sense. For example, if the boys play touch football, the best kid usually plays quarterback and is one of the captains. Then the next-best kid is usually the captain of the other team, and they choose by height, ability, and sometimes friendship.

Captains will pick their own teams. They shouldn't be micromanaged. If your son doesn't get chosen right away, he has to deal with it. What shouldn't happen is your kid being made fun of for being unathletic. It's cool that he's trying, so he deserves a spot.

Again, this isn't your cue to take over choosing the teams for the boys. I want you to understand this, so if something is taking a turn south you know exactly what battle to choose. In general, no parent should talk to the boys about how they're choosing the teams. If you do, people are entitled to tell you that you're micromanaging and the boys won't take you seriously. But you can intervene when the boys use the choosing process to make one kid feel like crap.

What if you're hanging out at the neighborhood park and you see a kid targeted? For example, maybe someone is purposely throwing a football at the kid's head. If you see this, call the perpetrator over to you. If you know his name, great, if not, yell, "Hey, kid in the red sweatshirt! Can you come here for a second?" Once he comes over, say something like, "It looks like you're purposely going after that kid, but there's no way I'm right, is there?" He mumbles. You respond with a warm sincere smile, "Good, I didn't think so."

WHAT IF YOUR KID ISN'T ATHLETIC OR DOESN'T CARE ABOUT SPORTS?

Sometime in early middle school, the kids figure out for themselves who will continue with sports and who won't. For those of you who don't have kids who are interested in sports, they'll go to PE a couple of times a week, and if they have problems with how kids or teachers are treating them there, you can refer back to the "Friendly Fire" and "Frontal Assault" chapters for help.

If you're an athlete yourself, it's going to be especially hard for you as a parent, but you're going to have to get your projection under control. If you don't, nothing good can come of it. Your child will resent you and pull away. There are lots of other activities he can get similar benefits from. He can experience working in a group toward a common goal, meet different people, and develop a work ethic while following a passion just as much in the theater, newspaper, or robotics club. He just needs to find something he's truly interested in. It may be good for him to spend his time doing something that isn't as supported in Boy World as sports are. He may even know this but doesn't want to explain it to you. The only thing to keep in mind is that it's important to teach your child that exercising is a good outlet for stress and keeps him healthy. Let him figure out what he likes to do. He'll find other interests. Promise.

There could also be another big difference between you and your child: drive. If you were a competitive athlete, maybe you were so driven because you had a tough home life and you gravitated toward a team as a second family. Maybe you grew up without a lot of educational opportunities, and athletics was your ticket out. Then you were successful and had kids, and they don't have such limited paths to opportunity.

Greg Taylor, a guy I went to high school with who played basketball, wrote me about his experience with his own child:

> *My son wants absolutely nothing to do with sports except to film or photograph them. I'm just happy that he enjoys doing something productive and is pretty good at it. For me, sports were a way to pay for college. As a friend once said, "He doesn't run and jump because he doesn't have to."*

WHY DO WE ENCOURAGE OUR KIDS TO PLAY SPORTS?

We aren't insane for getting our children involved in organized sports. We may doubt our sanity when we're waking up at 6:00 on a Sunday morning, but it's great for our kids for the following reasons:

1. They develop friendships around a common interest that doesn't involve a screen.
2. They get at least some of their energy out.
3. They develop a work ethic, no matter how talented they are.

4. They develop relationships with people they might never have met otherwise.
5. They test their abilities, focus, confidence, and concentration in stressful situations.
6. They learn to lose honorably.
7. They learn to win honorably.
8. They develop the physical habit and tolerance of getting through difficult and sustained challenges.
9. Sports (or a particular sport) is so engrained in our culture and community identity that involving our children is part of who we are and what we do.
10. They create a foundation for a lifetime habit of exercise and eating well.

Parents benefit too. For every crazy, yelling, horrible parent we shrink away from (and tell our spouses or friends about when we get home or in a text while we're watching them fly off the handle), we meet a hundred really great parents. These people cheer for our kids and console them when they have setbacks. They volunteer to pick up our children and take them home. If we aren't there, they take care of our kids when they get injured. We get to watch good coaches become role models for our kids and people our children don't want to disappoint on and off the field.

I think what's shocking for many of us is how something so incredibly positive can metamorphose into something that's its complete opposite. After a lot of discussion with my boy editors about what to share with you and how, I think it comes down to this: I may write things in this chapter that will make you very worried for your child if he plays sports. You may freak out a little. As always, the boys don't want you to freak out. They just don't want you to be naive because when things go wrong in this arena, they can go really wrong.

Some sports have so much social status in our overall culture and the ALMB that they can wreck a boy's sense of honor and responsibility to others. This experience can make him feel entitled to go after his inferiors, inflate his ego, convince him to cheat or dumb himself down, and believe he's nothing without his athletic accomplishments.

Here's where we get to the part where I put this on you. No matter how athletically talented your son is, you are the person most able to raise him to believe that his talents and the social status given to him because he plays a particular sport don't exempt him from the written and unwritten rules of treating people with dignity. You are the person who must show him that sports are only one part of who he is. He is more.

YELLING

We yell. Yes, we do. Even if you think you don't, you do. If you don't believe me, ask your spouse or a good friend. Better yet, record the next game your child plays. After the game, listen to what was recorded on the audio. At the start of the game you could remember what you're doing and try to stay on your best behavior, but I'm betting you'll forget at some point. And some yelling is great. But you have to follow the noncrazy parents' rules of yelling.

- *Know the rules of the game:* If you don't know the rules, ask someone who does. Don't yell, "Why is that a penalty!!!!!????" pretending to figure it out by yelling at the ref.
- *Understand that you're making noise to be part of the noise, not to convey a message:* Boys need to hear support in moments of frustration and success.
- *No yelling personal insults:* Don't yell at individual players something like, "Hey, 23, you suck!"
- *Recognize that your child can't hear the very important strategic tip you're screaming at him:* Even if he can, he's most likely to be distracted by his annoyance with you for having no idea what you're talking about and by thinking about how you couldn't follow your own advice either. Leave the coaching to the coach.

It's good for you to show noncrazy enthusiasm! If you're into it, know the league, follow the sport professionally, take your son and his friends to a game, and yell (according to the rules above) along with all the other fans. This is the good embarrassment I talked about in the beginning of the book.

After the game, some boys like their parents to leave and some like them to stay. You may want to leave because you're freezing and your butt is numb. No matter what kind of son you have or what the outcome of the game is, make eye contact afterwards that communicates, *I'm here. If you need me, let me know.*

TIME TO STEP UP

In one of my earlier books, *Queen Bee Moms and Kingpin Dads,* I go into great detail about parents as coaches, which is a great way to be involved in your child's life and get to know his friends. I'm not going to go into great detail here, but suffice it to say, coaching your child's team also has its challenges. I get a lot of emails from parents who are either coaching or sitting on the sidelines when they see another parent losing it, and they don't know what to do. Here's a typical one:

> *I was coaching my son's sixth-grade basketball game, and the other parent-coach was screaming at the kids—his own players. It made everyone really uncomfortable, and I didn't know what to do. Should I have said something? I didn't, and now I feel terrible about it. But at the time I thought, since they were his kids, I didn't have a right to speak up.*

As a coach yourself, you're in a position of authority, and one of your responsibilities is to uphold good sportsmanship for adults and kids alike. If you see another coach who isn't doing that, you have to be smart about dealing with the situation. You don't want to speak to the coach in public or when he's fired up because he'll get reactive and defensive. You don't want the kids having even more validation than they already have that adults are crazy and immature. During the next break, speak to the ref privately and express your concern, in the hope that he'll address the problem. If the ref doesn't do anything, talk to your own players after the game and tell them what it felt like for you to watch and listen to the other coach. Ask them if they want to talk about it. Don't excuse the coach's behavior by saying something like, "He got excited." Instead, call it what it was—an adult treating children with disrespect. After the game, write to the governing board about what you and your players experienced at the game. If you have the opportunity to play that team again, talk to the ref before the game, tell him your experience with the opposing coach, and ask what you can expect if it happens again.

If you're a parent sitting on the sidelines or the bleachers, and you see another parent losing it, you can still do something. I'm not talking about going over and screaming at them or wagging your finger at them, because some parents may be so wrapped up in the game that they don't realize what they're doing. But if it persists, then you need to say something to the coach. Then he or she needs to handle it.

TRYOUTS

At a certain level of competitive play, your child will have to prove he's good enough to make the team. For a lot of reasons, sometimes he won't make it. So what do you say to your child if that happens? He probably doesn't want to talk about it at length with you. Don't keep asking him if he's okay or if he wants to talk about it. Limit what you say to, "I'm really sorry. I'll talk about it if you want to." Later you can float the idea that you'll support him if he wants to try out again or you can practice with him. This isn't just about being cut from playing. It's also about being denied a part of his identity or what he wanted his identity to be, and it's also about being separated from his friends. Here's some advice from fourth- and fifth-grade boys:

My parents would probably try to comfort me, which I hate. So keep talking to your son really short. I don't really care if I get cut from a team, as long as the people on that team are still friends with me.
—Nick, 10

It'd be helpful if the parent would go back to a time when you were excluded and tell them what you did. Something bad to say would be, "I heard from a little birdie that you were cut from the team. I'm going to try to get you back on." —Zack, 11

Don't say, "You should have made it, you're better than everyone."
—Dominic, 11

Again, this is one of those easy-to-project moments.

He didn't make the golf team. He was close, but was cut. I told him he had to find something he was passionate about in high school . . . something that he could be involved in. A few months later, he came home and told us he joined the bowling team, it was a no-cut sport . . . I hate bowling alleys. But I have met wonderful parents of the other bowlers and made new friends. But I had to work on a positive attitude; I had to truly release my vision. —Sharon

It's hard to know when it's a good idea to push and prod a little if your son doesn't make the team. It's so easy for him to say, "No, I'm fine," but don't simply take his word for it. It's okay for him to sulk for a little while. But after a week, look for other evidence that he is working harder to prepare for the next tryouts or that he's moving on. Is he connecting to other interests or groups that are positive for him?

What Do You Say to Other Parents?

If your kid doesn't make the cut but his close friend does, congratulate the other parent when you see him or her in person because that parent will feel awkward around you and not know what to say. It's not like other parents can come up to you and say, "Hey, my kid made the team, and so sorry your kid didn't." I mean, they could, and for some situations that remark would be fine. But if they know your kid is really disappointed, it'll be harder for them to broach the subject. If you really like the parent whose kid made the team, disconnect your friendship from the sidelines. After all, somewhere between the carpooling and the orange slices, you all may have become good friends—which has nothing to do with your kids. Don't sell that possibility short. If you really want to include the kids, why not get tickets for a college game? That'll make it more comfortable for everyone.

He Made It

If your kid makes the cut, of course you're going to be really happy and proud of him. But also know what that means. The moment he makes the cut he's joining an established culture with its own set of specific unwritten rules. As a new player, he's going to want to be part of the team—on and off the field. If his friends don't make the team, they could react by trying to cut him down in other ways. Just be aware that this could be a challenge for him.

There are a few aspects of his team experience that would be good for you to pick up on. Do the players respect the authority of the captain? Does the captain exercise his authority fairly? How seriously do players take practice? Has your son been asked to sign a behavioral contract about not drinking or about how he conducts himself as a representative of the team? Have you been asked to sign a parental behavioral contract (pretty much the same set of rules)? Read both contracts and discuss them with him because, whatever he thinks about those rules, if he's on the team he's agreeing to them. And so are you.

WHAT IF HE'S REALLY GOOD?

Unless you're asked, don't talk to other parents about the elite teams and out-of-state competitions that you're going to. If your son is really good—so good that his talent clearly sets him apart—you have a responsibility to teach him how to handle the social power that comes with that talent. I know you know he doesn't have the right to treat other people badly because he's athletically talented. But the reality is, being good at things, especially sports, often gives boys an asshole pass. Your son is going to be sent signals that in the ALMB it's okay to be an ass when you're really good at something because people are less likely to hold you accountable for bad behavior. The result is that he's encouraged and enabled to become an ass, and we don't need more of those.

Talent all too often doesn't give a boy anything but a bad attitude. Hard work gives a boy strong character. The reality is that reaching the highest levels of athletics is about work ethic and intelligence. Lots of guys are talented. Even if your son is the best in his school or league or state, there are most likely hundreds if not thousands of other kids who are better than he is. Your goal as a parent is to show him that however good he is, he needs to show the kids coming up after him what it looks like to combine talent with hard work. If he sees you doing anything similar, you're giving him a powerful incentive to stay humble and work hard.

YOUR NINTH-GRADER MAKES VARSITY

You may have the experience of having your ninth-grade son make varsity. Of course, any parent is going to be very proud of their son for this accomplishment. But I've met many parents who are so proud of their son that they fail to realize the obvious: their fourteen-year-old son will now be socializing with boys who are seventeen and eighteen years old. If your son makes varsity at a young age, I guarantee you that he'll grow up faster, and it begins the moment he makes the team.

If he plays a fall sport like football or soccer, his introduction to high school will be largely through his experiences on varsity. For example, he's probably never hung out with junior and senior guys in a locker room, where his fourteen-year-old self will be changing around boys who have gone through puberty and are waving their penises around. And unless he's been hanging out in people's houses drinking, hooking up with girls, and driving around with his friends when he was in eighth grade, he's probably not accustomed to the social situations that come along with being on varsity, let alone high school in general. Now combine all that with the possibility that your son is playing an ALMB sport and suddenly has the huge social status that comes with those sports. Is it worth it? Yes, probably, but the least you can do is be aware of what you're sending him into, and frankly you owe it to him to help him through the process.

If everything goes well, the older boys will look out for him. These are the guys you want your son building relationships with. But if he's socializing with them, that also means the following: he's going to get into a car with a lot more kids than seat belts; older girls will pay more attention to him; and quite possibly there'll be one or two guys on his team who think it's a great idea to get your son to binge-drink or hook up with a hot older girl so they can make fun of him later.*

If things don't go well, there may be one or two guys who believe they have a right to haze younger players, which can be frightening, humiliating, and very possibly physically dangerous. If the captain of the team doesn't endorse the hazing but doesn't have the ability to stand up to his teammates, your son will also experience what it's like to depend on a leader who fails him. And I haven't even

---

*I promise you that I spend a lot of time on this in *The Guide*, where your son, no matter what position he's in—freshman, team captain, etc.—can get specific advice about how to handle himself.

started with the emotional and psychological impact on your son when coaches look the other way or are powerless to stop it.

I'm not telling you this so that you'll decide to bar your son from ever going out with these guys. I just don't want your understandable pride that he made the team to blind you to the very real consequences that may not be so readily apparent. You do need to know that your pride may very well stop him from talking to you about what's really going on because he doesn't want to worry or disappoint you. You need to be ready to be his safe haven where he can experience these challenges and know you're there for guidance and support.

Think of it this way. As a young man, he'll have to make decisions about what kinds of groups he wants to belong to and associate with. He needs to know how to handle himself with people who intimidate him or who have more authority and power than he does. What he learns now impacts how he holds his own and manages himself with his "superiors" in college if he continues on a team or joins a club or fraternity. In the workplace, he'll use the same skills with a boss. If you can help him while he's still under your roof, these later encounters will be easier for him.

THE LOCKER ROOM

When your son plays competitive sports, he'll be spending a lot of time in locker rooms. High school locker rooms have complex, unwritten rules that no boy inherently knows. He has to learn these rules without looking like he doesn't know them.

For example, some teams shower together. Some teams don't. But for any player, it's intimidating. What is generally true is that younger boys don't like changing in front of older boys. This makes things very difficult if you're a younger boy who needs to put on compression shorts or a cup. Many younger boys change in the stalls. Why they're doing that is obvious to the older boys, who just see huge red targets on their backs. The guys who want to make a point of it love to say things like, "What's the problem? You only have one ball?" Some older boys will make a point of walking around with their penises out. Some will get hard to freak out the other guys. The only thing they can say to that is some version of "Put that away." Most coaches don't hang out in locker rooms. They may walk through. They may be there for a short time to deliver a message or give out new uniforms, but this really is the boys' domain.

At the least, it's a good idea to get your son more comfortable being around other naked guys and helping him learn some locker-room etiquette. So dads, take your kid to the Y, the neighborhood rec center, or the public pool. He doesn't have to get naked. He just needs to become accustomed to being around naked hairy guys and get a chance to assimilate locker-room culture. There's nothing to be scared of unless someone is inappropriate to him. And the chances of that are substantially less likely than any harassment he'd get in the high school locker room.

IF HE BECOMES A CAPTAIN OR TEAM LEADER

Congratulate your son if he's made captain, because the way he has conducted himself has given his teammates faith and confidence that he's fair, levelheaded, and reliable. But now that he has his position, have one talk with him about what this means to you. As in something like this:

"I'm incredibly proud that your team has chosen you to lead them. But now that you're in an official leadership position, things can get tricky. Your responsibility isn't only to keep the players focused through the ups and downs of the season. It's also to keep all your players safe. Sometimes people, even friends, will test you about this. But the moment you accepted this position you accepted that responsibility."

You don't need to go into specifics here unless he asks, because he'll know what you're referring to. If he does have problems (and every captain does), his responsibility is to raise the issue with the player. If that doesn't address the problem, then it's part of what he signed up for as a leader to ask for help. Even if he's not the captain, he still needs to support the overall ideals of the team.

COACHING: THE GOOD, THE BAD, AND THE UGLY

As I write this, I have a few years under my belt with my boys on teams. My children have had vastly different experiences. My younger son, Roane, has always had great coaches. When he was five, he began playing soccer. His coaches were two enthusiastic dads who knew the game and loved each and every kid. At eight, he moved up to a more competitive league and had an amazing coach who worked with kids who wanted more focused competition. He was fair, worked the kids hard, and greatly improved their skills. After our recent move, Roane has continued to have great coaches who have good relationships with the parents, work the kids hard, teach them how to be competitive, and demand good sportsmanship from both the players and the parents. Not surprisingly, Roane has blossomed under their direction, loves playing soccer, and has developed the social skills to go up to a group of kids on a field and get in their game.

My older son, Elijah, hasn't been so lucky. His first team sport was also soccer, and he had two back-to-back, horrible parent-coaches. The first one screamed at the kids (they were six), didn't know how to coach, and was rude to the parents. The next coach played favorites and allowed the kids to be mean to their teammates. They lost virtually every game because the kids were so nasty to one another.

At the end of the season, we put Elijah in martial arts. He loved it, but he was incredibly shy about joining any pickup soccer, football, or basketball games at the neighborhood playground, while his brother confidently got in the game.

I was a competitive athlete and wanted Elijah to have the experience of working hard with a team guided by a great coach. From personal experience, I knew how positive this can be and how good it would be for him. But I lay low, hoping another opportunity would come up. Recently he played intramural basketball and had a nice coach who encouraged him to keep playing. The other parents helped us sign him up to play in a local league.

When I met the new basketball coach, I felt like we'd won the coaching lottery. She is tough and skilled, she loves the kids, she works them hard, she holds them to a high standard, and she makes it absolutely clear to all the parents that she won't tolerate any craziness from us either. A few games ago, she lost her temper at the opposing coach during a game. Immediately afterwards, she emailed all the parents to apologize for her behavior, acknowledge that it wasn't good role-modeling for the boys, and promise to talk to them about it at practice.

You know what I also love about her? My son values her respect, and he's a little afraid of her. So when my son is tempted to do something dangerous, bad, or below the standards we and she have set for him, he'll think twice before doing it.

Let me give a few more small but meaningful examples of good coaches who understand the leverage they have and their ability to teach their players what they stand for and what they demand of each player as a member of the team. In the "No Man's Land" chapter, I introduced Steve, Andrew's basketball coach. He shared more of his experiences with me:

I had one kid who was by far the most talented kid on our team, but every time he'd be on the verge of starting he'd get into trouble. It killed me, but I didn't start him. When my players make big mistakes, I do everything I can to keep them on the team. But that doesn't mean they get privileges. On game day they may not get to wear their game jersey. When they really mess up, I have them do lots of manual labor in order to earn their way back on. There's a line where, if it comes to the point that a kid isn't interested in making changes and following the rules and his actions are detrimental, he has to go. But it's a really difficult decision. I believe most bad things on teams don't happen, would never have happened, if the coaches held the kids to these standards.

Here's another one that I particularly love because of what I write later in this chapter about lacrosse. It's worth Googling and watching the video because it's so great. In August 2012, Mac Breedlove, a lacrosse player traveling with his team on a Southwest flight, was forced to read a public apology after his coaches caught him cutting in line during the boarding process. The coaches coordinated with the flight crew to bring Breedlove to the front of the plane and have him speak into the intercom system. Breedlove read from a prepared statement:

During the boarding process, I took advantage of this airline's kindness. I hope you will all find it in your hearts to forgive me, for I am just a young man that thinks I'm smarter than I am. Enjoy your flight, and remember to fly Southwest, because they let my coach do this to me.

Coaching: The Good

Coaches are probably the first (and maybe only) adults parents will allow to yell at their kid while they stand to the side and watch. This can take some getting used to.

It's important to distinguish between a tough coach who's hard on your kids and one who crosses the line. I think this is what it comes down to. Good coaches know how to motivate boys by appealing to the best of Boy World, the intense desire in boys to be part of a team and recognized for courage and hard work. Coaches can be hard, but if they're fair (which means equally tough on all the players), the boys will more than rise to their expectations. These coaches may really rub you the wrong way. They can make the boys practice so hard that they're miserable. They may not give your child the playing time you'd like, but the greater good of having your son around someone like this is more than worth the pine time.

Coaching: The Bad

We hear so much about bad coaches, and although there's a range of behavior, they exhibit a combination of the following characteristics:

1. Singling out a player or group of players and insulting them
2. Looking the other way when one of his players is violent or abusive to another person
3. Excusing bad behavior in a star player because he wants him to play
4. Practicing without breaks and without water in a way that puts players at physical risk
5. Comparing the players to girls when they're failing in his eyes
6. Not articulating his expectations clearly (or at all) and then blaming the player and/or his parents when they don't act according to these unspoken demands.

Coaching: The Ugly

One of the coaches would call us faggots and picked on this one kid all the time. Nobody did anything because they didn't want to be called a faggot either. —Jack, 16

When your son has a coach like this, it usually feels like there's absolutely nothing you or he can do except put up with it or quit. Those aren't your only options.

One of your possible advantages is that you'll see the coach interact with the players during the games. This is an advantage you don't have with teachers because you're almost never going to have the opportunity to see a teacher teach like you regularly see a coach coach. If you're unhappy with the way the coach is acting during the games, ask your son, "Are you feeling any of this in practice? Is this as bad as it appears?" To be fair, coaches can yell at their players during a game and then later more calmly explain why they got so upset. As a parent, you won't know this. That's why you have to ask your son.

If you have information that the coach is abusive, you can handle it in the same way you would talk to a bullying teacher (see page 234). You're going to ask to meet with the person at a mutually convenient time. You're going to prepare by using SEAL yourself, ideally in collaboration with your son. You're going to present the evidence you have and ask the coach if he believes that it accurately represents the facts. You're going to watch his body language and listen to not only the content of his words but his tone to determine if he's taking you seriously. No matter how intimidating the person is or how much social power he has in your community, you need to meet with him once. If he blows you off, then you can go over his head.

How to Get Through the Necessary but Incredibly Uncomfortable SEAL with a Bad or Abusive Coach

Set Up: Don't communicate with the coach about any of your intentions right before, during, or after a game. Contacting him by email is probably best. If both parents are available and won't get fired for leaving work, they both need to meet with the coach. If possible, try to meet somewhere other than his office, on neutral ground.

You *(explaining)*: Hi, Coach, thanks for meeting with us. As I said in my email, we'd like to talk about Brian's experience on your team.

Coach *(pushing back)*: Okay . . . *(Awkward silence. You wish you weren't there.)*

You *(explaining)*: Brian has always loved playing baseball and wants to work hard for you. But he's also really angry about how some of the guys are treating him and some other kids and feels that you're backing them up.

COACH *(pushing back)*: My players don't haze.

YOU *(explaining)*: Brian has told us that he can't change in the locker room without the kids messing with him. He's also telling us that you're making fun of him for it.

COACH *(pushing back)*: I think you're taking this a little too seriously. The boys mess around. I have great relationships with my players. They respect me. I love every player on my team. But I can't control everything they do. Is that all?

YOU *(explaining)*: I'm not getting the sense that you're listening. My kid wants to play his best for you. He also doesn't feel like you're looking out for him. I'm not asking you to coddle him. I'm asking you to keep him and all the other boys safe.

COACH *(pushing back)*: Look, I don't know what you're talking about, but I'll look into it.

YOU *(affirming)*: Thanks. I really appreciate it. Brian didn't want me to talk to you about this because he thinks you'll be angry with him. But I know you care about these boys, so I was willing to take the chance.

If your son's coach responds as this coach does, he probably has no intention of addressing your concerns seriously. In that case, your SEAL is probably more about having a record that you went to him to discuss your concerns. These coaches are also notoriously sexist, so in their presence both parents have to model the utmost respect for each other. Moms, no crying and getting "emotional." Dads, no laughing along with the coach if he says something you really don't agree with. Keep yourself calm, collected, and focused on the goal of coming across as someone he can't manipulate or dismiss.

YOUR KID WANTS TO QUIT

Your son doesn't wake up randomly one morning and decide he wants to quit. It doesn't matter whether it's football, lacrosse, badminton, music, or theater. Whenever a person gives up something to which they've dedicated years and sustained effort, it feels like losing their identity. Quitting is also often perceived as directly correlated with poor character and mental and physical weakness. Even if your son doesn't feel that way, most boys believe their parents feel this way. He also knows the sacrifices you've made. It's part of why this can be such an incredibly difficult decision for him. But staying with something that makes him unhappy will only make him more miserable.

The tricky thing about wanting to give something up is that it's inevitable that he'll go through a phase where he wants to give up but he should still stick with it. The only way he'll be able to figure out what's best is if he goes through an intense process of self-reflection and assessment of the overall situation. What often makes that too difficult for a boy to do is the disappointment he knows you'll feel. For parents, their son's decision to quit a team or activity can also feel like a reflection of their parenting. If he quits, you're bad parents because you've raised a quitter. If he stays, you're good parents because he's perseverant. This isn't true, but it's often what people believe.

Quitting often has nothing to do with actually playing the sport. Guys don't quit over the extra drill or the push-ups. They quit because they give up on their coach. They quit because their parents put unbearable pressure on them. They quit because the guys on the team are horrible to each other or other people. But since boys are so reluctant to tell us what's really going on, it's easy to fall back on what you, as the parent, assume.

If your son wants to quit, these are good questions to ask him to think about (just don't ask them all at once):

"Okay, you must have a really good reason for wanting to stop. Can I ask if that reason is hard to tell me, and why it's hard to tell me? Is it because you're worried about what I'll think about you? Or are you worried about what I'll think about other people on the team and I'll want to do something about it?"

Based on his answers, the questions he needs to answer for himself are: "Do I love the sport and hate the team? Is it worth transferring schools? Could I play at a club level and be happy?"

Here's a common way a boy tells his parents that he wants to quit and how he reacts to their responses:

BOY: I don't know if I want to do this anymore.

MOM: What are you talking about? Why?

BOY: I don't know. It's just not worth it.

MOM: Why? I am really not getting this.

BOY: Mom, it's not that big a deal. I'm just done.

MOM: You need to explain this beyond you feel like quitting. You have such potential. You'd be giving up everything you've worked so hard for. What if you change your mind? You can't go back . . .

BOY: Just forget I brought it up. *(Silence in the car. He stares out the window and puts his earbuds in. He's sitting in that car feeling so stupid that he thought it'd be a good idea to talk to her.)*

MOM: What's going on with you? *(He looks at her and doesn't know what to say.)*

This boy is torn between walking away and telling his mom everything. Partly he wants to tell her because he knows she'll feel so guilty if she knows the truth. But another little part of him wants to tell her just because she's his mom. All he can do is look away, struggling between the 90 percent of himself that desperately wants to keep his mouth shut and the 10 percent that wants to tell her.

Finally, he can't keep it inside anymore. He tells her. The previous Friday, after a solid month of being treated like shit, a guy on the team was held down after practice while four guys shaved his head because he didn't have enough "team spirit." He was one of the guys who held him down. He didn't want to, but he did. He'll never forget how the other guys laughed while the kid fought them, down on his knees. He tells his mother that the coach knew it was going to happen and conveniently left the locker room right before the guy was forced down to the floor.

First and foremost, this isn't boys "horsing" around. Having your head shaved against your will is terrifying. You're being held down, so you're at the mercy of your determined tormentors, and having your neck exposed in the presence of a sharp object can instinctually trigger a flight-or-fight response. This isn't what team spirit is based on. It's what tyranny is based on.

Boys believe there are three likely outcomes to telling their parents about an incident like this:

1. The parents will be outraged and insist on immediately calling the principal, the coach, or the shaved kid's parents, or all three.
2. The parents won't like what happened, but they'll want their son to keep quiet and let it blow over.
3. The parents won't see why their son is so upset because, technically, no one got hurt. An ALMB dad may also react by accusing his son of being weak or too sensitive.

All three of these outcomes feel terrible to boys. If the parent forces him to report the incident, he worries that he'll be accused of snitching. He's also going to have to admit that he participated. If the parent wants him to keep quiet, he now realizes that his parent is too scared or passive to do the right thing. If the parent dismisses the incident as a prank, an instance of "guys will be guys," the boy will have confirmation of what he's probably known for some time: that the ALMB controls his parent.

Here's how you can help your son if he tells you about something like this. Remind him of the difference between snitching and reporting. People snitch to get someone in trouble; people report to right a wrong. He's only in this situation because the guys did it and the coach permitted it by leaving.

He has to report it to the person at school whom he trusts the most and who has the most power. He's going to write a letter using SEAL and email it to this trusted person. Make sure he says where it happened, when it happened, who was there as a bystander, and who was there as a participant—including him. Describe the actions of the coach. If your son is asked to meet with this authority in person, you'll go with him as backup. Don't send him in there alone.

If he doesn't do this, he's going to carry this experience around with him for a long time. He's going to feel less of a man. The team will also suffer, because true team cohesion and "spirit" can only be developed through trust and love.

This is Brendon Ayanbadejo, a former linebacker for the Baltimore Ravens, pictured with a NoH8 (No Hate) tattoo.

The NFL epitomizes American masculinity and personifies the ALMB. Ayanbadejo personifies the NFL. Ripped? Check. Tall? Check. Handsome? Check. Straight? Check. Athletic? Check. But Ayanbadejo didn't let the ALMB trap him into being a shell of a man. In high school he was active in theater and politics and lived with his mom in an apartment on UC Santa Cruz's campus, where he was surrounded by many different kinds of people. He also happened to play football.

In 2009 Brendon became one of the first athletes from a major American professional sports team to speak out in support of same-sex marriage. It wasn't easy.

> *"If I was walking by, and they [the players] wanted to be immature and make comments, I'd keep walking," said Ayanbadejo, who has a 1-year-old son and a 6-year-old daughter with his longtime girl-friend. "If they wanted to be real men and have conversations, I would have, but no one did." (New York Times, September 14, 2012)*

Real men have conversations? Exactly. When Ayanbadejo heard gay slurs from his teammates, this is what he did:

> *I just drop a little something in their ear, and hopefully it lets them see a little bit wider that those words are harmful. They go, "I didn't mean it like that." I just tell them, "If you didn't mean it like that, then don't say it." (USA Today, September 12, 2012)*

This is the power of professional sports at its best. That a professional athlete who participates in the most popular sport in the United States, and whose size and strength embody male physical power, stepped forward to defend gay people is, in a word, stunning. He's showing that men who personify everything we glorify about masculinity can shatter the confining limitations of the ALMB by using its own power.

Let's use this example at your son's school. Imagine a person getting up to announce the next meeting of the Gay Alliance or whatever cause people generally blow off or don't think applies to them. Is the person you're thinking of the political girl who almost everyone rolls their eyes at or tunes out when she speaks? Now imagine that instead of her it's one of the best athletes in the school making the announcement, a guy who looks like a high school version of Brendon Ayanbadejo. Who would have more power to change public opinion?

If your son has this kind of power within your community, just think for a moment about how he can become someone who is a truly ethical and transformational leader, not just to his peers but to adults as well. The power of sports to transform people's thinking can't be overstated. But people's personal experiences with sports and the culture of athletics can be very messy and disappointing. It really isn't about the sport itself but about the social entitlement and power we give the guys who play.

LAXBROS

I can't remember the precise moment "laxbros" came into my life. It just seemed that one day a lot of guys showed up to school with perfectly layered longish hair while being completely oblivious to everyone else around them—unless they were saying something obnoxious to someone outside their group. Their behavior reminded me of a group of eighth-grade mean girls who had suddenly been transformed into high school guys. I do remember the first time I went to a lacrosse game between two highly competitive teams on the East Coast and saw the parents. I distinctly remember a mom with fake breasts wearing a tight white T-shirt with her son's school name embroidered in madras and a short khaki skirt, gossiping about female students at her son's school. I remember the dads talking to each other about the "market." While they chatted, their coach was screaming at their sons about what useless little girls they were.

If you live on some parts of the East Coast and send your child to a private school (bonus if it's a boarding school) or a public school with a high tax base, it may feel to you like laxbro (lacrosse) culture has been around for generations. If you live in the Midwest, it probably seems like all of a sudden lacrosse has become this really popular competitive sport. You may have noticed your son talking about laxbros, and if he's into it he may be wearing different clothes, cutting his hair in a way that seems to mimic a current teen-girl heartthrob (not true), and using words like "spoon," "laxho," "lax

sesh," and "bra." To recognize the laxbro uniform, here's the definition from Urban Dictionary:

1. Headwear: Trucker hats, backwards college hats, goofy winter hats
   (i.e., puff balls and ear flaps)
2. Hair: The longer the better, the wavier the better (a wavy "lettuce"
   out the backside of the helmet or cap)
3. Shirts: Bright-colored polos, youth league T-shirts, pinnies, or
   skins
4. Shorts: Plaid/madras, seersucker, long team shorts
5. Footwear: Rainbow, Reef, or Turf shoes with high black socks
6. Accessories: Hemp bracelets/necklace, shooting string or sidewall
   lace bracelets, Ray-Ban, Arnette, or Oakley shades, lax-themed
   tattoos (i.e., crossed sticks on calf)

Some other helpful descriptions from Urban Dictionary:

Every Laxbro has a pseudonym like El Diablo or Sea Bass or something cool in lax like that. If you're not constantly holding your stick
and getting women to think you're super hot just because you're a
laxbro, then you're probably not a laxbro.

They get all the girls and can bang anyone they want.
   Bro: Yo come here let's bang.
   Girl: Of course, you're a hot lax bro.

High school guys in middle-class and wealthy high schools know
that laxbros currently get the prize for being the biggest douchebags in Boy World. Somehow a really interesting, challenging sport
often played by great guys became infected with a tribal culture of
rampant entitlement, dismissal of all other opinions, using women,
unapologetic hazing, a belief in their own importance in the overall
social hierarchy, and an adamant refusal to admit any of this is true.
Plus, laxbro parents (as opposed to parents of lacrosse players) back

up this crappy attitude and steadfastly believe that lax will be the key to getting their son into an elite college and a job in the financial sector after graduation so they can make huge amounts of money and have no life beyond being rich, super-stressed, and emotionally stunted.

This isn't to say that other sports can't have arrogant, obnoxious guys. For example, in the Midwest and North it's been hockey, and in the South and Texas (and everywhere else) it's football. In cities and some areas of the Midwest, it's basketball. All these guys get high social status and are often treated better because of their participation in the sport. But there's never been a "white and rich" sport so filled with players who want to come across as entitled and disrespectful as today's generation of lacrosse players. And there's never been a group of parents who are stereotyped so quickly by high school boys and girls as desperate social climbers who enable their sons' bad behavior and then deny and protect their sons when this bad behavior becomes public.

Lacrosse coaches and players will tell you that the best players don't like laxbro culture. While I promised the coaches and players that I wouldn't reveal their names, I did talk to many of them—including guys who attend Division I schools. Here's what one of them said:

> *These kids often do not represent the good players who play for the love of the game, but rather those who use the game as a social mechanism. These kids find false confidence in the simple fact that they play lacrosse and cast a bad shadow on others who play. It's not much different from football meatheads or any other popular sport. These douche athletes don't really get it and get a free pass from those on their team because they're normal to them while it's tough to see how exclusive the group can be to an outsider. Unfortunately, the upper-middle-class preppy rich kid stereotype has this same sense of exclusivity, and when combined with playing a sport comprised of many rich white kids, it can create a super-douche.*

You can see the problem within this last quote. Laxbros get a free pass from the lacrosse players on their team. But as soon as someone says "It's normal," "It's what we've always done," or "It's tradition," you and your son must both have the integrity and courage to ask why. Why is it normal and therefore acceptable that the laxbro guys get to act like this? Even if your son plays lacrosse and thinks laxbros are stupid and genuinely dislikes these guys, when he says nothing he goes along with it. People associate your son with them and a sport he loves.

Again, this is no different from what happens in other sports. Players cover for other players. The only difference here is the preponderance of really rich white kids playing lacrosse. And really rich kids often have really rich parents who are used to getting their way and getting their children out of trouble when they clearly deserve to get in trouble.

If your son wants to or is currently playing lacrosse, I'm asking you to be aware of what he may be getting himself into. He may need to work on some skills to combat this mentality. I'm not saying he has to stop wearing madras and his pinneys. If he thinks his "lettuce" looks good, then by all means let him rock that hairstyle. But I'm saying he has to man up and demand better from these guys and from himself.

LAXBROS ARE NOT THE ONLY CULPRITS

Some of the guys who are helping me with this book think my house is going to be firebombed for talking about laxbro culture. But really, this isn't only about lacrosse. As I've said, all sports teams have the potential to encourage boys to abuse other kids. But the ones that fit into the ALMB are by far the most susceptible to this. Any athlete is more likely to feel entitled and be abusive if a few circumstances come together—say, he's good enough to be on the team but not good enough that his talent and ability set him apart; his team has high social status in his school; his coach is perceived as above the law by other adults, "motivates" his players by humiliating them, and looks the other way when players humiliate each other, even encouraging them to do so; his team is part of the history and traditions of his school; and his parents are so proud of his participation on the team that they excuse his bad behavior.

As I write this, soccer players in California are facing charges of forced sexual penetration of teammates and the victims are accusing the coach of knowing what was happening. In Georgia a football student is facing the same charge. In Ohio football players laughingly recorded themselves recently as they talked about a girl who was sexually assaulted at a party by their teammates while their coaches go after the victim's credibility. I've listened to parents excusing the behavior of these boys or saying that it was stupid, they were messing around, or it was just a fluke.

In these situations, the hypocrisy and denial of the adults is glaring, and it has been and will continue to be the most difficult part of my work. Please hear me on this: no matter how "nice" a school you send your child to, it can have this problem. Throughout my career I have seen heads of prestigious schools, coaches, and other people in positions of authority turn their backs on the emotional and physical safety of their kids. It's happening right now. Kids, including the most entitled and abusive athletes, don't go after other kids unless they know that adult "leaders" in their school don't or can't hold them accountable.

It doesn't have to be this way. In the book *Season of Life*, Joe Ehrman, a former NFL defensive lineman and volunteer high school coach, is described as he begins the football season with his players.

> *What is our job? he asked.*
> *To love us, the boys yelled back.*
> *And what is your job? he shot back.*
> *To love each other, the boys responded.*

With Joe standing by his side, Biff, the six-foot-three, 300-pound head coach, gathered the boys around him and said:

I don't care if you're big, small, huge muscles or no muscles, never even played football or star of the team—I don't care about any of that stuff. If you're here, then you're one of us, and we love you. Simple as that. We're going to go through this as a team . . . a community. This is the only place in your whole life where you're going to be together and work together with a group as diverse as this— racially, socially, economically, you name it. It's a beautiful thing to be together like this . . . so enjoy it. Make the most of this. It's yours. The relationships you make here . . . you will always have them . . . for the rest of your life.

This is what all of our sons deserve.

16

Outward Bound

I t should go without saying that everyone has the right to be treated with dignity. You don't have to be a member of a certain religion or political party to have the basic human decency to respect another person's right to exist in this world.

As I wrote earlier, homophobia is much more than a matter of "tolerating" or "accepting" homosexuality. Homophobia is one of the cornerstones of the lessons boys learn about what kind of men they're allowed to be—men who speak out in the face of cruelty or men who contribute to the cruelty by saying nothing or joining in. This isn't something you can take a neutral position about. If you believe every person has the inherent right to be treated with dignity and you acknowledge that you have to educate children in a manner that actually reflects boys' lives, you have to take a stand against homophobia—just as you should about racism, sexism, and any other form of bigotry.

If you're a parent, talk to your son tonight before he goes to bed or on the way to school tomorrow. Don't worry if you've never talked to him about this before and he's very confused by your sudden focus. Assure him it's nothing he's done that's made you want to say something on the subject. You've just been thinking about these issues and want to make sure he knows what you think.

If you're a teacher or coach, the next time you meet with your kids take five minutes to say something like, "I just want to make sure you understand that each one of you has the right to be in my class (or on this team) and feel safe. If you don't, please tell me, because it's my responsibility to make sure you do. If something's happened in the past that I missed or if I made a mistake, I want to know. I need to know."

You may notice that I do not always use the pronoun "she" in talking about boys' love interests. I'm doing this because not all guys are straight, and it's only fair to write this book for and about all guys—regardless of who they're sexually attracted to.

It's just a basic issue of what's right. And the fact is, gay guys experience the same insecurities, fears, highs, and lows in their romantic lives as straight boys—except for one thing. It's worse. Not only do they have to come to terms with their sexuality, but they have to do so in an environment where they're uncertain at best about whether people are going to accept them and where there will always be people who really believe they have the right to make them miserable. Even more annoying and potentially dangerous are the adults who are supposed to protect their well-being and keep them safe, but who back up the homophobic kids or do nothing about their abuse (which is the same thing).

A few of the guys who have helped me on this book are gay and have a lot of straight guy friends, and I've asked them to share what they think is most important for you to know. Ian, a junior from Bexley, Ohio, is out with his family and in school.

> I'm tired of the stigma that comes with being gay, like the feeling that I'm that typical "girls' gay best friend." It's just not who I am. Of course I have lots of friends who are girls, but I'm not begging them to go shopping and cry over The Notebook. . . . I hate how people expect me to know everything about musicals and Broadway.

I've also asked Matt, also a junior, who's out only to his best friend and his dad, to share what it was like to realize that he's gay.

> The fear starts when you realize that feeling, no matter how small, that you're attracted to the same sex. You can't shake it off. You try

to convince yourself that it's silly. "I'm just confused," I told myself.
I couldn't be gay; I couldn't be what many around me regarded as
being wrong and perverse. And since countless people use "gay,"
"homo," and "fag" as insults and as a substitute for "stupid" or
"lame," it seemed like everyone hated who I was. I was scared of
being myself around my closest friends, my own family, my parents,
the most important people in my life.

This is why it matters when people carelessly use the word "gay"
or any word like it to put someone down, or when they use it to
mean "stupid" and then assure everyone else that it doesn't matter,
"it's just what we say." As Matt said, the callous use of these words
makes guys like him feel like they're hated for just being themselves.
And then they have to put up with the people who say it and who
refuse to take responsibility for what they're doing.

As a parent, you need to educate your child about kids who are
in the closet. You need to make them aware that they may have close
friends, guys who they may deeply respect and like, who are also terrified to reveal their truth. So as you read Ian's and Matt's words, do
so knowing that someone you care about is probably going through
what they describe.

I just couldn't hold it in anymore. One night I texted one of my best
friends. I took about ten minutes to type the words and send them.
"I'm gay." Send. She wrote me back telling me that she loved me
no matter what. The weight that was lifted off of my shoulders was
incredible. After a week I told my dad. We both sat down, and I just
couldn't get the words out. Finally, I counted to three and told him.
His face turned into one of deep understanding, and he hugged me
tighter than he ever had before. I realize that my case is different
than most. I've heard of people who have gotten kicked out after
telling their parents, which was one of the reasons I was so terri-
fied to come out to my dad. But telling those two people made the
biggest difference in the world, it helped me believe that I might be
able to live a regular life. But coming out is a personal choice. I came

out to two people in the space of a week, but haven't come out to anyone else since then, and it has been six months.

I also asked Ian to write this letter.

Dear (Possibly) Gay High Schooler,

I don't know whether or not you're out, but we must acknowledge that other people may see us as inferior to them. If you come out, you may lose a couple friends, and on top of that, people who weren't your friends before may use you as a target for attack.

If you have straight, male friends, and you're afraid to tell them that you're gay, you're not crazy. I was terrified to come out to my straight friends. I prepared by deeply thinking about what I would do if they decided that they couldn't be my friends anymore. My first male friend I came out to looked at me as if I was about to pounce on him and force him to make out with me. For the next month he didn't answer any of my calls or texts, and wouldn't talk to me at school. After a month I finally got a hold of him and asked him if he wasn't responding because I was gay, and bluntly he said, "Kinda . . . yeah." But now, three years later, we're just as good of friends as before I told him, and the experience gave me ideas on how to come out to other straight friends.

You should go into it knowing there's a possibility of losing a friend after the talk. Be as calm as you can, and tell them in private. Also, don't take anything he says right after you tell him to heart, because he will likely be surprised like, "So . . . you like dick?" or "I'm straight . . . just to let you know." After this exchange, give him space and let him come back to you. He will probably need time to register what just happened before he can develop thoughts on it, so it may take a day, a month, a year, or he may never get over it.

In the case of losing a friend, you must trudge on and roll with the punches. There's no clock ticking down the time until things get better, so you must make it better for yourself. Embrace who you are, and absorb the attacks because that makes you more masculine than them. Now, when embracing who you are, you don't have to

*swing your hips when you walk and go shopping every weekend if
that's not your thing. Be whatever gay you want to be; you should
be the one defining how "gay" applies to you, because the moment
where you're defined by your sexual orientation is when people see
you as "that gay kid." If you're miserable, hang in there, because
I guarantee that someone loves you. You're worth something, and
don't let anyone tell you otherwise.*

> *I wish you the best,*
> *Ian*

I hope you can see from what Ian and Matt say that being gay isn't a "preference." No one, especially in his teen years, prefers to be something that could possibly make his parents and friends reject him. No one would choose to be something that puts a bull's-eye on his back.

Regarding people who say being gay is against their religion, if that's how they interpret their religion, then there's no arguing with that. I've had students get Bibles from their lockers to show me where it says homosexuality is a sin. But that's not the issue. Freedom of religion, your belief that something is a sin or not, doesn't give you the freedom to take away the rights of others. That's what the problem really is—using religion to excuse degrading or abusing gay kids. Unfortunately, religious teachings and values have been used to discriminate against people of other races, ethnicities, and religions for generations. I know there's nothing new there. I know you know that. But that fact doesn't make it right or mean that we should just accept it.

So while this issue is still being politicized, I'm asking you to teach your son or the boys in your care to uphold the basic dignity of all guys—and I'm asking you to do it as a defining point of what it means to be a man.

And when it comes to being a man, there's another challenge that our society does a very poor job of preparing boys to deal with: girls.

17

Girl World

How do you argue with a girl who's either delusional, unwilling to listen, or always thinks she's right? —Victor, 17

Sometimes you know what you did that pissed a girl off, and all you can say to yourself is, What was I thinking? And then other times it's like, What? I don't get it. Why? —Tyler, 15

Usually girls hold grudges, so you should probably avoid girls for the rest of the week. —Billy, 11

It's indisputable that your son needs to develop deep, meaningful relationships with girls for the same reasons it's important for your son to have deep, meaningful relationships with anyone. Being able to argue, compete, date, collaborate, and work with someone who is different from yourself is essential to being a human being who helps make the world a better place. The ability to have functional personal, professional, academic, and romantic relationships with girls and women is an overlooked and specific skill set that must be taught and reinforced.

It's also true that regardless of his age, background, sexual preference, or type of school he attends, your son's social and personal universe doesn't exist in a vacuum; it always exists in concert with

Girl World. But Boy World and the ALMB convince boys that not only do they not need the skills to develop meaningful relationships with girls, but if they do have them, they're being disloyal to the "bro code" and are less of a man.

By the time your son is in high school, he'll probably have already seen a boy treat a girl in such a degrading way that it'd make your stomach turn. He may be the boy who's doing it. He may be standing next to the boy and laughing. He may be helplessly watching but looking like he's fine with what's going on. Either way, seeing a girl being abused might make him feel depressed, angry, sad, helpless, and insecure. Even if he wants to intervene and "do the right thing," he may have no idea how to go about it. He may throw a punch and get in trouble for it. He may speak out and face devastating social consequences. Maybe he does nothing and he unwittingly becomes part of our culture of not helping each other out when it's called for. How do you want your son to respond to a given situation? Are you giving him the foundation to even begin to think about it?

Usually boys won't tell you how they and their friends and peers treat girls, or how girls treat them. Your son won't magically reveal to you what other adults are telling him about girls (including within your own family). You could be the most pro-girl, gender-aware parent on the planet, and your son could still have role models who convince him to treat girls disrespectfully or to say nothing when other boys do that in front of him. For every one of us, saying and doing nothing is unacceptable, because the disrespectful treatment of girls and women has a direct impact not only on the quality of our personal relationships but often on our collective sense of emotional and physical well-being.

Way back in chapter 1, I talked about the unwritten rules for guys. Of course, there's an unwritten rulebook for girls that has just as much influence on them as the ALMB does on guys. I've written extensively about this in *Queen Bees and Wannabes,* but here are the basics. Just as Boy World works to limit how boys express their emotions, Girl World acts in a similar way and has a similar impact on the way girls interact with your son. And that immobile face that boys are told to always wear? Of course girls have their own face that just as powerfully guides their behavior.

TOO SEXY TOO SOON

For years we looked at Barbie and wrung our hands about how bad she was for girls' body image and self-esteem. But just like boys' dolls have become increasingly gendered, so have those sold to girls. Below is a picture of Mattel's Monster High toys—one of the most aggressively marketed toys for girls. The difference between Barbie and the Monster High dolls is that Barbie portrays a woman. The Monster High dolls portray girls. When girls play with Barbie, she gives them a message about what women should look like. That's a problem, but Monster High dolls and their previous incarnations, like the Bratz dolls, teach girls what they should look like and act like right now.

When I ask five- and six-year-old boys and girls to act like these dolls, they walk around swinging their hips, gossiping, and talking about fashion, with their faces frozen in that weird semi-smile you see pictured here. It should be no surprise that today girls dress and act more "teenlike" (i.e., sexier) at earlier ages. Take a minute and really look at the unwritten Girl World rules in this picture. This is what I see. No matter what, girls should be sexy and super-skinny. Whether she's upset, happy, or depressed, she always keeps that look on her face. Even if she's dead or a monster, she has to look anorexic, she must have long straight hair (no matter what her race is—note that the girl on the right is Mattel's version of a black or Latina girl). Lastly, she must have a boyfriend who literally keeps her apart from her friends (that's the guy with the green hair who's holding Cleo, the Egyptian mummy girl, to the left).

Sometimes there are also written rules. Here are descriptions of Cleo taken from the Mattel website:

Cleo does her best to look fabulous and she wants everyone to know it.

Translation: girls should keep up with the latest fashion and show their high self-esteem and self-confidence by rubbing their fabulousness in other girls' faces (which also implies that she should put other girls down for not being as fabulous as she is).

She is very competitive and like all competitive people this can cause its problems.

Read the last sentence again. Would anyone ever tell boys, "Competition causes problems"? Of course not. Yet girls are still told to hide their competitiveness and competence and focus on conforming to the ideal girl everyone loves—perfectly skinny, just enough curves, always cute, and never uptight.

Boys know that girls are under pressure to conform to this image. They also know that adults are concerned about it—for girls.

But it's not all about body image. This message contributes to and then combines with others that I describe below to frame and control how girls and women believe they are allowed to think, act, and react to other people. In this chapter, I'm focusing on their experiences with men outside their own families—from their friends and boyfriends to the men they fleetingly interact with on the street.

THE MESSAGE

In writing this book, I've asked boys what adults say to them about girls. Boys tell me that adults don't say much beyond two general statements: "Never lay your hands on a female" and "Be a gentleman." The problem is that both of these value statements don't acknowledge boys' reality. Telling your son to "be a gentleman" is like telling him to "always do his best." It's too vague and is often reduced to the most basic appearance of treating women and girls with respect. In addition, the precise definition of "being a gentleman" is completely dependent on how the adults around your son define such a notion through their own behavior. Without a real discussion, "be a gentleman" is an empty platitude.

Meanwhile, the underlying message of "never lay your hands on a female" is that boys shouldn't hit girls because they're the weaker sex, not because hitting someone beyond defending yourself is unethical. While it's both laudable and obligatory, telling our sons not to hit girls is still complicated, not in the least because doing so inherently establishes a sense of difference and power. It also contributes to a dynamic that allows some girls to believe not only that they have the right to relentlessly attack some boys, both verbally and physically, but that they can get away with it.

Look at what Aaron has to say:

When girls scream at me and push me, I just bottle up my anger. My
dad always says I can't hit girls, but it's so wrong that they just get

to do whatever they want to me and I just have to take it. A week ago, when I was walking back after a football game, this girl got right up into my face. I just kept walking, but she wouldn't stop yelling at me. I didn't say this, but what I really wanted to do was say, "Just leave me alone, bitch." But I can't do that, because then she'll really freak out, I'll get into trouble, and nothing will happen to her. I just smile and try to get away from her as fast as possible, but it makes me so mad. —Aaron, 16

Aaron knows he can't hit a girl. We don't want him hitting a girl. Obviously that's good. He's being a gentleman because he's not engaging. But he's rightfully angry. He has a right to demand that the girl leave him alone. He shouldn't have to stifle his feelings and just put a smile on his face.

As boys get older, our advice seems to only get worse. By high school, most of the boys I work with tell me that adults have said these four things to them about girls:

1. Don't get her pregnant.
2. Don't get an STD.
3. Don't do anything stupid.
4. If you do anything stupid, don't get caught.

And then there are the even worse variations:

5. Just let them think you agree and then do whatever you want.
6. Always control women. That's what they want even if they won't admit it.
7. Treat them like dirt and they'll stick to you like mud.
8. Have fun on Saturday and abort by Sunday.

As I've said before, even if your son doesn't go along with these degrading ideas, they still have an impact on him. Adults (including "feminist" women) joke all the time about how men should say they agree with women when in fact they don't. It doesn't give women any actual power for men to placate women by saying, "Yes, dear." I don't know about you, but the men I've interacted with who love to joke about this, who say that their wife "wears the pants," have always turned out to be the most sexist. There are also self-described feminist women who condone this behavior; I really don't agree. Men, if you disagree with a woman, say so. Just do it in the way I've outlined—treating yourself and the other person with dignity. Women, we have to be able to hear men disagree with us without dismissing their competence.

But any of these catchphrases pales in comparison to variations 5 through 8. Imagine being a twelve-year old boy hanging out with a couple of friends at his house, hearing his older brother say, "Have fun on Saturday and abort by Sunday," and seeing his friends laugh, wide-eyed in apparent agreement. Do you really think he would confront any of them? No.

What I've seen time and time again is that by the time boys are in high school, they've either been convinced to tacitly agree with such ideas or have come to think there's nothing they can do about them. By the time they're eleven, they can be playing an online video game and stay mute as older boys call girl gamers "fat sluts." So what to do? In the absence of any specifically positive information on how to handle this situation, a boy will base his attitudes toward and behavior with girls not only on what his peer and media cultures tell him but also on the nature of his relationships with the important adults in his life. Specifically, is the boy close to a man who treats women with dignity and respects women in positions of authority? Is the boy close to a woman who holds him accountable as a man of honor and is comfortable asserting her authority with him?

For better and for worse, the relationships that boys have with women are the most important. Having a mother, sister, aunt, or teacher whom he takes seriously and who respects how she conducts herself matters to a boy. It's the difference between a boy who doesn't see girls as human beings and callously laughs at their humiliation and a boy who literally can't imagine behaving that way.

WHO'S DISRESPECTING WHOM?

The problem with girls is that they're crazy, said Martin.

Martin and twelve other sixth-grade boys and I had been talking for an hour about all the things that made their lives difficult and confusing when it came to girls, women in general, and their mothers in particular. We'd discussed what to do when their mothers got their periods ("She warns me that she may be a little grumpy," said Tyler, "so don't take it personally, and my dad says just get of the house"), sisters snitching on them, and their absolute certainty that girls in their school "never" get into trouble and boys "always" get unfairly blamed. But our time was up. The girls were waiting outside the door to come back into the classroom. As the girls were walking in, Martin said, "Ask the girls! We need to talk to the girls!"

I asked Ms. Margo Johnson, their (wonderful) teacher, and she agreed. As the girls seated themselves, I asked them if they wanted to join our conversation. I reminded them of the terms of engagement (no personal attacks and listening prepared to be changed by what they heard) and then said to the girls that the boys wanted to discuss how boys and girls got along in the grade.

I wish I had a picture of the girls' faces—their expressions embodied "bring it" and "be careful what you wish for."

Martin, throwing caution to the wind, said, "Girls are always screaming at us for no reason. We can't do anything without you getting mad at us." Five girls' hands shot up. "Yes, Carla?" I said to a girl with two braids. Carla put her hand down, folded her arms on her desk, and said, "The problem is that the boys in this class have a very negative attitude." I didn't understand what she meant by "negative attitude," so I asked her to clarify it for me.

"A girl can't say anything to a boy without him being perverted. When we're at recess and we want a ball, I say to Martin, 'Can you give me that ball?' Martin says, 'You want my balls? Hey, guys, Carla wants my balls!' If I asked for a stick, he'd say I want to touch his stick. And all the other boys just laugh. They're always doing things like this. They snap our bras. They make comments. That's why I get mad. That's why I think they're annoying. That's what I mean by their negative attitude."

I looked at the girls. All were nodding.

"Martin?"

Martin grinned.

The girls rolled their eyes.

When girls are dealing with the "perverted" boy during recess, in the hallway, or while waiting for the bus, it's not funny.* It's exhausting, it's annoying, it's rude, and it can be sexual harassment. Meanwhile, Martin thinks he's hilarious and actively seeks out the support of the other boys. Those boys, in turn, usually feel that they have to go along with him or else be labeled as being on the "girls' side," which can come across as an act of treason to the other boys.

Now imagine that you're Martin and you've gotten in trouble because the girls complained. You'll try to defend yourself, but you'll look like a jackass to the outside world. Your parents won't think it's funny. (Even if they think the school is overreacting, they'll still be mad at you.) Your teachers won't think it's funny. Your principal won't either. You'll be left excusing your behavior by saying, "You had to be there." You'll think girls are stupid and take things way too seriously. Which is why we now turn to humor and girls.

As previously discussed in chapter 11, humor has an almost religious significance and power in Boy World. But humor can also make things very complicated. For all its wonderful ability to forge friendships, lighten unfortunate circumstances, and even be wielded as a weapon in exposing the cruel, humor can also be used to brutally demean, marginalize, and dehumanize those who are different. It just as easily can be both a cure-all and a tool of oppression.

You need to convey to your son that people (girls in this context) have different definitions of what's funny and what it's acceptable to

---

*Just like when you were younger, there's always a pervy boy in your child's school.

tease them about.* It goes back to what I told you in the "Friendly Fire" chapter. Your son has his own boundaries about what he thinks is funny and what he can be teased about. He also has the right to have those boundaries respected. Your son has the ethical obligation to be aware of when he may have stepped over someone else's boundaries.

Tell your son that at some point, without meaning to, it's likely he will tease a girl and she'll get upset. And just like boys trying to talk to girls, girls can have a hard time telling a boy when he's over the line.† With confidence, you can tell a boy that a girl, like anyone, really doesn't like it when someone consistently points out her flaws or weaknesses—especially in front of other people—and then tells her she's being uptight or laughs when she says she wants the person to stop. This doesn't mean he can't joke around with a girl, but he can't do it all the time, and it can't be in public. If a girl tells him to stop, he needs to shut up.

When boys go over the line, they can be extremely defensive and reactive. Some of them are also pretty good at it—in other words, they're highly capable of making a girl even angrier than she already was. When I asked girls to tell me the most common and infuriating disrespectful comments boys make to them, this is what they told me:

> *"Relax."*
> *"Don't worry about it."*
> *"Calm down."*
> *"Settle down."*
> *"You wouldn't understand. You wouldn't get it."*
> *"Okay, okay, fine, whatever you say."*

---

*In *The Guide*, I decode for boys how they can tell from girls' reactions how funny girls really think they are.

†Keep in mind that teaching him about these dynamics and differences in personal boundaries is exactly the same message you want to convey as he gets older about how he gives sexual attention to someone or how he respects his and other people's sexual boundaries.

"Why are you in such a bad mood?"

"I'm sorry" (said insincerely, usually with no idea what he's apologizing for and obviously pretending to apologize only because he wants her to stop talking).

"You're being totally irrational."

"Talk to me when you aren't having your period."

"Why do you have to be such a bitch?"

"Make me a sandwich" (or any comment regarding women's role in the house).

CHECK YOUR BAGGAGE

Has someone said any of these things to you? How have you handled it?

Have you said things like this to get your way in an argument?

Does your son see what you're doing?

This is what I say to boys to get them to think differently: No one makes these comments to genuinely address a problem with a girl. According to my editors, a boy or man uses these phrases under five conditions:

1. When he doesn't care about the girl or what she thinks about him

2. When he's in an argument and he wants a quick, easy way to put a girl down, shut her up, or distract her

3. Because he has no respect for women and thinks it's funny to remind them of that

4. Because he knows he's lost an argument

5. Because he realizes he's wrong and so he says these things as a way to "save" himself

In the worst cases, if a guy resorts to saying something so blatantly sexist, then he doesn't have the real power to confront the girl on the merits of what they're arguing about in the first place. When guys say things like this in front of an audience (like his friends), his agenda is more about humiliating and infuriating the girl.

> *We do know that saying these things makes girls mad. Either the guy has no intention of resolving the conflict and only wants people to think that he's making an effort, or he just hasn't dealt with girls enough, making him completely clueless about how girls work. There's also a possibility that, if the conversation happens in public, the guy will want to seem either in control or careless about the whole thing, leading to comments such as "Make me a sandwich" or "Talk to me when you aren't on your period." By extension, this could also be a way to make the girl go away because of the humiliation, but this is a simple quick-fix, as down the road the problem will be much, much bigger, because so will her anger. —Matt, 17*

> *I have a guy friend who makes sexist comments and always puts girls down, and I know he's kidding, but he says it all the time, so I wonder if maybe he isn't kidding. So I asked him if he was, and he said, "No, well, sort of." —Molly, 16*

There's no such thing as "sort of kidding." Either you're kidding or you're not. Molly is struggling because this guy is a friend of hers, but "sort of" doesn't have a baseline of respect for a girl (which Molly happens to be). That's a tough thing to admit to yourself, never mind bringing up with a friend, who'll probably respond with even more put-downs. This is exactly the situation where girls keep their anger inside, blow up about something small, and then get further dismissed and ridiculed for being dramatic. Often it's one comment— even a comment the guy has made a hundred times before—that's just one comment too many and the girl explodes. To the guy, he's not behaving any differently from how he's behaved before. Here's the moment when a guy needs to stop himself from automatically blowing off the girl for "overreacting." He needs to realize that this girl is actually getting her courage up to say how she feels and for that reason needs to be respected. If he can control himself and really hear her, it can go from either or both of them feeling like this is a no-win situation to one where they resolve the conflict.

TALKING ABOUT "THAT TIME OF THE MONTH" ISN'T JUST FOR GIRLS

Women: don't you remember how infuriating it was when boys made fun of you for getting your period? Help every girl out by educating your boys. Explain menstruation to your son just as you would with your daughter—except you can obviously skip the part about it happening to him too. You can either wait for your sons to ask you about it or take the initiative when your son is about ten. Or, as in my case, your sons will find your tampons on their own, fill them with water, and have a tampon fight throughout the house. Tampons are expensive, and you can't have your son using them for battles because when you need them you need them. He also needs to know that sometimes you may get a little grumpy, and you're entitled to feel grumpy, but it's not the end of the world.

Men: if there are no women in the house, you have to cover the subject. You're more than capable of explaining all of the above to boys and telling them they can't embarrass girls about having their periods.

You know what's so funny about guys? They constantly bring up having your period if they think you're being moody or they want to shut you up, but the second you actually talk about having your period or needing a tampon, they totally freak out and run away. —Kimber, 16

YOUR SON HAS A SEXIST ASS MOMENT

"Be quiet, woman." It was said in a half-mocking, joking, let-me-see-what-kind-of-reaction-I can-get-from-my-mom-now tone of voice. I don't think my son had any idea what he was in for. Without real-izing what I was doing, my head whipped around, my hands shook, my eyes narrowed, and as I spoke the intensity of my voice scared even me.

"Don't you ever, *ever* say that to me again. I am your mother. You will treat me with respect. And you will never say that to another woman or girl. Are you clear?"

His eyes widened as he backed away from me. "Okay, okay. Sorry."

I've blocked out exactly when or which one of my sons said this to me, but whichever one it was, he was about eight. He'd never heard my husband or any of my male friends say that or anything like it to me, but he'd picked it up somewhere—in the neighbor-hood, at school, on some screen. Instantly, I was overcome with dis-belief (there's no way my child just said that to me), but mostly I felt betrayed.

Why betrayed? Because in that one moment my own child, the boy I loved dearly and who had never seen his father disrespect me, morphed into every sexist man I've dealt with. All the feelings I've learned to live with as a girl and a woman, from the boys in high school who ridiculed me for not being good enough or smart enough to every guy who ever said something rude to me in the street or pa-tronized me in a meeting, came right back up. But it was coming from my son. When I became a mother of boys, it never occurred to me that a son of mine would do that. The feeling went from shock, to betrayal, to anger, to a sense of failure.

I believe that most mothers of sons will have the experience of their sons "trying out" the sexism they see around them. They could be mimicking what they see in the media, how they see girls treated within their peer group, or how the men in your family treat you. When it happens, especially if our boys have seen us bear the brunt of male disrespect, it's so painful to admit that we don't talk about it or even acknowledge to ourselves that it happened.

There are distinct moments in our parenting lives that matter. This is one of them. As I've said before, mothers must be authority figures to their sons. But I also realize how terribly difficult it can be to claim that authority in the moment when it's being challenged. When we experience the cascade of emotions that these moments can bring on in us (not just in mothers but in female teachers too, by the way)—shock, betrayal, anger, failure—in that moment we can lose our words. In our silence or weak responses, we may seem to accept that it's okay to disrespect women or that we don't have the fortitude to stop it.

It's not good enough for a boy's father to step in and say, "Don't speak to your mother like that." Sure, it's better than the dad backing the boy up, but if you don't stand up for yourself, then the only reason your son won't openly disrespect you again is because of his respect for the authority and power of the man who is protecting you. Your son may not talk to you like that again, but he won't respect you. Likewise, it'll be that much more normal and acceptable for him to transfer his disrespect for you to other girls and women.

Ideally, a mother would begin this process when her sons are younger. If you're reading this, have an older son (I'd say twelve and up, or even younger if he's a big kid and aggressive), and are realizing that this is a problem for you, you need a strategy to effectively change the relationship dynamic between the two of you (and maybe the rest of your family). Because there's a world of difference between a boy testing you when he's younger, smaller, and physically weaker than you and when he's a young man whose challenge can come across as a true physical threat or who knows he can blow you off with "Mom, there's nothing you can do." If you're in that situation, this is truly something you can't handle on your own. You have to get help to figure out how you got to this place with your son and to create a plan for standing your ground while taking care of your physical and emotional safety.

DEALING WITH OTHER SEXIST ASSES

Right before I moved from Washington, DC, to Boulder, Colorado, I was walking with my boys in Bethesda, Maryland, an upscale suburban DC neighborhood. As we stepped out to cross the street in a pedestrian crosswalk, a green Subaru station wagon blew through the walkway. As I grabbed Elijah and pulled him back to the sidewalk, we could hear the driver screaming, "Get your kids out of the street, bitch!" Then we watched him run the stop sign and stop about fifteen feet away from us at a red light. For a few moments, the three of us caught our breath and I thanked God that Elijah hadn't been hit. But then I looked over at the Subaru, which was still sitting there waiting for the light to change.

As a woman, you'll have moments when a man goes out of his way to communicate how much he hates women and he'll direct that hatred at you. Now, you may be thinking, *You never know what can happen in that situation, so it's better to say nothing to that guy.* If that's what you feel most comfortable doing, then that's totally fine. But every situation is different, as is every woman. Some women will fight back, some will want to walk away, some will want to say something but lose their words. However you respond, what I'm asking you to do is not let the moment go without saying something to your child.

In my case, my anger about this man almost killing my child propelled me right over to the car. In it were two white middle-aged men. After I told the driver that he'd almost killed my child and then disrespected me, he cussed me out again. So I then asked the guy in the passenger seat if he was okay hanging out with a guy who cussed out mothers in front of their children. He said nothing, refusing to look at me. The driver called me some more names, and then the light turned green and they sped off. I didn't have my phone with me or I'd have taken a picture of his plate number and called the police.

But as I walked back to my sons, I was confused and sad. This wasn't like the guy in the car next to you who flips you off. I know what to say in that situation. I turn to my sons and emphatically state, "You see that man? You aren't going to grow up to be that kind of man." What do you say to your boys when they see that kind of disrespect? I think you say something like, "That was scary. I was really angry that that man almost hurt you. I can't believe he said those things to me. What do you think?"

Keep in mind that my sons were relatively young at the time, and both were shorter than me. I doubt the Subaru driver would have said those things to me now, when Elijah, my twelve-year-old son, is five-eleven and looks like he's sixteen (yes, he grew six inches in a year). If you ever get into a situation where your son will want to defend you, you need to honor his feelings but keep him out of it. Respond the way you think is most appropriate for the situation and then say something like, "Let this guy be an ass to me because I don't want you taking the chance of getting in trouble for what he's doing." You need to demonstrate some power.

These are the big overarching issues for women: the media's image of girls, dealing with the not funny perverted guy, and the struggle to claim women's authority when it's being challenged by their sons or other men in their lives. These dynamics are often invisibly influencing what goes on between people. But the daily reality for your son is different. The last thing on his mind is whatever he philosophically believes about women and why he believes it. Instead, he's likely to be focused on issues with girls, like what he should do if a group of Mean Girls gang up on him, how much he wants to destroy his younger brother for telling you he has a crush on someone, or licking his wounds after getting dumped. And you need to figure out what to do if your high school son suddenly falls head over heels in love with someone you think has the personality of a wet dishrag, or if you have the hilarious but truly uncomfortable experience of turning on the light in your family room at 2:00 AM to find your son and someone else "chillin'" on the couch.

18

Girl Troubles

There was a gang of bullies at our school that was all girls. I'd always see them gang up on a guy for no reason. Adults don't take it seriously because they think that boys can never be bullied by girls. They think it's not the way of the universe. —Nick, 11

I once had a girlfriend who went totally nuts and crazy because I wasn't reaching her "expectations." For some reason she thought that the idea of having a boyfriend would be a Cinderella story come true. And she was so pissed off that she just ignored me, avoided eye contact, everything, all for some test to see if I really cared for her! Like where is the logic in that?!? If I didn't care for her, I would've never asked her out! —Luke, 15

I have a friend that sweet-talked this chick for two months on his phone, she caves in, goes to his house, and gives him "favors," then he kicks her out of his house. She starts talking about having a relationship, and he promptly deletes her from his phone. All my friends love this guy, we all want to be like him, he gets what he wants, and there are no consequences. And I guess that's how guys think about girls. —Cole, 16

HERE ARE THE THINGS THE BOYS WANT YOU TO KNOW ABOUT GIRLS:

- When a girl is mad at a boy, she'll get other girls to gang up on him.
- If she doesn't gang up on him, she won't tell him what's wrong until she explodes—usually in public.
- Boys get in trouble for everything, and girls never get in trouble for anything.*
- Girls are all about double standards. For example, when girls complain about boys calling girls sluts, bitches, whores, and worse, boys don't respect or even understand those complaints when they hear girls do it too.
- Sometimes a good girlfriend can make life way better.
- Boys have a very hard time taking girls seriously if the girls they see act less competent than they are and/or are obsessed with their weight or clothes.

HERE'S WHAT I WANT YOU TO KNOW ABOUT BOYS AND GIRLS:

- Boys, like anyone else, often minimize the impact of their behavior on others. Boys can be bewildered or even hurt when girls get angry with them because they forget or don't comprehend what they did.
- Whatever interest your son has in girls is completely fine now and forever. That means he could be girl-crazy, sometimes interested, falling for only one girl hard, not interested right now, or never interested.

---

*Point out to him that sometimes he's going to be blamed for something he didn't do and sometimes it'll go the other way—he'll get off when he shouldn't have.

- Most boys believe that most of their male peers are way more comfortable with girls than they are.
- Most boys will have their heart broken.
- Everyone has different "sexpectations." Your job is to teach your son to know and listen to both his own expectations and those of the person he's sexually interacting with.
- Just because a boy grew up in Boy World doesn't mean he wants all of the sexual attention that comes his way. The same thing goes for every person he has any kind of sexual interaction with.

GIRL TROUBLES IN ELEMENTARY SCHOOL

Girl troubles can start way before anyone hits puberty. And while many people are aware of girls' aggression with each other or boys bullying each other, we often don't pay attention when young girls are doing it to young boys. Maybe it's because the girls are cute. Maybe the way girls are aggressive is so quiet compared to how loud boys can be, it's easier to see what the boys are doing. While not taking away anything a boy can do to a girl, it's important for adults to acknowledge that girls can be mean to boys.

To show you what boys believe about boy-girl conflicts, I asked my elementary-age boy editors the following questions and included their most common responses.

How Do Fights Start with a Girl?

It starts with one girl. She'll get mad at you, and then she'll tell her friend, who tells others. It gets worse and worse. And sometimes you don't know what you did. And they won't talk to you. But whatever you did, you have to apologize and sound all responsible and take the blame. But no, I don't mean it. Well, if they're angry, I don't mean it. If they're sad, then I probably mean it. —Brian, 11

But what if you really disagree? What if you're mad at the girl too?

Boys have a special place where they stow away their feelings.
—Nathan, 12

There's no point in confronting a girl when she's angry with you
because it's always three or four of them against one of you. It's al-
ways going to be this way because all of this stuff happens at recess,
and guys aren't going to want to help you because, if they did, then
they wouldn't be able to run around. What would you rather do? Play
dodgeball or confront four angry girls who will just get angry with
you for backing up the guy? —Troy, 12

Would you ever tell your side of the story? Like what if you were guilty of
some of the things she's mad about but not all the things?

The only time, maybe, is if a teacher gets involved, because that's
another level. Then maybe I'd say why. But you don't want it to go to
that level. Because overnight the whole grade can turn on you. (In-
cluding the boys?) If the boy doesn't have a lot of guy support, yes,
it can happen. —Max, 11

How do you comfort each other in these situations?

When we talk to them later, we put down the girl or we agree with
everything the guy is saying. You tell him how terrible she is and she
does this to other guys. —Taylor, 12

I was at my son Roane's soccer game when "Ben" sat down next to
me. Ben was in fifth grade at a small public school where girls greatly
outnumbered boys in his class. He sat down next to me because he'd
heard I dealt with Mean Girls, and he needed some advice. We pulled
our folding chairs away from the parents and talked for a few minutes. Ben had every reason to be frustrated. He was dealing with an
entrenched group of Mean Girls in his grade. They gossiped, excluded
people, refused to speak to him, pushed him, or accused him of being
immature if he didn't agree with their opinions on other people.

If your son is in a similar logistical school environment, please know that no matter how "good" the school is, if your son is out-numbered like this, there'll likely be problems. Exacerbating Ben's situation was that most of the kids had gone to that school since kindergarten, so the students felt stuck with their roles, reputations, and friend groups. It also meant that Queen Bees could solidify their power and probably wouldn't have any threats of insurrection until they got to middle school. To Ben, those girls seemed omnipotent, especially when he didn't think the adults took the girls' behavior seriously.

How do you help Ben or any boy who is up against Mean Girls? First, remind him that he's not weak to be bothered and angered by the girls. He also has every right to be frustrated at the adults for not holding the girls accountable. Second, because he's in elementary school, you need to tell the teacher what he's experiencing, including the fact that he doesn't think the adults care. Third, he needs to decide how to interact with the girls. Again, because he's younger, you probably have more ability to influence him. Use SEAL to map out your strategy, but if it's your own son you're helping, I want you to think first about what you know about him. If he's good at not letting people get to him, if he's a good athlete or gets along with boys, then he may only need your affirmation and support.

If he doesn't have at least one of these characteristics, he's more exposed to the girls going after him, especially during recess or anytime he's on the playground. If that's the case, then he needs more support from the teachers or he needs to use SEAL to prepare something to say to the girls, as in, "I'm not sure why you can't understand why I don't like what you're doing to me (or x person). You never leave me alone, and it's really boring."* But no matter what he does, remind him that the girls are going to feel no choice but to have the last word. For example, they could laugh at him, roll their eyes, call him a "mama's boy"—whatever is going to annoy him the

---

*Queen Bee girls *hate* being called boring. You want the boy to use words that strip the girls of their power in this situation, but to avoid bad words or other language that would give the girls a reason to go to the teacher and get him in trouble.

most. That doesn't mean he hasn't been successful in standing up to these girls.

If your son doesn't retaliate, chances are you won't know about this. But if he does, chances are you will find out, because you'll get a call from the school. Do you know how he can get into trouble? Imagine this has been going on with the girls for a while and the adults haven't been paying attention to it. Now it's PE or recess,* and the girls are playing dodgeball with your son.† Let's be honest. If you were him, wouldn't you be tempted to bean that ball at those girls' heads? If you're successful and the girls complain, then you get into trouble and that's your proof that "boys always get into trouble and the girls never do."

What Do You Do When Boys Put Girls Down?

How would you respond if your son said something like, "Black people are really lazy"? Wouldn't you be angry? Embarrassed? Wouldn't you say something to him? What's the difference between him using a racist stereotype and saying that girls are really stupid, only care about clothes and makeup, or are bad athletes? Your son will have a perfect rebuttal if you challenge him. "You don't know these girls at my school. That's the way they are." You can't take away someone's experience, but you can say that his personal experience doesn't reflect the reality of all girls, and you should advise him not to make generalized, blanket statements—even if he hears girls doing it in reference to boys.

---

*For many boys, the threat of recess being taken away from them as punishment is an ever-present reality. Recess is precious. They want to be running, playing, jumping, kicking, and throwing, not arguing with girls. Once a boy is in the game, he can be fairly sure that the Mean Girls won't stop the game to go after him.

†I know that many schools don't allow kids to play dodgeball anymore. Even if that's the case at your child's school, there's always going to be a ball you can throw at someone's head during a game.

Girls on the Team

Have you ever seen one or two girls on your son's fourth-, fifth-, or sixth-grade sports team? As we look from the sidelines, we often miss what's going on between the kids. Usually there's at least one boy who's already so threatened that he has to undermine her with snarky comments that the coaches and parents can't hear.

Our boys need to learn how to compete against girls without being obnoxious about it or refusing to put themselves in the situation. (Remember those AP courses I talked about in chapter 2?) This isn't about who's better than whom. It's about being secure enough to compete with girls, whether against them or side-by-side.

If you keep it short and sweet, you can use the situation to make sure your son knows you're thinking about what it's like for this girl. On the way home from practice, you can say:

> You: How do you think it is for Maya being the only girl on your team?
>
> Your son: I don't know. Fine.
>
> You: I'm asking because sometimes there can be a guy who likes to put girls down. Some girls are really good at standing up to that kind of treatment, but it can also be really hard. If anyone is going after her, at least I'd like you to tell her privately that you don't agree with the guy. I get that, if you say something in front of the other guys, they may accuse you of defending her because you like her. You don't have to be her friend, but you have to have her back. She's on the team like everyone else on the team.

Getting Outplayed or Beaten by a Girl

No matter how you've raised him, getting beaten by a girl can be embarrassing for a boy. Boys see no upside to competing when the best-case scenario is having nobody care because they were supposed to win anyway and the worst-case scenario is getting laughed at for losing when they weren't "supposed" to. If the boy is a big smack-talker, it's going to be even more painful for him, which could make him smack-talk even more.

Our boys need to learn how to own a loss graciously. That starts with realizing that it doesn't matter who they lose to. A loss to a girl, or anyone for that matter, should also drive them to work harder instead of blaming the circumstances. What's frustrating to girls, and highly ironic, is that the guys who are the most outspoken about girls not being real competition are the same guys who gloat the most about their victories over girls. If you see your son behaving this way or making these kinds of comments, you have to stop it. And dads, your words mean a lot here. No putting down girls or other boys who are beaten by girls. Of course, the boys can slam girls when you're not around, but your son still knows what's expected of him, and the thought of you hearing him may make him a little less loud and proud when it comes out of his mouth.

MIDDLE SCHOOL

Have you seen seventh- and eighth-grade girls and then looked at seventh- and eighth-grade boys? With the exception of one or two outlier guys who are shaving by fourteen, if you were an average middle school boy, with scrawny legs and arms and getting random erections during the day, wouldn't you be intimidated by girls? I'm a woman, and way older than eighth-grade girls, but those girls still intimidate *me*.

You could teach middle school boys multiple courses on girls and women's imagery in the media, and they'd still look at the girls in their lives—who want nothing to do with them and who hook up with boys two years older—and think you're insane for thinking they have any gender privilege in this situation.

Some of the topics I'm covering here may not be relevant to

your child until junior or senior year of high school—or they may suddenly be relevant in seventh grade.

Crushes

Picture the following. You're feeling very happy that you've managed to get everyone around the table to eat dinner together. The phones are off, you're eating healthy, and no one is arguing, when one of your children gets a smirk on his face.

> YOUR YOUNGER CHILD: Mom, by the way, John likes Sophia!
> YOUR OLDER CHILD, JOHN (*death-staring at his sibling*): Shut up.
> YOU (*thinking John has never ever said one word about girls, and not being able to help yourself*): What? Who's Sophia? (*your voice conveying way too much enthusiasm*)
> JOHN (*still death-staring at his sibling*): (*no response*)
> YOU: Do I know her?
> JOHN: There's nothing to talk about.
> YOU (*in your desperation and curiosity turning to the snitch, the child who started this whole thing*): What's she like?
> JOHN: (*stares at his food in misery*)

Please understand that you just got worked by your younger child. If this happens, here's what I suggest that you say instead: *"If John wants to tell me about this, then he will. It's his decision to tell me, not yours. If he needs my help figuring things out, I'll be here for him. But who he likes is private."*

This is what respecting privacy looks like to your child. You're also showing that your other child can't manipulate you. If you want any chance of having John tell you anything about this girl, he needs to see that you understand why he doesn't want to tell you. And you're never going to force it out of him, like this father did:

> *My friend's brother did this at the dinner table. The dad wouldn't let him leave the table until he'd told him about the girl. This is horrible.*

It creates a hostile environment and makes the child feel he has no power. —Phillip, 16

CHECK YOUR BAGGAGE

Remember your first crush. Did that person like you back? Why did you like that person? Did you tell anyone about it? Is your heart beating a little faster just thinking about it now? Empathize.

Aggressive Girls

Countless mothers say to me, "I can't believe how aggressive girls are today! When I was in middle school, I'd never even think to go after boys like the girls in my son's class do today."

You may have heard other parents say things like that. You may have even said it yourself. This is especially true if you don't have daughters and therefore aren't around a lot of girls. It's common for girls in middle school (and sometimes elementary school too) to pick one or two boys out of the grade to be "the cute boy" and then call, text, and generally pay huge, unrelenting amounts of attention to this boy. It's also common for those girls to fight over this boy or to try to make him choose one girl over another. The boy reacts to all this attention in one of two ways: either he becomes incredibly arrogant and remains that way until someone breaks his heart, or he's overwhelmed and runs away.

Much of the girls' behavior is developmentally appropriate, even though it can be unnerving to the moms of these boys. As boys and girls go through adolescence, they're trying out ways to sexually express themselves and seeing what kinds of reactions they're getting. That's not wrong or bad. It just feels really weird when your child is the one receiving that attention.

Where it can get complicated is that, by eighth grade, if not seventh, there will probably be some girls in your son's school who have significant problems and are sexually acting out because of them. Those girls can really get parents' hackles up—so much so that they forget that they're the adults and it's a thirteen-year-old girl they're gossiping about. It's also not uncommon for that gossip to get back to the girl. So I'm asking you to be mindful about a couple of things. Even if you aren't using the words "slut" or "slutty" (although plenty of parents do) to describe these girls, remember that girls are coming into their sexuality in a world that is constantly seeking to exploit it. Some of these girls have adults in their lives who have betrayed them. Incest, physical abuse, alcohol and drug abuse, and neglect are all common backgrounds for these girls—in some of the wealthiest communities in this country, by the way.

CHECK YOUR BAGGAGE

Why are these girls freaking you out? Do you think your son can't protect himself? What is it that you want to protect him from?

If people are talking about this girl, stop that talk. If you want your son to stand up to cruelty, then you need to do it too. All you need to say is, "I don't feel comfortable talking about this girl like this." If you want to add, "We shouldn't be calling eighth-grade girls tramps or sluts or saying they look like prostitutes," that would be awesome.

Calling the Bluff

In the eighth grade we were playing an away basketball game, and we had to use the girls' locker room to change. We had just gotten there, we were still in our coats and ties, when two girls accidentally came in. One of the kids on our team yelled, "Show us your boobs!" They walked out, but a few minutes later they both came back and flashed us. There were two or three seconds of total shock, and then everyone totally lost it, high-fiving each other. The kid who had said,

"Show us your boobs," was in the bathroom, so he missed it and was furious at us because no one took pictures or video with their phones. —Will, 20

I posted this quote on my Facebook page, and it caused strong reactions from the parents and educators who regularly read my posts. Most people believed that what the girls did was terrible and something they would soon regret. But I see this as a very complex situation, especially if it comes to the attention of parents or school administrators. Here is the closest we can get to understanding the "facts."

The girls knew the boys were in their locker room because there was a sign on the door that said VISITING TEAM. They went in knowing there was a very good chance they would see partially clothed or naked boys.* Then the boy tried to do the equivalent of cat-calling a woman on the street. The girls decided to "talk back" by flashing the boys. It's debatable the extent to which their actions were actually inverting the power dynamic or serving as a good way for them to assert themselves. I think the reason the girls felt the freedom to do it was because it was a group of boys they didn't have to see every day.

Here's the big issue. This generation of teen girls knows that anything they do could be easily recorded. It seems only logical that those girls made the decision to flash those boys understanding that there was a reasonable possibility that a boy would happen to have his phone out and be able to take a picture of them in the two seconds their breasts were exposed. But here's where it gets confusing. It's possible that the girls didn't think about it when they walked back into the locker room. James Everitt, principal of Sacred Heart Preparatory in Atherton, California, shares his perspective:

Technology diminishes the amount of time that an administrator has to craft a thoughtful and purposeful response that helps the stu-

---

*If the roles were reversed and the girls were changing in a boys' locker room and two boys had "accidentally" walked in, they'd probably have gotten into trouble and no one would have believed it was an accident.

dents, boys and girls, grow and mature. Often, parents are on the phone to the school before the administrator even finds out that an event occurred. Second, schools are under a tremendous amount of scrutiny and risk when dealing with any behavior that might indicate sexual harassment or bullying. An effective school administrator wants sufficient time with the boys and the girls to discuss the reasons behind their behavior and to tease out if there was, in fact, intent to harass. The behavior that Will describes is, of course, inappropriate for both groups, but it's perfectly consistent with the ways in which young people try on different identities and manage school social hierarchies. It would be ideal to shift our response from a strictly disciplinary mind-set into a growth mind-set, keeping before us the very real needs of adolescent maturing. Our young people live in a media culture that promotes sexual aggression and rewards risky behavior. Perhaps we might begin to help our students navigate these difficult waters with real skills and healthy models of maturing.

A different situation that looks similar is when girls do things like this when they're drunk and/or too insecure to say no to a large group of guys (see Fruit Cup Girl, page 341). Most of these situations aren't proud moments for the girls because groups of guys talk, coerce, or force them to demean themselves.

All of this means that you need to include in your son's mobile phone rules, "Don't take photos of naked or half-naked girls. No, not even if they flash you." And yes, this is yet another example of how weird it is to be a parent raising children today.

LANDMINE!

Don't say, "You may hate them now, but you won't soon."

And don't say, "Boys and girls can't be friends." Also resist smiling when he argues with you and saying something like, "You'll see." By reacting this way, you're contributing to the general assumption that boys and girls can't have meaningful friendships with each other without being romantic or sexual. So, sure, it may turn out that one person likes another person more than as a friend, but when a parent says that to a child, it comes across as not respecting the friendship. You want your son to have strong friendships with girls, so don't be so quick to sexualize them. And don't say, "I told you so," if it turns out that you're right in this one instance.

Really Aggressive Girls

I discovered texts + photos from a fourteen-year-old girl on my son's phone that looked like they came from a gynecological exam. I texted back and told her I was the mom and that she was better than this. She actually wrote back and said, "Oh, I'm a different person now. That was just a bad phase." She'd sent the text two days prior (sigh . . .). —Kelly

I'm sorry, but Kelly's quote made me laugh out loud. Kelly did such a good thing by acting as a mother to the girl and telling her she was "better than this." Good stuff. But you have to love a girl who assures a mom that she was in a bad phase two days ago but she's over it now.

If you find out that your son is receiving this kind of text, reread the sexting section in chapter 9. But the important thing here is to do what Kelly did. In a nonjudgmental way (i.e., not coming across like you think she's a tramp or stupid), communicate to the girl what her standards should be for herself.

How Do You Explain to Boys Why Some Girls Act Less Intelligent Than They Actually Are?

When I was twelve, I remember wondering why girls had to act so fake around guys. They would stand around in clusters and scream and giggle and shoot looks over at some guy. Maybe one of their friends would come over and give you a message. If they act like

*that now, I would think they were trying to hook up. It's obvious.
No one acts like that much of a moron unless they want to hook up.*
—*Patrick, 16*

Have you ever heard a girl or woman sneeze in a way that sounds like she's a small cat? Do you remember, when you were a teen, seeing a girl you knew was really smart act incredibly stupid and incompetent around guys? Do you remember women going to college parties and doing that? Would one of those women be staring back at you if you looked in the mirror right now?*

When a girl acts like this, I call it Fruit Cup Girl—after a sixth-grade girl I taught many years ago who pretended during lunch that she couldn't open the top of a fruit cup so she could ask the guy she liked to do it for her.

*I think guys are partly responsible for FCG, because somehow girls
understand or believe that guys tend to like dumb girls and girls
want guys to like them, so it makes us want to slip back into the Fruit
Cup persona.* —*Emily G., 16*

There is a spectrum of Fruit Cup Girl-ness, and almost all women have found ourselves on it at some point in our lives. But no one ever has to literally explain how to be Fruit Cup Girl. Girls just know because of those unwritten rules of Girl World.

In the short term, it can feel like there are real benefits to being Fruit Cup Girl. It gives a girl a "script" that makes it easy to get the boy's attention. But there are some serious negatives: guys won't take FCG seriously, and other girls judge her for being stupid or slutty. Why do they do this? Because FCG makes them really uncomfortable. On the one hand, they're jealous of the attention FCG is getting from the boys. On the other hand, they know guys don't respect her (which of course doesn't stop some of them from hooking up with her). Girls hate her for making "attractive" girls look so stupid and

---

*There'd be one staring at me if I looked too.

shallow. They wonder, do you have to hide who you really are, what you really believe, for guys to be sexually attractive to you?

As girls get older, they usually believe it's too immature to act like FCG, so they need an excuse. That's where drinking and drugs come in. As long as a girl has a drink in her hand, she has an excuse to be FCG. The metamorphosis from Fruit Cup Girl to Solo Cup Girl sets the stage for girls to use alcohol and drugs as justification for acting sexy stupid. In no way does it mean that she's responsible for someone sexually harassing or assaulting her. Instead, it's a setup where she loses no matter what.

Boys do this too—they just don't get so criticized for it. Or even if they do, that criticism doesn't impact their social status the way it will for a girl. So when a boy takes off his shirt for no reason (and uses it for his FB profile pic) or gets really loud around girls? He's doing the same thing Fruit Cup Girl is doing. Boys just call him "That Guy."

HIGH SCHOOL

What if your son or another guy around him complains, "Why do girls wear tight clothing if they don't want the attention?" Here's what you can say:

"Many girls do want guys' attention, but there's a big difference between appreciating an attractive girl and treating her like she's stupid or a slab of meat. When girls wear revealing clothes, don't make the assumption that they want to have sex. Wanting to feel sexy is not the same as wanting to have sex with you."

And why do girls get mad at boys for calling them "slut," "bitch," or "whore" when they call each other the same thing all the time?

The girls at my school are incredible. They're such hypocrites. They call each other sluts, whores, and bitches all the time, but the minute a guy does it they freak out. I'm not going to just take that. Someone needs to tell them how full of it they are. Someone needs to be honest. —Paul, 17

Paul's right that it's hypocritical for girls to call each other these words and then get angry with guys when they do it. But that being true doesn't make it right for guys to do it. It just gives boys an easy excuse. Girls also believe that it's way more disrespectful and degrading when guys use these words than when girls do because girls usually use these words only with their closest friends—who presumably can tell the difference between good teasing and malicious teasing. (More or less the same reasons apply here that I outlined earlier as to why white guys shouldn't try to use wannabe black slang with their blacks friends, regardless of how they might think their black friends talk to other black kids.)

Since we're talking about sluts and whores, let's take a moment to address the it's-just-what-we-say-it-doesn't-matter defense that both guys and girls use. Similar to using the word "gay" as an everyday way to put someone down, people use the words "bitch," "slut," and "whore" to put down girls. And if they really want to insult a boy they call him a bitch. This is the background I explain to my students:

Historically the word "slut" (or any word like it) refers to a woman who's only valued for sex and has no right to an opinion. Historically the word "bitch" is used against women for being too opinionated. Both words are about denying women the right to speak. Both words are particularly powerful against girls because of two characteristics: these words quickly shut a girl down, and they make her feel either terrible about herself or incredibly angry. From a guy's perspective, using these words can also make girls act in very strange ways.

For example, you know how some girls can take forever to get ready, constantly changing clothes but never satisfied with how they look? It's easy to assume that these moments prove that girls are inherently obsessed with their looks. They're pressured into behaving this way, however, and that's not what's really going on. Instead, girls are trying to figure out a complex equation: how to look sexy without coming off as slutty (being and feeling attractive while avoiding being trashed by other girls for being too slutty). So they'll try to achieve the impossible by pleasing both girls and guys, two groups with competing agendas.

> *We dress to catch one person's attention, but as a result make everyone else notice and flip out. I don't think the balance is just hard to strike; I think it's impossible.* —Maureen, 18

Doesn't Bother Me Girl

There's one more girl I want you to remember from when you were a teen. This was the cute girl who always sided with the boys when girls complained about them being sexist and rude. Naturally, boys (especially the sexist rude ones) loved this girl and used her as justification to dismiss the other complaining girls.

This girl is not only frustrating to other girls, but she messes with their brains. So when you combine the trifecta of Fruit Cup Girl, Doesn't Bother Me Girl, and the constant need to balance wanting to be attractive with not being slutty, girls can really struggle to be honest with themselves about what they want, let alone communicate that clearly to anyone else. When you add on being told by the boys to "relax" and "calm down," there should be no confusion about why girls can give mixed messages to boys.

You don't have to explain all of this, all at one time, but it's important that your sons hear from you that girls can struggle to communicate clearly. That doesn't mean they're stupid. It means they're growing up being given a lot of confusing and contradictory messages that may take a while for them to sort out.

Definition of Terms

There are a few terms that regularly come up in my discussions with high school boys that are important for you to know. In fact, if your son is regularly using a word with his friends and you can't figure out what he means, just go to Urban Dictionary's website and search for the word there. I'm sure you'll be able to figure it out in a minute.

Stalking: This word used to only apply to someone being obsessed with another person he or she doesn't know or barely knows. Stalkers were scary and to be avoided at all costs. Now both girls and guys commonly use the word to negatively label someone they don't like who's attracted to them. Of course, the old kind of stalking still exists—so you need to pay attention to tone and context when this term is used.

Creeping: Usually defined as a form of stalking or hitting on a girl.

Dating: Being in a relationship that other people know about.

Hooking up: "Hooking up" means different things to different people. It could be anything from kissing to having sex or anything in between. But in the moment when a guy tells other people that he hooked up with someone, there's an assumption that everyone is in agreement about exactly what he means.

Dibs: This is a way for guys to communicate their interest in someone when there's a good possibility that they're competing for the same person with another guy and they want to minimize conflict. Or they want to annoy or assert power over another guy in such a way that the other guy isn't allowed to get mad. Of course, what dibs doesn't take into consideration is that the girl's choice trumps any dibs that are called; she has the final call.

Wingmen: I use the term "wingman" to describe a friend who backs him up when he really needs it—but many guys almost exclusively use the term "wingman" to refer to a friend who helps them hook up.

Friends with benefits: A sexual relationship with no time requirements or obligations. Its easy appearance is exactly why it's so confusing. In a "friends with benefits" relationship, there's an implicit understanding that neither party wants, or will ever want, more in the relationship. Some people are comfortable having a sexual relationship without commitment. But then there are people who say they agree to having a "friends with benefits" relationship but really want more. They just don't want to admit it. What's not cool is to know that about the person, or have a pretty good suspicion that's in fact what's going on, and use them anyway.

The Friend Zone

The Friend Zone: A state of being where a male inadvertently becomes a "platonic friend" of an attractive female with whom he was trying to initiate a romantic relationship. Females have been rumored to arrive in the Friend Zone, but reports are unsubstantiated.
—Urban Dictionary

Chances are pretty good that your son will land in the Friend Zone at some point. So if you notice that he's pining away for one of his friends, you can ask him if he wants to talk about it, but remember, you're now treading on very sensitive terrain. Don't say any clichés like, "If she can't see how special you are, then she doesn't deserve you anyway." Instead, hear him out, empathize, and then, if you must give advice, just tell him not to wait around for her. But, really, this is a topic boys don't want to talk to any adult about. That's what friends are for.

Bad Boys: The Boy World Version of Fruit Cup Girl

As a parent, you want to raise a boy who is respectful to women. But one of the most frustrating things about being a decent guy is seeing "Bad Boys" get hot girls. Boys don't treat girls disrespectfully simply for the heck of it. They act that way because they've been given a lot of powerful messaging that treating girls badly will make girls want them more. Think of clichés like "Nice guys finish last" or "Treat girls like dirt and they'll stick to you like mud."

Bad Boys, like Fruit Cup Girls, are people falling back on behavior they believe will get them attention from the opposite sex, plus they've bought the message of male entitlement. And sometimes it works. Situations like the one Cole describes at the beginning of the chapter—where a guy treats a girl badly and not only gets rewarded for it but is treated as though he's "even cooler" as a result—aren't unusual. It's easy to see why some guys come to believe that being attractive to women means adopting a disrespectful attitude.

If you want to talk to your son about this, wait until an obvious moment presents itself. When it does, you should have one or two masculine role models in mind who don't pander to the Bad Boy "treat them like dirt" cliché. There are men who are comfortable in their masculinity without being asses. You just need to point them out to your son. And do not under any circumstances bring up a boy who is the current teen heartthrob.

LANDMINE!

There is nothing worse than parents saying to their son, "You're so handsome and nice. I'm sure you'll have no problem if you just be yourself."

Relationships

You don't want to know everything about your son's dating life. Do you want to know what he's thinking about doing with the person he's attracted to? Do you want to know exactly what he did on your couch the other night when you were out? No. But of course, you do need to know if he's hurting, if he's worried about an STD, or if he's in a relationship that's so messed up that he needs guidance (either from you or from someone you trust and respect who can help him). The key is knowing how to walk that line between giving him the space to grow and make his own choices, on the one hand, and making sure he has the support and firm guidelines he'll need when things get rough, on the other.

That's easier said than done. The first intense relationships can be over the top. If your son is dating someone, chances are it's going to be crazy-intense. Manipulation, jealousy, extreme swings of affection, hatred, selfishness, and sacrifice are the norm. It's often excruciating for me to watch my students go through this process, and they're not even my kids. But this is how your child will learn to ask himself the tough questions about what he needs in a partner and what he can willingly give to a partner without losing himself in the process.

Don't fool yourself. These relationships matter. They set up the patterns and expectations that your son will take with him as he becomes an adult.

Things Not to Say to a High School Boy About Dating

"Think with your other head."
"You're too young for a serious relationship."
"Don't get whipped."
"Are you going over to X person's house again?"
"It's always good to keep your options open."
"There's no need to be so exclusive at this time of life."
"You don't really know the difference between love and lust."
"It's not like you're going to marry them."

Should Girls Be Allowed in His Bedroom?

No.

What Do I Do When I Find Him on the Couch in the Basement with a Girl?

You can't make it easy for him. Just because I said that you shouldn't let him have girls in his bedroom doesn't mean your son isn't going to get some action. Or want to get some action. And try really hard to get some action.

Here are my rules:

"You can't hang out with your girlfriend for hours on end in your bedroom. So I'm going to make it easy for you and just make a rule that she can't be in your room. If you break this rule, you deal with the consequences. I've educated you about contraception and STDs and listening to what other people want and why it can be hard for people to clearly communicate when sex is on the horizon. I know I can't guide you any more than that. These are your decisions to make. You're educated, and you know what my expectations are."

And then, after the horribly embarrassing moment for everyone when you catch them on the couch, you say, *"I'm going to turn around and give you a few minutes to get your clothes on."* After they're dressed, sit them down in the kitchen and say something like, *"Since you put me in the position of walking in on you, I'm now going to put you in the position of listening to me about sex."* And then you are going to calmly tell them what your values are in a way that doesn't shame them and sets clear expectations for their future behavior.

They're Joined at the Hip and You Want a Saw

You may have started out liking the girl your son brought home. But after a few weeks, the sight of her makes you want to lock the door. You know that teens have intense relationships, but do they really have to be so sickening? First, try your hardest to limit your passive-aggressive and sarcastic comments to your friends, your parents, your in-laws, or whoever you parent with. If they're all over each other, then you can tell your child specifically what you do and don't feel comfortable with them doing in front of you. Like holding hands—no problem. Sitting on laps—problem. Hand across shoulder—no problem. Nuzzling, hand under her shirt—problem. If he doesn't listen to you, then feel free to talk to them the next time they're together at your house. Of course, that's embarrassing to him. But you told him privately and he didn't make the requested changes, so you don't have a choice but to talk to them together.

If the problem is that they're spending all their time together, you need to set aside some designated family time. You can acknowledge to him that you know he'd rather be with this person, who's welcome in your house other times, but the time you designate as family time needs to be respected. In addition, you shouldn't let this new relationship become his excuse to neglect schoolwork, abandon other commitments, or neglect his friends.

> *Family night. I don't like it, but there's no way I am getting out of it.*
> *—Owen, 17*

You Don't Like the Person He's in a Relationship With

It doesn't really matter why. It could be that this person comes across as a wet dishrag, or maybe kind of fake, or you really don't know why you don't like this person but you just don't. Think about this like I've asked you to think about the judgments you make about your son's friends. He needs to have different relationships in which he learns what he wants and needs in an intimate relationship. There will be some duds along the way. Your single biggest goal is not to make this look like a choice between the person he's in love with and you. If you do that, you make it much harder for him to see any possible problems in the relationship. He will stay with the person longer, and he won't tell you if and when he needs help. And even if he breaks up with this person, the next one will probably be very similar.

The Princess Problem

> *I never say anything concerning my girlfriend's faults. I really try to treat her like a princess. I would never want to say anything that would upset her. But she has no problem pointing out what she perceives as my flaws. She says things with no remorse, like "You have a huge ego" or "Nobody is as smart as you," in that sarcastic tone we all love. The other day I told her I didn't like when she said stuff like that, and it was maybe the first fight we really had. She thought I was being just a little too touchy. Am I? —Jake, 17*

I hadn't focused on this "Princess" problem until it kept coming up when the guys talked about problems with their girlfriends. Princess messaging teaches girls that guys should treat them as delicate weaklings. But here's the irony. If the Princess doesn't get what she wants, she's entitled to turn into an angry, spoiled brat who can bully the guy into getting her way. Or, as Luke described it at the beginning of the chapter, giving him the silent treatment.

If you're reading this and disagreeing with me because you want to raise polite boys who treat women like queens, I'm challenging you to really think about what that means to you and your values in raising boys. Boys can hold doors for girls. They can even pay for the first couple of dates. But this generation of girls can hear these Princess messages and take them to mean that boys trying to be polite must give in to their demands. Wrong. A boy can be a girl's hero—as when he stands up to guys (including his friends) who are disrespectful to her—but if a boy is expected to pay for everything (and by the way, going into serious debt this way is just stupid) or to treat a girl like a delicate flower, that just encourages her to be incompetent, spoiled, and superficial.

For guys, it's not so great either. Guys who buy into this often feel that they can't argue with the Princess. They can also never admit any weakness or failure. But that's not reality. Being the knight in shining armor may look good, but it's impossible to keep up all the time. Once in a while, sure. Just not all the time.

He Wants to Be the Savior

High school boys can be incredibly romantic. So if your son gets involved with a girl who has problems—maybe she's depressed, or comes from an abusive home, or has a parent with a drinking or drug problem—he can really get in over his head.

If this happens to your son, take a step back and realize that it's coming from a good place. He cares about this girl and wants to help her. And getting into an unhealthy relationship that teaches you how to manage personal boundaries with another person is a common rite of passage. In the long run, this could be a good learning experience for him. In the short run, you could easily worry yourself sick. So here's what I suggest you say:

"I know how much you care for her and how important you are to her. And you can help her, but to do that you also have to take care of yourself. That means not talking to her all night and maintaining other important relationships in your life, like your friends and family. If she's threatening herself or the relationship because of things you do to take care of yourself, I really want you to think about that. You can't fix her problems for her. She has to do it—with the help and support of the right people, but it can't be all on you. It's not what she needs, and it's not fair to you. If you're feeling that she is getting worse or that the relationship is out of control, can you please consider talking to someone who specializes in (whatever she's dealing with) so you can come up with a plan to help her and keep yourself strong?"

He's Dating a Much Younger Girl

Understandably, parents can get a little freaked out if their son is dating someone much younger than he is in high school. I think concern is reasonable in one situation: your son has high social status, he doesn't have strong friendships with girls, and when you see them together she seems to be focused on pleasing him. These are the older boys who consistently hook up with and use younger girls because they can't handle being in an equal relationship. But your chances of seeing this girl around your son are very low because he won't want to be seen with her in "public" (meaning you).

The other kind of older teen who dates younger girls is the opposite of the guy above. This guy usually has very little experience with girls, he may be a little physically immature or shy, and girls his age are intimidating or not interested in him. This boy almost always falls hard. He usually idealizes the girl and idealizes their relationship. If her parents disapprove of the age gap, he will do everything and anything he can to prove that he's honorable. If she breaks up with him (as is usually the case), he'll be devastated. He won't understand why; he'll want to talk to her for closure, may have a hard time not "bumping" into her, and may come out the other end a little bitter. Your job is to let him feel the sadness and rejection but be clear that he needs to honor the breakup. And if possible, work with him to not assume that people he dates will betray him.

He's Dating an Older Girl

It used to be that junior and senior girls in high school would never date freshman or sophomore boys. Never. It still isn't nearly as common as older boys dating younger girls, but some of the stigma has worn off.* An older girl can hit on and hook up with a physically mature freshman without her reputation suffering. If you're the parent of this boy, it's really important to acknowledge that while this experience may be exciting and flattering and increases his social status (especially among the kids in his own grade), hanging out with an older girl means he'll be in situations with other older kids. There's a lot of pressure on younger boys in this kind of situation to always say yes. How could a boy say no to the sexual advances of an older girl? Remind him that he does have that right, and he can exercise that right like girls have done forever—lying and distracting. As in, "I have to leave with my friends. And if I don't get down there soon, they'll come looking for me. Oh, they just texted me now. I really have to go."

He Gets Her Pregnant

Whenever I'm leaving at night, my mom says to me, "Don't bring me back any grandchildren." —Eric, 17

Because we tell teen boys so often not to get girls pregnant, it's only fair to talk to them about what happens if they do. Whatever your position on abortion, and whatever ultimately happens with the

---

*One of my favorite boarding schools had an "informal tradition" where the night before the students left for winter holidays, the senior girls would hook up with the freshman boys with a clear understanding that there were no future obligations.

pregnancy, give your son permission to feel the mixture of feelings he's probably experiencing, like anxiety, joy, and sadness. But also be clear that you expect him to support the financial future of his child if necessary—and then make sure to reemphasize your love and your support at his taking responsibility. Any boy dealing with an unplanned pregnancy is going to have his world turned upside down and will be grappling with powerful emotions, including fear, uncertainty, and probably a certain amount of shame. He's going to need to know you're there for him.

Heartbreak

A couple of months ago, I broke up with my girlfriend. She was the first girl I had ever fallen in love with. I had always told myself that love wasn't possible in high school and it was simply infatuation with this girl. We kept going until I found out she cheated on me. But she didn't just cheat on me once. She cheated on me with three people. I ended it with her, without ever cursing or yelling at her. I simply ended it and haven't talked to her since. I treated her like a princess.* I was a junior, and she was a freshman (not tooting my own horn), but I'm a good-looking guy and frankly, people didn't even know why I went for her because I could have done better. But yet I loved her. I still can't fall asleep many nights just thinking about it. I've done what most guys try to do to get over the past GF and hooked up with a couple of other girls, and that hasn't helped at all. I feel empty, and that sounds so lame and stupid, but it's true. I honestly feel like I'm missing something. Don't get me wrong. I don't love her anymore. Actually, I despise her with every fiber of my body, but for some reason it won't stop hurting when I think about it. How do I get over this girl? —Lance, 17

Here are the general things I tell a guy who's been betrayed or rejected (after I thank him for trusting me enough to ask for my advice):

---

*See—this Princess thing is a problem.

1. You can't control who you fall for or why. Honestly, it could be pheromones.
2. You can't force yourself to stop having feelings for someone, even if they did something really bad to you. This isn't because you're stupid or blinded by love or lust. Most likely it's because the person had some really good qualities and that was the reason you fell for that person. It just so happens that the person also had some other qualities that could really bring you down.
3. You can love someone who doesn't deserve it.
4. You can love someone and that still doesn't mean you should be in a relationship with that person.

Ease into it. You can say, "Hey, have you been seeing (X) girl?" Then maybe you can get an answer out of him. —Grant, 16

I was dating a girl for fifteen months, but when I broke up with her, my parents had no idea. —Tony, 16

If He Doesn't Understand That the Girl Has Rejected Him, Should I Tell Him?

Yes. If he's telling you that she's not calling him back, or she's answering him vaguely, then you can tell him it's a possibility that she may not be that into him. Yes, it's harsh, but it's better that he hears that from you than if he continues to pursue her until she either embarrasses him in public or gets weirded out. But this is a really uncomfortable conversation to have with your son, so it's fully covered in *The Guide*.

ABUSIVE RELATIONSHIPS

Have you ever been attracted to someone you didn't really like? Gone to a party and stayed later than you wanted to because a friend didn't want to leave? Gotten into a car with someone you knew you shouldn't be with but did it anyway? Most of us have had experiences like these. It's not because we're weak or stupid. It's because, in the moment we make the decision, we come up with a logical reason to explain to ourselves that what we're doing makes sense.

This is pretty much the same reason why people find themselves in really messed-up relationships. In the moment, we want it to work out. No one's relationship deteriorates overnight. It happens gradually, after we've become invested in the relationship and the person. After we know the good sides of the person as well as the bad.

Think about it in your own life. Most of us know of at least one relationship that is so messed up that it makes no sense to us why the person who's treated like dirt doesn't leave. You may have wondered the same thing about a relationship you've been in yourself. Everyone, no matter what their age, can get into a seriously messed-up relationship. And everyone includes guys the age of your son. I know we most often hear that girls are the victims in abusive relationships and guys are the perpetrators, but here are some recent statistics* that show a different picture.

- 44 percent of perpetrators of psychological teen dating violence (TVD) are male; 56 percent are female
- 76 percent of perpetrators of sexual TDV are male; 24 percent are female

So guys can be both the abused and the abuser, and it doesn't do any good to argue about who is abused more, girls or guys. What matters is to recognize that people who are in these relationships need help. And the guys represented in those statistics are in an even more complicated situation than girls in their position. Remember, adults talk to girls about relationships. They give books to girls, who often read those books, and most of those books have a section on how to recognize and get out of an abusive relationship. While it's

*Josephine Korchmaros, Michele Ybarra, Jennifer Langhinrichsen-Rohling, Danah Boyd, and Amanda Lenhart, "Perpetration of Teen Dating Violence in a Networked Society," *Journal of Cyberpsychology, Behavior, and Social Networking*, 2013.

really difficult for girls to talk about being abused, they don't feel stripped of their femininity when they do.

When guys are abused, they feel like they're literally stripped of their manhood. It doesn't help that their friends are probably relentlessly teasing them about how "whipped" they are, even if that teasing is a cover for their genuine concern. If your son is ever on the receiving end of abuse, you're probably going to have a lot of emotional reactions: confusion, anger at the girl, guilt because you believe that somehow you caused it to happen, and helplessness because you can't just tell your son to stop seeing her. Again, these are feelings to share with your partner, a sibling, or a close friend. Don't make your son feel like you're forcing him to break up with her. But do remind him of the following:

1. Just because you're in love with someone doesn't mean you should be in a relationship with that person.
2. People who are abusive, no matter their sex and age, are usually highly socially intelligent and manipulative. That means they know exactly what to say and do to control you and keep you in the relationship.
3. You're always entitled to your feelings and perspective. Abusers are amazingly good at getting you to question yourself. They'll literally make you doubt your sanity or grind you down so that you give in.

If you're increasingly frustrated because he won't leave or they keep getting back together, remember that it's impossible to fall out of love overnight, even when the person you love treats you like dirt. An abuser can make you feel like the most special person in the world, so you tend to focus on the abuser's good qualities and minimize the manipulating parts. Getting out of an abusive relationship is a process.*

---

*Two good resources for teens and abusive relationships are Love Is Not Abuse (loveisnotabuse.com) and Break the Cycle (breakthecycle.com).

What If Your Son Is the Abuser?

I have a friend who has been dating this girl for about a year. It's like they're married—the really f——ed-up kind. I like him, but he has a temper, and when he's angry he can be pretty mean. But he's never mean to me like that. We're all in this group of friends of guys and girls, and the girls now hate him, and they aren't friends with her either. It's so complicated. He never hits her, but it's like she's his slave and he can do anything to her. I don't really get why she stays with him. He makes fun of her all the time, he puts her down. She has to tell him where she is all the time. It's crazy, but if you ever bring it up with him, he just blows you off. Once in a while, she tries to break up with him, but then she always goes back to him. —Aiden, 16

Abusers aren't out of control when they're mean. Even if they're drunk or high or having a really bad day, they only abuse people they can get away with abusing. They have complete control over who they go after and how. That's why you may never see this part of an abuser's personality. But just because you don't see it doesn't mean it's not happening. I've had students who were abusing their girlfriends, and if I hadn't known about it, I wouldn't have believed it. But the people who do know are his friends. So my guy editors suggest that if you suspect abuse is going on, you can ask the friends of the person you suspect in the following way:

If his mom or dad came up to me privately and said, "I'm worried about how Dave is treating Sarah. You don't have to tell me all the details, but can you tell me if my gut is right?," then I'd tell them. —Grant, 15

The Dark Side

I walked into this bedroom at a party, and there was this girl who had passed out, and guys were taking pictures of her so it looked

*like she was giving them blowjobs. They'd pull up her shirt. It was
bad. They'd move her around from guy to guy, and most of the guys
were laughing their asses off. I stood there for a few minutes, not
sure what to do. I left. I didn't know what to do. —Kyle, 16*

*Some senior guys painted on their cars RAPE PROSTITUTES—CLASS OF
2012 RULZ! and then drove onto the school campus. We have little
kids who go to our school, and when the parents complained and
I tried to discipline them, my house was vandalized with FUCK THE
DEAN. —anonymous high school administrator*

How do I talk to my son about sexual assault? I imagine this isn't a
question you've asked yourself or even want to think applies to your
life in any way. As a parent, I don't want to do it either, but we have
to face facts. There isn't a neighborhood in this country that doesn't
have girls and boys who have been sexually assaulted by other boys
and men. You know this. None of us are raised outside the culture
of rape. Everyone knows someone who has been raped, even if they
haven't told us. We may have been sexually assaulted ourselves, and
if we were, it most likely happened when we were young. There's a
culture of silence around these horrible acts, so when it's our turn to
teach our children about these issues, we don't even think about it
until it's too late. And even if we did want to talk about it, we don't
know how.

How do we bring boys into a conversation knowing that some
of them have the potential to callously disregard the most basic
human rights of another person? How do we talk to them about
the possibility that they could witness or even participate in a scenario like Kyle described? That they might be the ones laughing
or taking pictures of the girl who had passed out? How do we acknowledge that, when perpetrators have social status, the pressure
on victims to recant their story is so overwhelming and we, the
adults, are so desperate to maintain our denial that we often rationalize a way to dismiss the entire incident?

"It's a fluke."
"It's a misunderstanding."
"Boys do stupid things."

These are still the most common reactions from parents to a boy who has sexually assaulted another child. If you send your child to a prestigious school with high social status in the community, you can't assume that the school will do the right thing when one of its students assaults another kid. There are some heads of private schools who are masters at getting out of situations like this to preserve the school's reputation. Or sometimes the head of the school or the deans want to do the right thing but aren't strong enough to challenge other authority figures in the school, like the athletic director or the school's religious leader.

What's amazing to me is how often parents won't give up on the belief that if they send their child to a certain school, these kinds of things won't happen because the other parents and the school leadership share their values. Yes, if you asked the staff at that school whether they condone their students raping other students, they'd say, "Of course not," and believe what they're saying, but they still excuse and look the other way when given information that this is a possibility or has already occurred. Never assume that really messed-up things don't happen and that your son might not be right in the middle of it.

It's really on you. You have to talk to your son at the latest when he's entering high school, and this is the way I'd do it:

"You may see things that are really messed up, and it'll be a real struggle to know what to do. This isn't something that happens to you only when you're a teen. This is a fact of life forever. It could be what a guy is doing to another guy or what a guy is doing to a girl. Girls can also be cruel to other girls and to boys. It could be at school, in the locker room, at a party, or in someone's house. In the first moments when you realize something's wrong, it's really easy to not believe what you're seeing or to convince yourself that it's not serious. Other people can try to convince you that nothing's wrong. Trust your gut. Or think about what

I'd think if I could see what's happening. If you can't speak out in that moment, I'm asking you to leave the room and call me or another adult you trust. Sometimes these things happen so fast that it's hard to really process what's happening. You can always tell me, and I can help you figure it out."

People love to advise bystanders to say, "How would you feel if this happened to your mother or sister?" "Motivating" boys to care about rape only because it could happen to "their" women is disrespectful to all women and to the boys and men who have been sexually assaulted. But this question also never stops the perpetrators. First, you have no idea what the perpetrator's relationship is with those women in his life, but it's not a huge leap to think he doesn't hold a great deal of respect for them. Second, these boys have dehumanized their victim. They don't care.

If you're worried that your son could do something like this, you can say:

"I don't like saying this to you, but I need to. I have a feeling that there's a possibility that some of the guys you're hanging out with could take sexual advantage of a girl (drinking or not), or even go after a guy to physically humiliate him. If you participate in this in any way— including laughing and taking pictures or commenting on whatever happened on Facebook or Twitter—I'll hold you accountable in the most serious way I can. I expect you to be a man who fundamentally recognizes that people can't be stripped of their dignity. I expect you to hold yourself accountable in the moment."

For the parents who are caught in the aftermath, unless your child is being criminally accused of rape or some kind of assault, please don't get caught up in definitions. You don't have to call it rape, sodomy, or sexual assault, and you don't have to invoke the legal system to say unequivocally to your child:

I love you. You are my son. That doesn't take away that your actions have hurt another person. You will, in various ways and times, have to come to terms with what you did. Through that process I will be by your side. But I will not deny what you have done, and I will deeply *reflect on how we got to this place. Anytime you would like to talk to me about this, I will be here.*

I know this isn't anything parents want to talk about with their son. I wish things were different. I wish that some boys wouldn't try to get away with assaulting other kids, that some parents wouldn't dismiss such assaults as one kid getting out of hand, that some administrators wouldn't forget that their primary responsibility is to keep their students safe. But your son lives in a world where all of this is possible. You have to be ready to stand for what is right.

The Final Word

YOU PROMISE...

- I will treat my son with dignity. That means taking his concerns seriously and not dismissing them as immature, hormonal, or trivial.
- I will act consistently with what I say. When I don't, I understand that earning his trust back will take time.
- I will not humiliate him in private or public.
- I will acknowledge and own when I have made a mistake. Not by saying, "People make mistakes or nobody's perfect," but by saying, "I was wrong and I'm sorry."
- I will teach him to express his emotions in emotionally healthy ways.
- I will hold him accountable when he doesn't treat someone else with dignity.
- I will support him wanting to ask for help and, when appropriate, talking to other adults about a problem.

HE PROMISES...

- To treat me with dignity by paying attention when I'm talking to him, respecting the family's rules, and not putting me down or being rude, either privately or in front of his friends.
- To give me the information I need to know to help him be safe.
- To be truthful in his words and actions. If he's not, he understands that earning my trust back will take time.
- To reflect our family values in his behavior toward all others.

Suggested Reading

Emily Bazelon, *Sticks and Stones: Defeating the Culture of Bullying and Re-discovering the Power of Character and Empathy* (New York: Random House, 2013).

Danah Boyd, *A Networked Self: Identity, Community, and Culture on Social Network Sites* (New York: Routledge Press, 2010).

Po Bronson and Ashley Merryman, *Nurtureshock: New Thinking About Children* (New York: Twelve, 2009).

————, *Top Dog* (New York: Twelve, 2013).

Ernest Cline, *Ready Player One* (New York: Crown, 2011).

Dave Cullen, *Columbine* (New York: Twelve, 2010).

James Garbarino, *Lost Boys: Why Our Sons Turn Violent and How We Can Save Them* (New York: Anchor Books, 2005).

Temple Grandin, *Different Not Less: Inspiring Stories of Achievement and Successful Employment from Adults with Autism, Asperger's, and ADHD* (Arlington TX: Future Horizons, 2012).

Michael Gurian, *The Purpose of Boys: Helping Our Sons Find Meaning, Significance, and Direction in Their Lives* (New York: Jossey-Bass, 2010).

Edward Hallowell, MD, *Driven to Distraction: Recognizing and Coping with Attention Deficit Disorder,* rev. ed. (New York: Anchor Books, 2011).

Sameer Hinduja and Justin Patchin, *School Climate 2.0* (Thousand Oaks, CA: Corwin Press, 2012).

Aaron James, *Assholes: A Theory* (New York: Doubleday, 2012).

Jackson Katz, *Leading Men: Presidential Campaigns and the Politics of Manhood* (Northampton, MA: Interlink Pub Group, 2012).

————, *The Macho Paradox: Why Some Men Hurt Women and How All Men Can Help* (Naperville, IL: Sourcebooks, 2006).

Michael Kimmel, *Guyland: The Perilous World Where Boys Become Men* (New York: Harper Perennial, 2009).

———, *Manhood in America: A Cultural History* (New York: Free Press, 1996).

Richard Lavoie, *It's So Much Work to Be Your Friend* (New York: Touchstone, 2005).

Jeffrey Marx, *Season of Life: A Football Star, a Boy, a Journey to Manhood* (New York: Simon & Schuster, 2004).

Jane McGonigal, *Reality Is Broken: Why Games Makes Us Better and How They Change the World* (New York: Penguin Press, 2011).

Pedro Noguera, *The Trouble with Black Boys . . . And Other Reflections on Race, Equity, and the Future of Public Education* (New York: Jossey-Bass, 2009).

William Pollack, *Real Boys: Rescuing Our Sons from the Myths of Boyhood* (New York: Random House, 1998).

John Elder Robison, *Look Me in the Eye: My Life with Asperger's* (New York: Crown, 2007).

Michael Sandel, *Justice: What's the Right Thing to Do* (New York: Farrar, Straus and Giroux, 2009).

Leonard Sax, *Boys Adrift: The Five Factors Driving the Growing Epidemic of Unmotivated Boys and Underachieving Young Men* (New York: Basic Books, 2009).

Ron Taffel, *Breaking Through to Teens: A New Psychotherapy for the New Adolescence* (New York: Guilford Press, 2005).

Michael Thompson, *It's a Boy! Your Son's Development from Birth to 18* (New York: Ballantine Books, 2009).

Michael Thompson and Daniel Kindlon, *Raising Cain: Protecting the Emotional Lives of Boys* (New York: Ballantine Books, 2000).

Anthony E. Wolf, *I'd Listen to My Parents If They'd Just Shut Up* (New York: William Morrow, 2011).

Acknowledgments

RYAN: Ms. Wiseman, Ms. Wiseman, are you going to put our names in the book?

ME: Yes, you'll be in the acknowledgments.

RYAN: All of us? You promise?

YOU: Of course. But we need to talk about what I sent you last week to review. What did you think?

WILL: It's okay.

ME: What does okay mean?

CHARLIE: It's fine.

ME: Really, what does that mean?

CONNOR: Well . . .

An awkward silence filled the room, which was really odd because up to that point these guys wouldn't stop talking.

ME: Guys . . . come on. Tell me what you think.

WILL: We don't really use the term "wingman" like you do. We only use it when we want to hook up with a girl and our buddy helps us out.

ME: Why didn't you tell me this before? That's all I've been writing for the last two weeks. I've sent you so many emails and no one said anything.

Fifteen pairs of shoulders shrugged.

ME: Let me explain something to you. As Ryan just asked, your name will now be in this book. My name is going to be on the cover of this book. You're now a part of this, and if I get this wrong because you won't tell me what you really think, then I'll look like an asshole and you'll look like an asshole.

JORDAN: Well . . . the whole chapter was sort of boring.

KENNEDY: Yeah, I didn't really get it.

ME: Thank you. Now we're getting somewhere.

I doubt many writers threaten to publicly embarrass the people who are helping them. And I realized shortly after this conversation that the boys had to trust me to tell me when I was wrong. Once we got over this hurdle, they never held back again. And for that, I am immensely grateful. So . . . to each and every one of my guy editors, thank you. Thank you for trusting me to do a good job and share what you really thought. Thank you for reaching out to one another. Thank you for taking the leap of faith that we could do this. Thank you for going to parties on a Saturday night and taking my questions with you and reporting back. Thank you for dragging other guys to meet with me. Thank you for meeting me early on a Saturday morning at the beginning of your summer vacation. Thank you for sharing aspects of yourself that you have always kept private. Thank you for making me laugh, learn, and remember why this book was so important to write. There were times in writing this book that I never wanted it to end, and that was because of you all.

The Editors

Andrew Karolidis, Andrew Seide, Aaron Hutchinson, Aaron Wilson, Abram Blau, AJ Dunham, Al Hernandez, Andrew Steggman, Anthony Conselatore, Anthony Kuhnriech, Antoine Oates, Antonio Guanes Gomes, Auguste Boova, Austin Howard, Ayon Basu, Ben Spear, Blair Ivory, Brian Firshing, Brian Tien-Street, Brian Wolfson, Bryan Devlieg, Byron Schaeffer, Case Van der Velde, Johnathan Calderson, Cameron Lowe, Calvin Phillips, Carol Krell, Charlie Schubert, CJ Burton, Christopher Hall, Christopher Fortenberry, Cody Phillips, Connor White, Cole Benit, Corey Campbell, David Colvey, Duncan Harvey, Erik Overdyk, Ethan Pacifico, Eric Biehm, Evan O'Leary, Forest Dearing, Guy Holloway, Graham Dick, Grant Wolf, Haris Ghayas, Harvey Robin, Hunter Gofus, Ian Brennan, Ian Kinslow, Ian Davis, Ian Dumas, Ian Tasiopulos, Jack Zwemer, Jack Tyler, Jack Oliver Pitchford, Jackson Crispin, Jacob Bibeau, Jacob Freund, Jacob

Schoifet, Jake Stein, Jason Benedict, Jarrett Bond, JD Birks, Jordan Noble, Justin Meyer, Josh Klein, Josh Murdy, Jude Druffel, Kennedy Kommor, Kevin Kopervas, Kevin Bengtsson, Kris Craiger, Landon Tillery, Lachlan Moore, Larkin Nickle, Luuk Kuiper, Najee Booker, Mathias Tucunduva, Matt Dias, Matthew Mullock, Max Guidry, Mendel Schwarz, Michael Birks, Michael Reikes, Mike McCalpin, Ned Oliver, Noah Hackman, Ondre Johnson, Owen Yaeger, Pedro Quirino, Raffaele Saposhnik, Ricky Coston, Riley Jamison, Robert Chen, Robbie Springfield, Ryan Perry, Ryan Baker, Sam Fishel, Samuel Burge, Sam Paplow, Sebastian Luna, Sebastian Medina-Tayac, Seondre Gambrell, Stanley Feeney, Stephen Goodly, Tristan Anderson, Troy Washington, Trevor Riley, Tyler Wells, Tucker Stas, Victor Chang, Victor Ruiz Fierro, Vincent Santos, Will Llewellyn, Will Melley, Will O'Malley, Grace Ishimwe, Will McAnulty, William Davis, Will Oldham, Winston Robinson, Wilson Walker, Alejandra Charrabe, Anna-Rogers Daub, Sarah Nugent, Corrine Asher, Natania Lipp, Annie Hall, Annie McCall, Antonia Smith, Carrie Anderson, Claire Sleigh, Crista Butler, Crystal Staebell, Emily Callahan, Molly Oliver, Emily Munch, Claire Dickinson, Emma Merrill, Georgina Eaton, Diana Perkins, Barbara Lannert, Grace Ohaus, Hannah Schmelzer, Melissa Vaz-Ayes, Hannah Scott, Anisha Datta, Izzy Gwozdz, Julia Sidman, Morgan Rogers-Daub, Adrienne Gallus, Teresa Davis, Kate Maguire, Elizabeth Beckman, Lenna Soltau, Ryley Van der Velde, Sarah Farnsworth, Alicia Furlan, Ellie Jay, Victoria Karem, Lizzie Dollar, Kasey Hemeon, David Keyer, Kimber Ludovico, Maddy Lyons, Mary Oliver, Maureen Lei, Gracie Parrish, Melody Estevez, Mia Henkebein, Michelle Dange, Paige McClellan, Pascale Bronder, Samantha Schweickhardt, Samantha Westrum, Sarah Bode, Sofi Sinozich, Jack Twomey, Matthew Disilva, Chris Baker, Chris Doyle, Christopher Esselman, George Isaacs, Isaac Keuber, Jack Tiedman, Jacob Hoffman, John Villanueva, Michael Borger, Nick Christensen, Noah Tuell, Parker Duff, Preston Luniewski, Tyler Lolla, Will Stern, Michael Webb, Coley Sullivan, Tyler Lolla, Alicia Furlan, Camden Donner, Farrah Staebell, Kacey Wheeler, Katie Hillebrand, Molly Speth, Sarah Camp, Tori Smith, Wambui Watene, Nico Adamo, Zack Anderson, Dante Chavez, Ryan Choi, Cole Emry, Saijai Kaushal, Brooks Lebow, Michael Maragakis, Wayne Nelms, Dylan Patel, Bennet Speicher, Essex Thayer, Jack Tortolani, and Jack Witherspoon.

The Parent Editors

Andy Meyer, David Horn, Sean Britt, Tim Katz, Christine Tiedemann, Heather McCubbin, Jennifer Zwember, Melissa Moore, Johanna Olson, Kyle Esh, Melissa Smith, Sharon Ney, Amy Hewitt, Christine Buchberger, Lynn Devlieg, Maria Grat, Mark Frega, Rana Clarke, and Steve Shapiro.

The Generational Bridge Editors (Guys in Their Twenties)

Max Neely Cohen, who literally made this book something I can be proud of. Will Pierce, who started out not at all sure if this was a good idea but stuck with me. And Charlie Kuhn, who joined this project at the exact right moment.

The initial outreach to the editors wouldn't have been possible without incredible teachers, administrators, coaches, and community leaders connecting me to the boys and, in some cases, girls. Thanks to my partner schools: Walden, Louisville Collegiate, Sophie B. Wright High School, Hynes Middle School, The Hill School, Millbrook, Haverford School, Gilman School, Bexley High School, Graded School (São Paulo, Brazil), Potomac Falls High School, Montgomery Blair, and Sidwell Friends. Thank you to the other schools where I presented to your students and they came forward to help. Thank you also to educational colleagues: Carey Faversham Goldstein, Susan Steinman, Linda Van Houten, Andre Perry, Sharon Clark, Margo Johnson, Michelle Douglas, Kirk Dolson, Jay Greytok, Officer Lindsey Wilson, Dan Feigin, David Swaney, Laura Morgan, Patty Manning and her staff at Cincinnati Children's Hospital, Janet Seide, and Eugenia Brady. Thank you also to my publisher, Crown, my editor Rick Horgan, Nathan Roberson, my über-editor Tina Constable, and Jim Levine and everyone at Levine Greenberg Literary Agency.

Thank you to my husband, James Edwards, who again made it possible for me to go into the writing cave. And thank you to my sons, Elijah and Roane Edwards, who showed absolutely no interest in the book—except for the chapter on video games. I completely respect their honesty and constant ability to give me so many opportunities to put my advice into practice.

Index

Dear Reader,

After finishing *Masterminds and Wingmen,* you might want to share some of what you've read with a boy in your life. Although I'd like to believe that most boys would love to talk about these issues, the reality is that any discussion may send him running in the opposite direction, horrified that you now think you have insight into his deepest thoughts. That's perfectly normal, but the truth is that even if he's too embarrassed to talk, he's probably dealing with some issues for which he could use guidance. It's also important that when he *does* need help, you have a shared degree of understanding and can communicate with each other.

For all of these reasons, I've written, in addition to *Masterminds and Wingmen,* a book specifically for middle and high school boys titled *The Guide: Managing Douchebags, Recruiting Wingmen, and Attracting Who You Want.*

Before I continue, let me explain why I'm using "douchebag" in the title. All boys will have experiences with other guys who are so rude, thoughtless, and arrogant that in our boys' minds there is no other word that describes them. "Douchebags" are a universal experience, and the bottom line is: we have to reach boys in ways that reflect their experiences.

Beyond dealing with douchebags, in *The Guide* I also cover such issues as:

- What happens when a boy is tired of covering for a friend who is getting him into trouble?
- How should he respond when a group of girls decides they hate him?
- How should he handle himself if he's stopped or pulled over by a police officer?
- How can he make amends and redeem himself when he screws up?

Boys want to grow and figure things out on their own, but every guy needs a wingman. *The Guide* is that wingman—it's always there for him when he needs it. When I was writing these books, I worked with hundreds of boys. Not only did they want to clue *you* in, but they also wanted to help their peers. *The Guide* is for them.

Together, these two books provide a foundation for you and the boy in your life to get the support you *each* need, communicate effectively with each other, and better tackle the challenges of Boy World. You can download *The Guide* as an ebook by going to my website, rosalindwiseman.com.

Best,
Rosalind Wiseman